Happy Birthday
Judith   1978

Mother + Father

Please
Love
Me.

OTHER BOOKS BY KEITH MILLER

The Taste of New Wine
A Second Touch
Habitation of Dragons
The Becomers

with Bruce Larson
The Edge of Adventure
Living the Adventure

Please Love Me.

**One woman's silent plea
for the miracle of intimacy**

Keith Miller

WORD BOOKS
PUBLISHER
4800 WEST WACO DRIVE
WACO, TEXAS
76703

PLEASE LOVE ME

Printed in the United States of America.
ISBN 0-87680-509-9
Library of Congress catalog card number: 77-89053

To
MARY-KEITH MILLER
*who continues to help me face
my dishonesty and psychological games*

Contents

Acknowledgements

BECAUSE THIS is a different kind of book from those I have tried to write—or even seen—I asked several people to read all or parts of it in manuscript form. Their suggestions were enormously helpful. Some I followed, some I did not. The opinions were so varied that I want to thank each of the following people who read this manuscript—without blaming them for material appearing in the final draft, which they thought should have been deleted: Bruce and Hazel Larson, Bob Flynn, Vester Hughes, Jr., Bob and Wendy Frahm, Chuck and Carolyn Huffman, Gene Warr, Brooks Goldsmith, Bob and Garnett Parker, Joan Allison, Ann Hutchinson, Tiny Hawn, Bill and Patty Woerner, Dorothy Glancy, Tom Luce, Jeanine Burdine, Fayteen Holman, and Mary-Keith Miller.

Joan Palmer not only typed the manuscript but helped keep the office (and the author) together during the writing of the book.

Although it is not customary to mention one's editor by name, I am compelled to say here that I have been amazed at the sensitivity and ability of my dear friend, Mary Ruth Howes, to understand and help interpret some of the complex emotions and ideas which are bound to get tangled up when a man tries to interpret the inner life of a woman in the first person singular. She may not have agreed with all that appears on these pages, but any clarity and coherence is largely due to her efforts as co-worker.

For the Reader

THIS IS A REAL story. I want to say that right off, since this account is so dramatic in some places and so prosaic in others that it might not be believable as fiction.

Occasionally in a generation it appears that a life is changed in such an unusual way that the struggles of that life reveal some of the problems of a whole society. When I first heard the rough outlines of the story you are about to read, I realized that it was not just the recounting of a remarkable and dramatic life, but that it spoke to some of the deepest frustrations and yearnings I have experienced and seen as I've traveled across America during the past few years.

To protect the privacy of certain persons, all the names, cities, institutions, and certain of the events and vocational identities following this preface have been changed. Any similarity of the names of persons actually used in this book to people living or dead is purely coincidental.

The individual on whose life the story is based is one of the most sensitive and courageous people I have ever known. After extensive conversations with her and others near her, I have tried to write as nearly as I could from her perspective.

Some religious people may be shocked at the frankness and vivid language with which the story is told. But this frankness is deliberate. For years we have strayed far from the honesty and directness of the biblical writers. They did not whitewash their heroes nor "clean up their stories" to make them acceptable to the religious reader, as we customarily do. Their message was and is that God meets men and women in the earthy events and language of real experience.

This story has been written for anyone anywhere who has cried out silently into the night, "Please love me."

KEITH MILLER
Port Aransas, Texas

PROLOGUE

THE WAY IT WAS
by Keith Miller

The Way It Was

"HELLO, KEITH!" It was the hostess letting me in the heavy double door of her entry hall. Smiling, I asked how she'd been as she guided me into the crowded living room. After looking around a few seconds, I edged through the shifting mass of talking faces to a corner and sat down in an empty chair. I didn't feel like talking to anyone.

I was miserable. My back ached and I felt sort of numb. In one way I didn't know if my life was over, or if there was going to be anything good left for me in the future. There was an awful gray feeling in my stomach—like maybe I might not make it through the depressed days I was going through—and that scared me. Now here I was in Chicago for another meeting, fourteen hundred miles from home and feeling very lonesome and out of place.

Sitting there on the edge of the party, I began to think about my life. I felt that I'd fouled up all my closest relationships, and for the first time I hadn't been able to make things right for everybody. Everything I'd touched had seemed to go wrong during the past two years. People appeared to be distant as I was becoming more and more isolated. As a professional speaker, I'd begun to feel like a "ten-dollar-a-plate-dinner," a traveling program in a world of strangers instead of a person. And the worst part was my faith in God had become gray and distant too. And I had no idea what to do about that.

Now I was at a party in Chicago with more strangers, most of whom I'd never met. Feeling as if I were looking at the party going on around me from a great distance, I glanced across the room again. People were laughing or talking and seemed to be saying nothing.

Bored and frustrated, I looked to my right. A couple had just sat down. I recognized the woman. She was Hedy Robinson, a very beautiful artist, from Lake Forest, just outside Chicago. We'd met and visited at one of her art shows. Although she had seemed then to be a very sensitive person, I didn't feel like talking to her now. She appeared to have life so "together" and mine was anything but. Hedy was with a tall man who was, I learned later, a doctor from Nebraska or somewhere. I started to say hello but she was talking to the man on the other side of her.

My mind turned inward and I began to think about the things I had to do during the next two weeks. Everything looked depressing and impossible. I'd said I'd speak to a convention about a subject which was furthest from my mind: Miracles. And I wasn't even sure what I believed about *God!* I felt myself withdrawing further.

Just then Hedy turned to me. "Hello, Keith, how are you?" She smiled, and as she spoke I remembered that her voice was always only a hoarse whisper. I looked at her and smiled. I'd forgotten how attractive she was. After we talked a few minutes, I asked her bluntly, "Hedy, what do you think about miracles? Do you believe in them?"

Surprised, but without blinking an eye she said, "Yes, I certainly do."

"Why?" I asked.

She looked at me curiously, "Do you really want to know?"

"Yes, I really do."

She looked again to see if I were serious. And then in her whisper-voice she began telling me the following almost unbelievable story which was to change my life and give me hope again.

"Let me begin," she said, "by telling you what happened one night four years ago which shocked me into taking an honest look at my life for the first time."

PART ONE

HEDY'S STORY —
THE BEGINNING

1. Dead on Arrival

I THINK IT ALL started late one Halloween night a few minutes after I'd said goodbye to friends who'd been with me for dinner. When the doorbell rang it startled me. I felt a sudden uneasiness and stood still to listen. Nothing. It was 1:30 in the morning but still Halloween. Who in the world could it be this late? My children had been out trick-or-treating and were spending the night with their father. So I was alone.

The bell rang again. It seemed loud and harsh in the silence. The front page account of the "winsome rapist" flashed into my mind. Then I shook my head. What an imagination! As I came through the swinging door in the dining room I smiled at myself in the hall mirror. Here I was, twenty-nine years old, an artist with a new career, two lovely daughters and a fresh chance for life and happiness. "Hedy," I said to myself, "quit being so afraid. You just can't believe you have the right to be happy, can you? Everyone else, but not *you*."

As soon as I opened the door and saw Danny looking down at me, my stomach tightened and my hand was cold on the brass door handle. I remembered our last meeting and I knew instinctively what he'd come for. His eyes were strange, and his half-glazed stare bored right into me. He was on something heavy.

He stood there waiting for me to let him in as I had a hundred times when we'd been lovers. Too scared to speak, I just shook my head. His eyes squinted into mine with frightening intensity for what seemed like twenty minutes, and then he brushed me aside as if I were a paper doll and stepped into the living room. Glancing at the remains of the party he hadn't been invited to, he raised his eyebrows. "Hmm, I see you've had company." I could tell he was trying desperately to cover his hurt.

His hands in his windbreaker pockets, Danny walked slowly around the living room, glancing at me. He looked around the room as if he were imagining the place filled with people laughing and having a good time. And then as I watched—terrified and not moving—his face seemed to harden. His eyes narrowed into a blank impersonal stare. I felt cold between my shoulder blades, felt a sudden rush of fear that he could actually kill me. I stood very still, watching him. He was chewing gum slowly. Looking at the fine blond hair across his forehead I couldn't help feeling tenderness in spite of my fear. He'd been such a gentle man, and though he was my age he seemed almost a boy now behind all his confusion. Surely he wouldn't hurt me.

He looked at me, apparently trying very hard to keep his eyes focused. "Hedy, I need to talk to you. . . . I've . . . I've found a way we can be together and—everything will be all right."

"Listen, Danny, I told you we're finished." I was speaking slowly, trying to keep my voice even, "I don't want to go out with you any more. We're a million miles apart now. And there's nothing else to talk about." I hoped my tone was steady, confident, because I wasn't at all.

The minutes dragged by in an unnatural quiet. My heart was beating so wildly that I thought surely he could hear it, but he only stared at me across the three feet that separated us. What was he thinking? What would he do?

But he only nodded his head a couple of times and smiled, shrugging his shoulders almost casually.

"Can I use your bathroom before I go?"

I nodded. My mind flooded with relief. He was going to go

home. But a few minutes later he came back—my loaded .38 caliber revolver in his hand!

His expression was cold again. The desperate, scared look he'd had a week before was gone—the night I'd told him it was all over. How much heroin had he had this time? And mixed with what? As I watched his eyes I knew he was capable of anything tonight—and tomorrow he might not even remember it.

"Hedy," he said softly, looking at the revolver and turning it slowly in his hand, "let's go out to the shooting range. I want to try out your gun and show you how to use it."

It was after midnight and if I screamed, probably no one would hear me. I just looked at him, trying not to panic, and shook my head.

He was standing about two feet from me and calmly raised the gun to the side of my neck.

"We're going for a ride in my car, Hedy, and I promise you this'll be the last time I'll try to talk to you."

As we walked out of the house into the darkness, the familiar smell of the damp grass and the cold fall night in Lake Forest sent a shiver through me. Instinctively I pulled my sweater around my shoulders. I had the eerie feeling I was in a TV movie. Only there were no cameras. This was really happening. As I saw his face in the light from the street lamp, it dawned on me that Danny actually *wanted* to kill me.

He opened the car door as he had so often, only this time his grip on my arm was like a steel tourniquet. "Don't try to get away, Hedy, I'm serious." The calm intensity of his words was more terrifying than if he'd screamed.

He started the car, staring straight ahead. I watched him, helpless, but fascinated. My thoughts didn't make sense. In spite of what was happening I was sorry for Danny. His fragile world had really cratered and was crumbling all around him: No job, no purpose, and after a year and a half of love and support, no Hedy. How was he paying for his drugs now?

Twenty minutes passed. We had left town and were driving very fast on an almost deserted two-lane highway. I didn't know where we were and Danny hadn't said a word so far. A sign flashed by in the headlights: "Dundee." The town was dark except for the night light in a closed gas station. In a few moments we were in the lonely countryside again. I was conscious of the dark shapes of trees flitting past on the left. Danny was staring straight down the road ahead. Finally he began to speak jerkily.

"Hedy, I've been thinking about it and I—I don't want to live without you. We can't seem to make it together." In the dim light from the dashboard I could see that his knuckles were white as he gripped the steering wheel. His right hand still had the gun in it. "I've been a loser all my life. Nothing's worked and I . . . know you're not happy either. So I've found something we can do." I saw a tear slipping slowly down his cheek.

"Hedy," he said, looking at me for the first time since we'd gotten in the car, "we're going to die together. And that way everything will be all right."

I looked at the speedometer and it was quickly passing eighty miles an hour. This had to be some kind of crazy nightmare! I couldn't move as I watched the car going faster and faster. Then suddenly a sharp curve appeared. The speedometer was at ninety-six miles an hour!

I heard myself screaming his name. Then we seemed to be floating off the highway on the curve. From the headlights I saw the outlines of the heavy stones.

"My god, a wall! No, Danny!"

*   *   *

I tried to open my eyes. The lids flickered. But nothing else moved. The world I looked out on was unfamiliar, blurred and undulating like an underwater movie. Was I dead or alive? Faces came and went above me. I was evidently lying in a bed. There were voices and the smell of alcohol, but I couldn't focus clearly. I tried to move my head, my hands, my toes. Nothing. Stone. And there was no pain. I must be dead. I tried to ask the faces where I was, but no sound came.

Moments—or eternities—later, I recognized a familiar face moving into focus out of the blur. It was Findley, my ex-husband. He looked frantic and helpless. I could tell he didn't know what to say and since I couldn't speak there was no way to ask him where I was, or what I was doing there. I thought, "Hedy, you've got to be dreaming—or you've been killed and this is the way it feels."

After a few minutes Findley said, "I guess you want to know what happened." In bits and pieces he gave me a full medical report: I had been pronounced dead on arrival at Wesley Memorial Hospital in Chicago, and had been in a coma for some time. My neck was broken, my throat was cut to the neck bone and crushed, my voice box was destroyed, my legs were fractured in several places, and I'd be paralyzed for life because of injuries to my back. But even if there hadn't been any spinal damage, I couldn't have walked because the ligaments in my right leg were virtually destroyed and both of my knees were smashed. Also, I'd never be able to talk again.

Findley stared toward the ceiling, avoiding looking at me. "How much better he does dealing with facts," I thought, "even awful ones, than he does facing his feelings."

"Frankly, Hedy, they say you have about a one percent chance to live, and I thought it was only fair to tell you in case there was anything you needed to do about it."

Do about it? What in the world could I *do* about it? I couldn't move or talk.

Paralyzed! Forever! Tears suddenly poured down my face. My first thought was that I'd misused and wasted any life I'd had in my headlong searching after—what *had* I been searching for so frantically anyway? I couldn't remember. Well, whatever it was, it didn't really matter any more.

As I lay there trying to think back over my life, I realized how totally selfish I'd been in so many ways. Now I was going to have to live with the fact that I couldn't do anything to make up for the past or even tell people that I'd realized and was sorry. I tried to shift my weight, wiggle my toes, but nothing—nothing moved. When I thought of my two little girls, seven and nine, and what an insensitive mother I had been, I cringed behind my useless face. Now, I'd never be able to make it up to them.

The feeling came over me in a wave that *I deserved what had happened*—that somehow God had worked out a way to get rid of me. And yet I'd even fouled that up.

As the hours moved imperceptibly into days in my frozen, timeless world, I lay motionless and silent. At first my mind refused to accept the doctor's verdict that I'd be paralyzed. But finally I realized it was true. My thoughts didn't change much after that except for the growing terror that I *might* live.

At times my mind would jump back and dwell on different days, places, people in my past who had meant so much in my life. I saw how I'd hidden the real Hedy from everyone, along with the intense search I was on. When I thought about that search, somehow my memories always included scenes with my father in them, and the aching feeling that whatever I'd been searching for, I hadn't found it. In the meantime I'd always worn a mask of pride to keep people from seeing my secret lonely searching, a mask which lied to the world: "Everything's fine with Hedy Robinson."

Being considered pretty and looking right had been one of my most important securities. Now I wished I'd been different. Why hadn't I let down my cool mask, invited some people inside and let them know I loved them? Why couldn't I risk telling someone what I was really like behind my face—in my heart, in my stomach? Now I couldn't, and *never would be able to!* Since I couldn't talk, I kept my face an expressionless mask. I thought about all of my beautiful friends. What if they let some of them in to see me? I would die.

The first day Findley brought the children to see me, they huddled nervously together in the corner and stared, obviously frightened. Their smiles were frozen on their little faces and I don't remember their blinking once. As I watched them out of the side of my eyes I had a knot in my stomach which moved up to my throat and stuck; then I felt it rolling out of my eyes in hot tears.

I ached to hold them, to tell them how sorry I was and that I knew now how much I'd let them down. But I'd never be able to put my arms around them or smooth their hair. They would go through life, not even knowing how I wanted to love them.

A wave of horror swept over me, which brought more tears and must have frightened the children, because they were quickly led away.

Then my mind became like a caged bird frantically trying to get out—to communicate in some way—to tell people I was in here and could listen to them and understand them: "For god's sake, somebody hear my thoughts!!! My brain was *not* damaged!" I began to scheme and try to speak with my eyes—as I had been able to do so well all my life in a room full of people. But now no one "heard."

Finally, after several weeks, my frantic efforts subsided and I began to wait for whatever it was that was coming. I heard enough scraps of conversation I wasn't supposed to hear to know there was no hope that I'd recover. I also heard that they were looking for a maintenance care facility where human vegetables were kept. But I wasn't a vegetable! Good lord, they were going to bury me alive with a bunch of eighty-year-old zombies! Suddenly I realized how much I *did* want to live.

My only escape from the terror of that future was to "think outside" the hospital room. I wondered where the people from my childhood were. My mother came, but she was so nervous and distraught the doctors thought it better for her not to come in after a few visits. My brother hadn't come to the hospital, even though we had seen each other every day for the past three months. And my father—my *father* hadn't come to see me either, and he worked within three miles of where I was. Even as I felt the hurt, and sensed my anger rising, I excused him.

My father. I began to cry as I thought of him. I'd tried so hard to get his attention. *That* was part of what I'd wanted, his loving attention. I realized that in some ways I'd spent my whole life working and searching for my father's love—*and he'd never even known it.*

My mind drifted back to my childhood.

PART TWO

GROWING UP

2. "Please Love Me, Daddy"

When I first started thinking back down the years, I felt a great resistance. My childhood was like a musty, locked room in the basement I didn't want to go in. At first I couldn't remember anything. Then I saw myself as a pinch-faced little girl who was so helplessly wrapped up in her own needs that she didn't have many friends. Her life seemed unattractive and boring. And she always saw herself as a victim of other people's sins and mistakes. But I had to think about my childhood—even if my self-centeredness made me look unattractive—in order to understand the drama in my life which was to follow.

THE GREEN BACKYARD in Libertyville on the outskirts of Chicago was filled with soft lights and the sound of men talking and laughing. Daddy was having another party. He sold houses, or something, and he had a real way with people. I loved to watch him talk and laugh with the other men. He was so tall and handsome.

It seemed to me that we had a party almost every night, with barbequed chickens, steaks, and plenty to drink—or rather *they* did. I was supposed to stay in my room. But sometimes I would tiptoe across the hall dragging my little blanket and watch them out the window, wishing I could be a part of things.

On this particular evening I sneaked outside and climbed the knobby old apple tree when no one was looking. I can still feel the bark scratching my thigh where my nighty had hiked up. Daddy's booming voice was easy to pick out above the others! He was over by the stable gate bragging on his new colt which had been born that morning. He raised horses in the white-fenced field behind our house.

Daddy opened the gate and picked up the little colt in his arms to show his friends. Putting it down, he turned to say something to them. The wobbly baby took a few hesitant steps and suddenly disappeared into the open cistern which was being fixed! Daddy dragged the feebly struggling little thing out of the hole and discovered its legs were broken. It would have to be put to sleep.

Then Daddy started to cry, and to walk back and forth, up and down, and then in circles. He didn't seem to care that the men were watching him or hearing him cry out loud. At first his hands weren't even covering his face.

Up in the apple tree watching, I wanted to cry too. My eyes hurt. I felt a lump in my throat as my own tears ran down my cheeks. I wanted to pat the side of his face and kiss his tears away. My arms ached to hold his strong blond head. But I didn't dare climb down. I wished that he'd walk towards me, look up, and take me down in his arms. But he turned and went the other way.

Daddy had never touched me, not that I could remember anyway. And I'd never seen him hug or even touch my mother, nor her him. He only seemed to be interested in his friends and his business. So I never knew exactly how I fit in as his daughter. But I loved him desperately and followed him everywhere I could when he was at home. I longed for him to say, "Hi, Hedy!" and open his arms for me to run into, or for him to catch me up, kiss me and throw me into the air, as I'd seen daddies do in the movies. But he never had. That night after the men had gone, I sneaked back in the house and lay awake till dawn, wondering how Daddy felt inside, and if he'd cry that way about me if I got hurt.

It didn't help that Loretta, my sister, who was two years older, seemed to have everything I wanted. She was relaxed and laughed and sang a lot, and didn't seem to be afraid that anything she might do could make anyone not like her. I can still see myself watching her through the living room window from behind the drapery as she ran out to the car when Daddy came home from work.

"Hi, Daddy!" bright and cheery.

And Daddy's booming answer, "Well, who've we got here? Hello, Baby!"

But I felt sick with jealousy because I was afraid to run out for fear he wouldn't greet me. So I waited, hating Loretta for being so natural when I felt awkward and couldn't ever get my feelings out.

On Friday nights Daddy took Loretta to the wrestling matches. I only got to go with them a couple of times. And I was so afraid I'd mess up my chance that I couldn't think of anything to say, while Loretta chattered away all evening. I hated myself for being so afraid, but couldn't do anything about it.

When I was six, my little brother Sam was born. I can't remember much about Sam as a child except he was happy, too, and got into everything. Like Loretta, he seemed to fall naturally into the family.

But my attention seemed always to be on my daddy. One time I came into the living room when his friends were there drinking beer. He'd told me to leave but I was hoping he'd forget, although I knew he could be harsh and sometimes had a violent temper. He decided to teach me a lesson about being where I wasn't supposed to be. So he lined up seven glasses of buttermilk, which I hated, on the table in front of his friends and made me drink every one. But I wouldn't cry. One of Daddy's friends clapped me on the back and said, "By damn, Hedy, you're as tough as scrap iron." And from then on that was my nickname, Scrap Iron. As I ran off and got sick, I could hear them snickering. I've never tasted buttermilk since.

From then on I became even more careful about letting my love put me in a position where I might get embarrassed or hurt—by him or anybody. It never occurred to me that outwardly I might be cold and not especially easy to love.

Who was this man whose love and approval I wanted so desperately? What did I have to *do* to win his love? As it was I lived in constant fear of doing something wrong that would make him mad at me.

My mother was very different from my father. But I didn't feel any closeness to her either. She tried hard. But so much of the time she seemed to be wanting other people's approval, which made me feel pushed to be perfect so I wouldn't embarrass her. She was constantly after me to look right, dress right, speak right, often correcting my English to the point of making me forget what I was saying.

Another of her habits kept me in a constant fear of failing to measure up. For instance, once, much later when I was running for cheerleader, I came home the day before the election. Excited but very much afraid I wouldn't be elected, I was greeted with, "I've told all my friends you're going to be the new cheerleader. You are running, aren't you?" My stomach tightened into a ball. What if I weren't elected! My face was already hot with the shame I'd feel if I didn't make it. I was so grateful when I did.

But whatever her interest in how I did, Mother didn't seem to really notice me unless I made a mistake. The rest of the time she appeared to be preoccupied with her own thoughts. So most of the time I was ill at ease with her, and in fact with everybody.

I can still remember how I felt as a child when guests came to our house. I would sit stiffly, saying nothing, trying to hold my head high and look confident as their grown-up conversations droned on around me. Listening to every word that was said, I wanted a hundred times to ask someone what they meant or what they thought or felt, but I couldn't. And when we moved into the dining room for dinner, I was terrified to eat for fear I'd do the wrong thing. So I made up my mind not to make any mistakes and to be the perfect, polite daughter.

But no matter how much I achieved, I never felt worthy. And behind my confident face I ached with loneliness, and the fear of being found out. What if people learned how hard I had to work to hide my faults and mistakes and to get my parents to notice me.

Although there were happy days when people came to our house with children my age, I spent much of the time alone. Loretta and I didn't have too much in common, and she didn't want to play much with me. I was too little. I was so private about my life for fear my inner thoughts would be wrong and unacceptable that my family often forgot about me—just when I was crying out for their attention.

One day when I was very small, everyone left and evidently forgot about me all day. It was raining outside and dreary. I went to the dining room table and dragged each chair into the living room. Since I was so tiny it took a long time. I went to each room in the house and pulled every chair I could move to the living room and lined them up in rows. Then I put on a costume of my mother's clothes and sang and danced for two hours in front of the empty chairs.

I remember another afternoon sitting out on the pasture fence alone, looking at the sky. The hot summer breeze fanned my tight skin, and my face felt hard as I made a decision. I said silently to my mother and daddy, "I'll get your attention all right! I'll do so well you'll have to notice me! I'll be a superstar *no matter what it takes or how long!* I'll show you!" I'd pay whatever price it took! And they'd be sorry they never loved me or noticed me. I felt the hot tears rising behind my eyes. But I couldn't afford to let them, or my true feelings, *ever* reach my face. The world might find out that I wasn't a superstar at all but only a little girl.

Since there was no way I could really "star" for my father, I became a tomboy, dressed in blue jeans when I could, and tried to do all the things that I thought he would have done when he was a little boy. Sometimes I wandered in the woods and through the neighborhood alone for hours. Other times I walked along the railroad tracks balancing like a circus performer on one silver rail in the summer sunshine. With my broomhandle balancing stick I could imagine thousands of cheering, adoring fans below. I would glance away from the rail and give them a grim smile—letting them know that I loved them and appreciated their love, but that risking my life for their entertainment was serious business.

Since I couldn't relate to my family very well, I turned to the neighbors to see what the rest of the world was like. There was my best friend Betty, whose mother sewed for her constantly. I liked Betty and wanted to be a real friend, but I didn't know how to go about it. When I went over to her house, she'd bring out the new dress her mother had made for her that week. I thought they were the most beautiful clothes I'd ever seen. And she always preened in them, like a prissy turkey gobbler. I almost hurt physically with jealousy and was speechless. Finally one day I blurted out: "Betty, I don't care *what* you wear!" and ran out. But I cared, oh how I cared! My love of beautiful clothes may have come from that experience of seeing Betty's dresses as a sign of her mother's love.

Another thing about Betty bothered me, that she always looked so feminine. I needed to be a tomboy to be like my father. But even at that early age, something else was stirring inside me. I was beginning to realize that I was very "girl," a lot more so than Betty, and I felt that it didn't have anything to do with our clothes. But it was very confusing at the time. Betty seemed to have everything I wanted but didn't have. Inside, behind my cool little poker face, I was miserable and helpless and wanted to punish all the Bettys in the world.

I began to get back at Betty by playing mean little tricks on her. Once I told her that my daddy's chicken medicine pellets were candy, and she was sick for several days. Another time I went too far. Betty and I were out playing in the field next door. I had brought along a small box of matches. Betty was very apprehensive: "Hedy, you'd better not play with matches in the field! You'll start a fire!"

Because she was afraid, I started striking matches and lighting the dry weeds. We'd watch them burn, but I'd stamp the fire out before the flames had a chance to spread. I was delighting in Betty's fearful fascination. After a little while I became bolder, just as a breeze came up. And this time I lighted a fire I couldn't put out! Betty started screaming, "I *told* you so! I *told* you so!" and ran home. I was really scared and took off for the creek where I hid in my secret place in the bushes.

By the time the fire department arrived, the whole field had burned black. I sneaked back to watch, and Betty's older brother came over and asked me what had happened. I shook my head and lied calmly, "I don't know why Betty did that. I told her not to play with matches in the field."

Betty was grounded for two weeks. And that night I went to the movies. But instead of enjoying it, I felt miserable and guilty, imagining Betty sitting at home by herself. I wanted to find a telephone and call her and send her a present or at least a note and tell her I was sorry. After the movie, I walked back and forth in front of her house wanting to go in and tell her I loved her. But I couldn't. I was too proud and too ashamed. Above all, I couldn't admit I was wrong, that I'd made a mistake.

Later that night I crept out of the house and slept in the back seat of the car, feeling very lonely, hoping my folks would miss me, get worried and come find me, but at the same time fearing that they wouldn't even know I was gone. And they didn't. I never did apologize to Betty. I couldn't. As horrible as it sounds, my fear of being rejected meant more than Betty's friendship. And she was almost the only friend I had! I moped around my private haunts in the neighborhood, aching with loneliness. She never mentioned the fire to me and I never knew what to say. So we pretended it had never happened.

This was the first time I remember getting away with something bad and feeling guilty. From then on I had a lot of secrets and bad feelings for things I did that no one knew about. I didn't know how to get rid of these feelings, or if anyone else had them. This made me even more secretive as I learned to live with guilt along with the fear of rejection and failure. And my fear of being found out caused me to bend and stretch the truth sometimes to protect the fragile little girl behind the confident Scrap Iron toughness.

I didn't know that I was gathering myself together to pay the price to win in the big world. But I had no tools to carve out a place for me out there. How could a skinny pigtailed little girl called Scrap Iron make it on her own in a grown-up's world?

3. A Ticket to the Stars

I SUPPOSE MOST HOUSES with children have a box of colored pencils and maybe a set of watercolors. But for me these things had special meaning. I can't remember when I didn't draw or paint. Once as a little girl about five, I came into the room where Mother was playing bridge to show her a picture I'd drawn. She looked at it and said, "That's nice, Hedy." I showed it to each of the other ladies and all of them said, "That's nice." That settled it. I drove everyone crazy from then on showing them my pictures.

And I could evidently draw well. By the time I was six or seven I realized I had found a way to get attention. I painted on everything I could find—rocks, wood scraps, the garage, the bathroom wall, behind my curtains, under my shoes and down my arms. I always had a paint brush or a pencil in my hand.

And I drew faces, faces everywhere. I wanted to fill the world with people I knew better than anyone else did. So I drew them from my imagination. Many were sad little-girl faces looking out of shadowy windows. But all of the faces looked gentle and loving. Because inside, with my loneliness, was a heart which was brimming with love for everyone and everything. I saw beauty in the ugliest people and could sit for hours hugging my knees and watching a field of spring flowers. I wanted to reach out and love all the people who hurt. But of course I didn't dare—they might not want me to. So I pretended I didn't care.

I had several other subjects I drew and painted again and again. I was fascinated with Indian teepees where whole families lived together with no walls between them. Also, for some reason which certainly didn't fit my early training, I kept painting monks, priests, missions and nuns.

When I drew or painted I seemed to disappear into my own private world. There I could create what I wanted. I could make life into the beautiful place I dreamed it could be, should be, *had* to be! I could paint castles and ladies. I could paint princes coming to rescue princesses and watch my dreams becoming real. The people I painted looked out at me with loving eyes, with understanding. I was always fascinated by people's eyes and learned very early to read much about their thoughts by watching their glances.

At last I could at least make *something* happen the way I wanted it to. Art was the first thing I had ever had that was really mine and didn't depend on anyone or anything outside me. No one knew the hours I spent alone drawing, redrawing, painting, looking at the way things were made, the way people smiled or frowned. I was fascinated by the shape and movement of people's bodies, their muscles, their hair, their breasts, the way they moved, flowing or tense. All these things became a part of me, a way to read people's real meanings and motives through their bodies and faces.

Painting became a familiar world of my own into which I could go for peace and to dream dreams. I imagined that someday I might be a fine artist. It was an exciting secret goal no one else knew about. Maybe life wasn't going to be so bad. The world seemed new and I began to think I was going to be O.K., even though I didn't feel loved. At least I had something.

Then out of nowhere, a lightning bolt crashed into my life, destroying everything that had been security in our home. Mother walked in one afternoon. I was seven years old and had just gotten home from school.

"Hedy," she said evenly, "Your father and I got a divorce today."

And I hadn't even known it was a possibility! Though we weren't affectionate, I thought all families were like ours.

My whole world changed.

A new neighborhood, a small home on Illinois Road in Lake Forest, new school, new teachers, and no Daddy in the house. For some reason he had stayed in Libertyville.

I felt even more "different" from other children. And more unworthy than ever because I was the only child I knew of in my class from a divorced family. We were living in one of the smallest homes in Lake Forest. And although we weren't starving, I knew that we must have less than anyone else because of all their big houses and cars and nice clothes. The only way the other children would like me, I decided, was for me to try to be the very best. So without anyone knowing it, I began to learn how to be the top one at everything I wanted to do.

In the third grade I got double promoted. By the fifth grade, when I had homework, I went home every afternoon and started doing it. At 10:00 P.M. I would start rewriting it, so that my handwriting would be perfect. Mother worked hard for a living, leaving before I got up and coming home tired in the evenings. Sam was with relatives part of that time and later was sent to live at the Kiwanis Club boys' home. Loretta was staying with Daddy. So I was pretty much on my own. I drew or painted pictures with all my reports and found that my art work made up for anything I might not have included. By concentrating on doing well in school I had a way not to think about the friends and things I didn't have that other kids did.

I was a fanatic about taking care of myself and the clothes I had. After putting the finishing touches on my homework, I washed the things I planned to wear the next day, shampooed my hair, straightened my room and went to bed. In the morning I got up early and ironed my clothes. Except for my own things, I wasn't too helpful around the house. Some mornings I did try to straighten up, often putting the dirty dishes in the oven and the dirty clothes in the bathtub behind the shower curtain, in case I found a new

friend to bring home from school. Then I'd walk to school, to try
to be the very best, the cleanest, the neatest, the smartest and the
prettiest in my class, and later in the whole school.

All this sounds like I was a real grim Cinderella. But that isn't
true. *No one* ever knew I was doing all this work, even my mother.
As a matter of fact, I didn't want *anyone* to know how hard I was
working to try to look good. And in grade school I was a real tomboy. I could outrun any boy in the school and played baseball,
basketball, soccer, everything. Though I didn't have any close
friends, I learned to remember people's names and get along with
other girls. I tried to be friendly with everyone.

But the class I really enjoyed was art. The teacher, Mrs. Jones,
liked me and believed in my work. She was the only one in
school I felt I didn't have to prove anything to, and I really worked
hard to please her. Having her kind eyes focused on me and seeing
her nod approval was like I could imagine a smile from God might
be.

In my class I got to illustrate most of the books which the other
kids reviewed, and later I painted the stage sets for the dramas. Mrs.
Jones entered my work in a contest at the Art Institute when I was
nine. When I won the contest I was thrilled and amazed. If it
hadn't been for art, I don't know what I'd have done, because I
still didn't have any close friends.

For a while after the divorce my father would come to get
Loretta and me occasionally for a day or two. The first weekend we spent with him was strange. He took us to a hotel in downtown Chicago. After checking in and going to the room, we sat
down on the beds and looked at each other, two little girls and a
daddy. Neither of us had any idea what had happened between
him and Mother or whether or not we had anything to do with the
divorce. We didn't know what to say, and the silence got very long.
I peeked at Daddy's face, and suddenly it occurred to me for the
first time that maybe he didn't know what to say or to do with us
either.

At last Loretta said, "I'm hungry. Can we go get something to
eat?"

Daddy brightened up and said, "Sure, let's go!"

He took us to an Italian restaurant. I remember not knowing what to order when the menu came and turning to him, my eyebrows raised in a question. He said, "Hedy, you need some pizza and a short beer." And that's what he ordered for me. The few other times we went to that restaurant, I always asked if I could have "pizza and a short beer." And he would let me.

But after a few months, Daddy drifted away from us, and we almost never saw him.

When I was about ten I started to take art lessons on Saturdays. I'd take the train to the Northwestern Station and then a bus the rest of the way to an art school near Lincoln Park. I felt very important getting to go by myself. After class I'd wander through the Lincoln Park Zoo and amusement park. Sometimes I'd sketch the live animals and the strange painted ones on the merry-go-round. I was a secret watcher and imagined this was my own park and zoo. Often I'd sit at the edge of Belmont Harbor and watch the birds as the evening sun mirrored the boats on the dark surface of the water. Before the sun went down I'd walk back to the bus line, my mind filled with pictures of what I'd seen.

Besides Lincoln Park and the secret invisible paths I walked through in our part of Lake Forest, I had another private "place" where I found some comfort with a kind of mystery which fascinated me. I spent many hours in my room alone. Behind the closed doors, so no one could make fun of me, I'd read the Bible and think about God, and even try to talk to Him. It was very mysterious. I looked all around the ceiling and wondered if He heard me.

Once in a while a girlfriend would ask me to spend the night and I'd get to go to church with her family on Sunday morning. And sometimes my grandmother took me. She was the one who'd given me the Bible. But although we weren't churchgoers, I was taught to be moral and honest for very practical reasons. Mother said "All nice girls tell the truth." If you didn't tell the truth, "What in the world will people think of you?" For a long time I thought that people would just know and never like you.

So I tried to be first in everything—and very honest too. I worked so hard during those years that I didn't fail very often. But since *total* honesty and success were expected, I had to hide anything which wasn't successful or honest, even from myself sometimes. All this secret but frantic trying didn't make for much of a life inside. I was always anxious and full of questions, but didn't know where to go with them.

When I look back on my childhood, I see a skinny little girl with a crooked smile looking nervously out at the world! I knew there must be someone who could understand me. There had to be help somewhere.

4. Out of a Cocoon

Trying to recall that part of my life having to do with boys and men was especially difficult. At first I blocked it all out and couldn't remember anything. Then I gradually saw again the bewildering and painful things which happened to me after the striking change in my appearance. As I finally remembered the events of those years, I wanted with everything in me to go back and shake myself into awareness. But of course that was impossible, so I could only continue to be amazed at my own naïveté.

A BIG CHANGE came over my life in the sixth grade. At first I couldn't understand what was happening. As I walked down the hall the first day that fall, several boys who had never spoken to me before said "Hi." I thought they had gotten more friendly over the summer.

But soon I found out that a lot of them were noticing me. When I'd smile at one of them, his face would get red or change somehow, and he would turn his eyes away. Some of the boys seemed unable to talk to me and acted nervous or bashful. I could tell that when they tried to talk, *they* felt something. And when they looked at me with that dreamy stare, *I* felt something which seemed to come from them through their eyes. It was warm, and it was directed toward *me*. And although I didn't know exactly what it was, I liked it.

After that first day at school I ran home and looked in the mirror. It was as if I were seeing myself for the first time. I'd always seen only my faults before. Now I saw that my lashes were really long! And my shoulder-length blonde hair had a soft glow I hadn't noticed before. My small nose seemed more normal-looking somehow. But my mouth had changed the most. It looked relaxed, the crooked self-conscious smile was gone, and my lips were more soft and full.

Backing away from the mirror, I squinted my eyes and opened them. I was very developed physically. It was as if I had been touched by a fairy godmother's wand that let me see something I simply couldn't believe. Was it possible that I was pretty? I felt like a butterfly in the spring just coming out of its cocoon.

In the days and weeks to come I was full of good feelings about life. Now the whole world had a sparkle to it. Hope and excitement filled the hours at school.

Boys! Here was an audience I'd never dreamed of. "And there must be a million of them!" I thought. Their paying attention to me was filling the emptiness which had been there since I could remember. Right away I knew this was not the same as the warmth I wanted from my mother and daddy. That was important, but this was exciting and mysterious. There was something very big and important about this thing with boys that had nothing to do with my parents. But it had something to do with closeness and not being so lonely.

I didn't really know any of the other kids, and because we never talked about personal things at home, I knew almost nothing about growing up or the way other young people felt about life or each other. So my new popularity was almost a dream come true, my dream of being discovered a princess in one of the fairytales I loved to think about.

I wasn't about to let anyone inside the little shell I had built, but the boys' feelings about me warmed the shell and made me feel much more like somebody, instead of nobody, though I was still

very lonely inside. And the more attention I got the more afraid I
was to let people come too close; then they'd know that I really
wasn't nearly as sharp inside as they seemed to think I was because
of my looks. If anyone saw the real me, the one who felt so unlovable and scared, I was sure I'd be ruined.

So I kept myself even more private and apart from other girls
than I had. Because of this I was never in on those top-secret girl-
talks in which I could have gotten the "truth behind the mystery"
of boys which sixth grade girls discuss so endlessly. If I'd had few
girl friends before, this new popularity with boys didn't help any.
And I never knew for sure what the girls really thought of me.

When I was twelve, something happened which looked like it
might take away my loneliness and give me a place. I transferred
to a different junior high school.

At first this school was a frightening new world. The other kids
seemed different, more cliquish, more careful about accepting
strangers. It was an exclusive private school to which my mother
got me a scholarship because of my grades. My feelings of not
fitting in ballooned. Where I'd come from, the girls had worn
sweaters and skirts. But in this new school they wore long sleeved
white blouses, buttoned all the way up and tied with a scarf underneath the collar. It didn't take long to find out my sweaters were
very wrong, and the other girls seemed to think I wore them because of my figure. They smiled and started saying, "Here comes
sweater girl." I could feel my face turning red. And to my mortification the nickname stuck. I changed my wardrobe as soon as I
could.

Many of the girls had grown up together. They knew each
other's brothers, sisters, parents, where they lived. I knew none of
these things about them and wasn't about to tell anyone about my
family. They seemed and looked younger than I did, which just
made me feel more different.

To try and find my place in this world, I became friendly, tried
to look calm and secure, and worked night and day at winning them
all. I spoke to each person I passed in the hall, feeling real warmth
and wanting to reach out to them.

Within a few months my hard work began to pay off. I was elected a cheerleader. At last I had a place, it seemed. Inside, though, I still didn't feel I belonged.

But the next year Bobby changed all that. He was the captain of the football team, and I'd noticed him the first day there. Bobby was the best-looking boy in school and, I thought, more mature. His voice sounded an octave lower to me, and his shoulders were broader.

Bobby had gone with Sylvia since they were little kids. Everyone said Sylvia was the prettiest girl in school, and her daddy was very rich. She wore very expensive clothes and seemed always to be cool and sure of herself. I heard they had broken up just before I came.

The minute I saw Bobby, something happened to me which had never happened before. My heart began to beat faster, my face got very flushed when I was close to him, and I felt sweet warm feelings all over. I was in love! But how was I going to get him to love me?

I had made sure he noticed me, which wasn't too hard, since I was the new girl in school. Now I would just happen to be around corners in the hall or outside classrooms I knew he would pass at certain times. At first Bobby was distant and I'd go home miserable, wondering how in the world I could get his attention, since I was too shy and too afraid of his rejection to do anything obvious.

Finally Bobby began to say "Hi." Then we'd walk between classes. And eventually he fell for me as hard as I had for him. We began going steady, and suddenly I was "in." I wore his I.D. bracelet on my arm and his silver football around my neck. I stood up straighter and girls became more friendly. I felt like I had more energy and courage in everything I did. It was like heaven to me.

Going steady in Lake Forest, at that age, consisted of having at least one long telephone call from Bobby on week nights. We'd talk about school work, teachers, other kids, the TV programs, the latest hit records. On weekends, steadies went to their girlfriends' houses to listen to records, watch television, drink cokes, and smooch. And on special occasions we'd walk down and get a hamburger and a malt, holding hands or maybe even with our arms around each other's waists. His mother or father would drive us to school dances, where we danced together the whole evening.

One night Bobby turned to me. "Hedy, I'm really proud of you. You're not only the prettiest and most stacked girl in school but you've got more friends than anyone else." I was so surprised by the last part of what he'd said that I almost couldn't hear the first. More friends than anyone? How could he think that, when the truth was, I wasn't sure I had any, though I knew all their names? But I wasn't close to any of them. Of course, I didn't tell that to Bobby.

Going steady with the most wanted boy in school let my feelings of being on the outside subside, though I was always aware of Sylvia in the background and was very jealous when she stopped Bobby to speak to him. I watched her like a hawk to see what she had and did, but never mentioned her name to Bobby or anyone else. I not only loved Bobby but I was grateful to him. He backed me up in anything I tried to do and really cared.

We'd been going steady for several months when I noticed a change taking place between us. He skipped calling a couple of nights, and then with no explanation quit calling at all. Every night I waited. I got an upset stomach and was cross and even more secretive at home. I began to cry myself to sleep wondering what I'd done and why he wasn't calling. Then he quit meeting me after classes.

For a couple of nights I imagined his coming to my window and asking me to run off and get married. I was really lovesick. Then I became embarrassed. "What will I do," I thought, "if I see him? Should I let him know I'm hurt or hide my feelings? What if I see him with Sylvia? I'm wearing his bracelet." I wanted to hide, to disappear, to die. I got indigestion and couldn't swallow very well. All I did was think about Bobby and worry all the time, trying to find some way to make things right again. Of course I didn't want anyone else to know my feelings or that Bobby wasn't seeing me any more. All of this took place within one school week.

The following Monday I walked out of the side door of the

school building and there was Bobby, leaning against a tree. He saw me coming through the door and didn't move. I walked over to him and said, "Hello, Bobby."

He looked me directly in the eye completely without emotion and said, "Hello, Hedy, what can I do for you?"

I felt the hot humiliating flush coming into my face. My stomach tightened as if I were going to throw up, and I couldn't stop the tears from coming to my eyes. I looked down, wanting the ground to open and take me in. But there was no place to hide. Bobby just stood there chewing on a piece of grass.

Finally I looked up and said through my tears, "Bobby . . . please . . . please tell me you love me." He had been looking directly at me with cold indifference. Now he looked at the ground. Very slowly and methodically he repeated the words, "Hedy . . . I . . . love . . . you." A complete monotone. If he had stabbed me it would have been easier. I just couldn't believe it.

In the next few weeks I became very depressed. I felt unattractive again and ashamed. I became superconscious of my inadequacies and what I did not have that other kids like Sylvia did. Since I didn't have enough clothes that looked nice for every day, I started simply staying away from school, sometimes one or two days a week. But eventually I got back to going regularly.

It was during that same year that something else very important happened. I had worked especially hard on a painting about the poem "Annabelle Lee" and entered it in a contest at the Art Institute. The painting won first prize, and someone offered to buy it! I could hardly believe it when I held the money in my hand. I looked at the fountain in Grant Park near the Institute that evening and saw my art emerging from the waters like a genie filling the sky, a genie who could almost magically bring me some of the things no one could give me.

At that moment art took on a whole new importance in my life. That glimpse of hope with the real evidence of the check for the painting gave me a slight surge of confidence. Whether people liked me wouldn't kill me now. I could paint and show them the beauty and love I had on the inside which I could pour out onto my canvases. I might even make a living at painting, but more important, I'd be safe from their hurts and rejection. I felt the tears of relief rising behind my eyes. I had a way out, and secretly I began to work harder with new hope.

But the following year my plans to be a great artist got sidetracked. At thirteen I was becoming increasingly aware of new feelings and of the fact that my body had really changed and developed. No one in my family seemed to have noticed.

I longed to ask my mother what it meant to be a woman, how babies were really born, and what did a girl do about the sexual feelings which went along with growing up? But I wouldn't dare. The only thing I'd ever asked about was the term "French kissing" I'd overheard at school. My mother was horrified, "Hedy! Things like French kissing are only for degenerates and perverts!"

Mother had never given me the faintest hint as to what was involved in any kind of relationship between women and men. And I'd missed most of the girl-talk, so my views about life were unbelievably idealistic even for a thirteen-year-old. But I didn't really look thirteen. I had the body of a nineteen-year-old and had picked up, by watching older girls, a "mysterious" and quiet way of looking at men and boys in the halls which made them pay immediate attention to me. I didn't know what kind of signals I might be sending out, since I didn't know what the world of men and women was like. But I knew that I could have a certain influence even over adults that was very real.

Except for going steady with Bobby, I'd had no close relationships with men or even boys. Bobby had been fun and exciting. But these new feelings were of a totally different order. And I had no way to find out what the new responses to me involved.

5. A Thirteen-Year-Old in Fantasyland

I SAID THAT no one in my family was aware that I was growing up, but that wasn't quite true. When I was thirteen I came home from school one day, ran up the steps into the living room and flopped on the couch. Then I noticed my mother looking at me thoughtfully.

"Stand up, Hedy." I did.

"Turn around."

She looked me over closely, then turned and stared out the window for a long, silent moment.

A day or two later she took me to a modeling school, telling them I was eighteen.

The glamour and excitement were wonderful to me. I was grateful that the school had a good program for new models, and I could get assignments to work my way through. From the first day I began to watch and learn from everyone who was good. Being so young and frightened and needing to succeed so much, I was an ideal student.

I had never realized how much was involved in just walking. I studied every gesture, every move. From the beginning I knew that some of the girls whose movements were perfect had something missing that I couldn't put my finger on. Others who went

49

through the same motions had a certain quality about their modeling which was alive, like electricity. Behind the precise movements was an inner flowing which couldn't really be seen, yet which was a part of every move, a sort of natural gracefulness. These were the models who were in constant demand.

For a while I was terrified that I wouldn't be any good. Then one day, one of my toughest instructors said in an offhand manner, "Hedy, you're as smooth as a damned jaguar." Evidently I had that something. After several months I posed for a composite of pictures. When the pictures were developed and sent to everyone in the business, my career was launched with one of the finest modeling agencies in Chicago.

If I had been a private person with the girls at school, I totally walled myself off from these beautiful and sophisticated eighteen to twenty-four-year olds. I listened to everything they talked about without seeming to listen at all. And what I heard about the men in the life I was coming into just made me more afraid and added to the thickness of my protective shell. Only a woman brought up in a strict atmosphere who can remember the uncertainty of being thirteen and totally inexperienced can imagine the panic I felt in trying to pass myself off as a worldly wise woman in the amoral fantasyland of the modeling world.

As I began to go out on assignments, I felt even more alone and frightened. There were a few fine people who helped and encouraged me and recommended me for the better assignments. But the protection of the accepted Lake Forest social rules was gone. Everything seemed raw and direct. Wide-eyed cameramen and clothing salesmen stared openly and made suggestive remarks. Several tried to get me to pose privately in the nude.

When suggestions like this—or for that matter, anything I didn't know how to handle—came up, I put on a very sophisticated look which seemed to say, "Yes, of course I understand what you're saying, but I'm a lady and live in another world from all this." I projected the cool prep school, social "in" look. But I also learned to kid in a knowing way, to become a part of what was happening wherever I was, while always keeping an inner distance. Before long, I felt that I was accepted by those I'd been around as a real professional—slightly modest but a lady. Looking back, I can see that with my need for attention and love, my great fear of discovery probably saved me from the immoral whirlpool so many young models are drawn into.

But life was exciting. Though it was hard for a thirteen-year-old, it was like being an actress in a glittering fairy story. One day I was in a bathing suit walking before the judges in a beauty contest. The next day might take me through the complicated and intense working out of a TV commercial. Another day I'd be modeling clothes. Designers often had cocktail parties in connection with their fashion shows. Never having had a drink, I didn't know what to order. But I accepted what was offered to me or asked for a drink I heard someone else order.

I soon discovered that having a drink calmed my anxiety and made me feel more confident. So when I went to interview for a job and a man would ask if I would like anything (meaning coffee, I later realized), I began to ask for a cocktail. I always subtly tried to show off my best features. And since I was only thinking about me and how I looked, I didn't realize that by asking for a drink I was practically sending a written invitation to men.

As time passed, I realized more and more how little I knew about men, how to relate to them and how they felt. Though I didn't understand the strength of the desire I saw in their eyes, I began to feel that I was walking a very dangerous line. But I thought it was just the way I looked and didn't see anything I could do about that. It didn't occur to me that I might be doing specific things to cause some of their responses.

As it was, when things got too scary, I'd claim I had a sick mother and was late, and I'd run for home. But finally the inevitable happened. I was called to an assignment for a prominent photographer whom I had noticed watching me on other jobs. He had a studio building a few miles outside the city. When I arrived I saw that I was the only model.

"Hi, Hedy, here are the clothes. Change in there." The photographer waved his huge cigar toward a dressing room door.

I took the clothes and walked into a nicely decorated room, with a good dressing table and mirror setup and a long couch against one wall.

I had just taken off my dress and bra when the door opened without warning, and the photographer came in. He was overweight, balding, fiftyish. I noticed his eyes seemed larger than usual behind his thick glasses. His coat was open and his tie was pulled down from his open white shirt collar. He looked sweaty.

Laying his cigar on the dressing table by the door he moved toward me carefully, like a huge pin-striped cat. Standing in my panties and garter belt with my dress clutched in front of me, all I could do was back up, my heart pounding. As the grotesque figure came closer to me clenching and unclenching his hands, I felt perspiration on my temples and looked frantically for a way out. But he was staying between the door and me in the narrow space. A scream rose in my throat, but I knew we were alone in the building. Then I felt the wall against my back. I was trapped!

Suddenly he stepped forward and grabbed me by the upper arm, pulling me next to his body. His sweaty hands went all over me. His cigar smell and body odor made me sick. His breathing was heavy and he seemed desperate, almost in pain. I'd never seen anyone like this. I didn't know what to do except struggle with every ounce of energy I had. But he was much stronger and held me tightly, moving me toward the couch. He threw us both down on it, and kept pawing at me.

I was terrified, but finally, as he struggled with his pants, I doubled my legs in a sudden movement and shoved him off on the floor with my feet.

We were both exhausted. He got up on his knees and looked at me almost surprised but very apologetically:

"Hedy, I'm sorry. I thought . . . you were so beautiful I just didn't realize . . . what I was doing."

Was everyone in the world crazy? I couldn't get the question out of my head on the way home. I'd almost been raped! If I had been, I'd never have been able to face myself again. Why did men have to be that way? How could I find out about living in a world of people I couldn't trust or even talk with about anything important? "Oh, dear God," I thought, "if I only had someone to turn to who could explain to me what's happening."

But there wasn't anyone. I certainly couldn't go to any of my high school friends. I would have been mortified if any of them ever knew I drank in my adult-world-after-hours career. They had no notion that the quiet little Hedy Franklin, who painted pictures of little girls, had to fight off men older than their fathers at night in order to earn some money and to help some with the family expenses. And I couldn't go to anyone in the modeling world. They'd know I was only an inexperienced kid.

I had kept my two worlds completely separate, but I knew it wouldn't work much longer. Sooner or later something had to give. On an assignment I might meet my English teacher coming out of a night club. Or my picture would be seen in an ad.

And how much longer could I play the adult game? Someone in my work would discover that I was so dumb I didn't know anything about men and sex—and that had almost happened today. I shuddered as I thought that maybe the next time someone would not be put off and *would* rape me. I had always dreamed of how romantic it would be to have a boy want me so much he had to have me. But it wasn't romantic at all to be attacked by an old man and possibly ruined for life—it was stark and ugly.

For the next few weeks I was extremely skittish about working with a man alone. But I soon regained my poise and confidence. Then a short time later, it happened.

Several of us were assigned to do the photography for an article on night life in Chicago. This particular evening we were in a very sophisticated night club and were to be part of the crowd during the interviewing of celebrities. A friend introduced me to a nice-looking man, about thirty, from Miami. The long scar across his cheek somehow added to rather than detracted from his good looks. As I was about to catch a cab home he offered to drop me off. I should have been wary, but I was a veteran model of two years.

I was going to spend the night with Loretta, who now had an

apartment in Wilmette, and gave him directions to her address. About a block before we reached her place, he pulled his Cadillac to the curb. It was a dark street with lots of trees. We'd been having a quiet drive and I was very relaxed. I turned and raised my eyebrows in a question, suspecting he was going to kiss me goodnight, which was perfectly all right with me. Sophisticated people always did that.

But as soon as I saw his eyes in the light of a lone passing car, I felt something completely different. The fears of the last two years throbbed in my head. Chill bumps ran down my arms and settled in my stomach. This man was unlike any I'd met. He was cold steel and meant business. Deliberately, he began to take off his coat. When I slipped my hand toward the door handle, he took a gun from his inner coat pocket and showed it to me very calmly. His meaning was absolutely clear.

He told me in specific detail what we were going to do. I heard the words at a distance, unable to move. I shook my head. My throat tightened and I didn't think I could speak. I heard myself almost gasp, "But I've never . . ." And then what happened was like a nightmare, one that I'd been dreaming for a year. The pain was sharp, but the fear and shame blotted it out. The thing I'd been terrified of had finally happened.

When it was over, I was crying. He pushed me toward the door. Somehow I got out and stumbled over the curb onto the dark sidewalk under the trees.

I stood in the shadows sobbing, trembling all over, my face in my hands in total shame as the car drove away. I thought I might be sick. Then somehow I made my way to my sister's apartment building and sat down on the front steps. Under the porchlight I noticed there was blood on my dress. I wanted to run in, wake Loretta and call the police. But then I realized my father would know. And I couldn't bear the shame of having him find out.

I began to cry again. How would I ever live, look people in the eye, trust anyone? Would people know by looking at me what had happened? I was ruined. That's all I could say over and over again through my tears, "You're *ruined*, Hedy, you're *ruined!*" I shook my head, hoping I'd wake up or that my mind was playing tricks on me and I'd discover it wasn't true.

Looking up at the stars, I wished there were someone, somewhere, to go to who would hold me and wipe my tears away and tell me I was still a worthwhile, decent girl. But I realized that there never would be such a person to forgive me and love me— because I could never dare tell *anyone* what had happened on this night. That was certain. And all the love and gentleness I'd been hiding away would never be able to be lavished on anyone. I saw a life of punishment, of solitary confinement inside myself for the crime of being—pretending to be—sophisticated in order to be the prettiest and the most successful. I cried out silently, "Why, oh dear God, why can't I be like other people and be loved and understood?"

I knew there must be some reason for going on with my life, but what could I find now? I knew no nice man would ever marry me after this. Maybe if my father never found out, I could at least spend my life working hard and finally make him proud of my success. But right then I only wanted some man to stand up for me, to fight for me. Life seemed so hopeless and confusing.

It was almost dawn when I faced the fact consciously that I didn't know what I was doing in this business of being beautiful and even less about getting attention and building relationships with men. I wanted desperately to go away and hide and never come back. But having no one to go to I could only go inside the darkness of myself, down the spiral staircase into the torture chamber of my own soul with my horrible secret. I locked up the budding young woman I'd become, or laid her to sleep somewhere deep down inside me. She was to lie curled there for a long time. And I closed the door on my secret—I thought—forever.

As I went inside my sister's house it was almost daybreak and my tears were dry. I realized that at fifteen I really wasn't a woman at all. But now I wasn't a little girl either. So where did I go? I had no place to go. But somehow I had to find a way to leave Chicago and Lake Forest.

6. World, Please Say I'm O.K.

RUNNING! I'D BEEN running so hard I was out of breath and my legs ached to stop. But I couldn't let "them" catch me. Part of me knew I was having a nightmare, but I was still afraid. Suddenly I came to a wall. It stretched to the horizons in both directions. What could I do? Nothing. I couldn't go on. But something said to me, "Go *through* the wall, Hedy!" I shouted, "I *can't* go on! Can't you *see?*" But since "they" were closing in, I finally shook my head and, feeling very foolish, stepped into the wall. And, miracle of miracles, I walked through it and was on the other side!

Then I was wide awake, perspiring all over.

As I lay in bed, I couldn't remember who was chasing me, but I realized I *could* go on with life even if it appeared impossible. I had to step into the next day, as impossible as it seemed to do.

In the weeks that followed the rape, I had to fight hard to hide the awful depression that draped my life like a cold wet shirt.

Fortunately, about that time my career began to sprout wings. Doors opened I hadn't expected. There were many calls for work: magazine covers came out with my picture on them, I posed for all kinds of advertisements, television commercials and series— there were even honors just for having my picture in the paper or being selected for a highly publicized assignment.

I had been studying for three years at the North Shore Little Theater two evenings a week to become an actress and learn how to use my voice. A TV director had told me that I needed to lower my voice to make it better for audio work. I loved acting and began to hope I could move into it professionally some day.

And I loved the glamour of my work. Through beauty contests, I was selected the "Sweetheart" of several organizations, like Miss Transworld Airways and Miss Transcon Van Lines. There were big receptions, national television interviews and shaking hands with hundreds and hundreds of people. From executives to the truck drivers, they all seemed to see me as the sweet innocent girl I wanted to be.

I was very grateful that they evidently liked me. It felt good to be elected and accepted by these crowds of men—something like meeting hundreds of fathers and brothers. Some were shy and some blushed. Most of the executives were courteous and treated me like a princess in white. It was glorious. But when I went home after one of these nights, I had the haunting suspicion, though I couldn't have put it into words, that all this was not really life either. These men loved what I seemed to represent: youth, beauty, sparkle. But inside I felt strangely tired and discouraged—tired and old.

One night as I thought back over my professional life, I wondered about my father. Did he know I was succeeding? Had he read or heard about me? I didn't know. But as I was dropping off to sleep I heard a voice echoing up from the basement of my mind, an aching, tearful voice of a lonely child saying, "Please Daddy, please love me!"

7. Some Other Kids at Last, and a New Career

"IsN'T THERE ANY *fun* in life?" It was a seemingly casual question I threw over my shoulder on the way out of the house going to the Little Theater. My mother looked surprised.

"What do you mean fun, Hedy? You ought to be ashamed. Anyone else your age would give anything to be where you are."

"Never mind, Mother, it was just a thought." As I walked down the front walk, I knew exactly what I'd meant. Would I ever find anyone my own age with my own teenage interests to relate to? The men I knew were fifteen to twenty years older, and the women at least five.

When I got to the Little Theater class that night, everyone was excited and chattering about something. After things quieted down, the director began to tell us that a rock and roll movie was going to be made in Chicago. Atlantic Studios was sending a producer and directors to interview young actresses for parts in the movie. As I sat on the floor with the others, hugging my knees, I was certain that announcement was going to change my life.

And it did. I was chosen for the female lead in the movie. All that I had worked and studied for could be used in acting. For the first time I found myself working with people approximately my own age. They were attractive, bright creative kids who were interested in the same things I was. And they were fun! They evidently had found a place for themselves and, most important, they seemed to be happy in it!

During breaks in the filming, we all gathered in the back room to talk, laugh, sing songs or listen to some of the rock musicians play new stuff they were working on. I remember looking around at the other kids one day and thinking: "Hedy, this is it. These people accept you as you are." It was a kind of family of neat, ambitious kids who seemed to understand each other. For the first time I relaxed with other people and felt comfortable and a sense of really belonging, as I listened to the stories of where they'd been and what had happened to them. But I was afraid to tell them much about me. Those days seemed like a dream come true. I couldn't wait to get to work every day, however early it was.

Then one day the film was completed, "in the can" as they said. And my "family" disappeared with casual goodbyes. But the goodbyes were not casual with me at all. For those weeks I had had a home, a place for me, with acceptance and the hope of friendships. Now it had disappeared overnight like a circus, leaving me alone again. I was restless and depressed for days, unable to get back to business as usual with my modeling.

The movie came out and was very popular. Before long people began to come to Lake Forest from Hollywood to interview me regarding movie contracts. Such excitement! Maybe if I could get to Hollywood, I'd find my "family" again and live with them for the rest of my life. They wouldn't judge me for tragedies or mistakes—their pasts were riddled with them.

Then one day a man came from Atlantic Studios who had discovered several of the famous actresses of our time. The best-known blonde of the past twenty years had been his protege. Not knowing anything about his personal relationship with the actress, I was awed that this man was coming to offer a contract to me.

My mother and I were very excited when he came to our house, and I left them alone so they could talk. On that hot summer day, I must have walked for hours down the familiar shaded sidewalks of Lake Forest. I looked at the houses I was passing and took special notice of the nice ones. I pictured the smug, stuck-up people inside who didn't understand or accept me—though now that the movie had come out some of them seemed to be nicer and even proud of me. As I walked along, I said silently to these people: "Some day when I have lots of money, I'm going to have a lovely home here, too, and I'll have more fine clothes than any of you. And when I do, I'm going to help people you don't pay any attention to, who can't afford nice things. I'm going to be the best homemaker in Lake Forest. You'll all be surprised! And then you'll see that I'm a fine woman and you'll love me."

As I stopped to cross the street to the Lake Forest College campus in the late afternoon traffic, my fantasy took off. . . . I was coming back from Hollywood to Chicago—to stay! At the airport at night, with the flash bulbs going off all around me, I could see my father standing in the front row of the crowd behind the police. He was smiling and looked so proud. I could see his lips forming some words. I thought he was saying, "I love you, Hedy," but I couldn't be sure. I stepped down from the plane to run to him . . .

Hoonk!! A car swerved and barely missed me as I had unconsciously stepped off the sidewalk into the traffic on Sheridan Road.

Instead of blushing, as I ordinarily would have at doing something stupid, I laughed when the angry woman motorist shouted at me. I was going to be free from all this. Walking through the green carefully mowed campus, I didn't even smile back at the looks or greetings of the college boys. They were not in my world. They were all "normal" and wanted to date and marry "normal" girls from "normal" homes. Surely in Hollywood I could find someone like me someday to fall in love with and marry. Then I'd have a family and a real place where I could share my life and not be afraid to love.

Marry! My gosh, I realized I hadn't even thought about the idea of marriage for months and months. I had learned in the most painful way to keep men very carefully at a distance. Most of the men I worked with were still much older than I. But I had learned the adult woman game of listening to them and asking questions which got them talking about themselves and their work. Since most of them were very self-centered, this kept them (and me) on safe ground. But it also meant that when other girls my age were learning about the teenage games of courting and having mad crushes in which they shared secrets and hopes and dreams with young men, I was learning almost nothing about these things.

As I walked back up the front steps to our house, I knew I was ready to leave home and find the pot of gold at the end of the rainbow, or whatever was out there beyond the mists of my childhood dreams. I was going to find a place where I could accept myself and live. I stopped with my hand on the front doorknob. "Hollywood," I said to the front door, "here I come."

PART THREE

HOLLYWOOD

8. Hollywood — Another Ride Home?

IT WAS A BEAUTIFUL September morning, almost my sixteenth birthday, and the smell of fall was in the air. I hadn't slept at all the night before—too excited. I'd kept looking at the clock every thirty minutes to see if it was time to get up. Finally the alarm went off, and I got up to finish my last-minute packing. I'd had a hard time deciding what clothes to take. What did a "future star" wear in Hollywood? Eventually, I packed everything, deciding that if any of it wasn't right I'd throw it away and buy new things. The potential salary the producer had mentioned seemed like a fortune to me.

Oh yes, I had to make sure I had his name, address and phone number in my purse—I'd already checked twice. He was going to be the only person I'd know in California, two thousand miles from home. And since I only had my airplane ticket to Los Angeles and a little expense money, he was a very important person. Although I'd learned to take a drink and look like I was at ease in any social situation, I'd always come home to mother's house and been a little girl when no one was looking. And never having been away from home, the idea of trying to get around alone in a strange city really frightened me. I unfolded the slip of paper for the third time. Yes, I had his address.

Everything seemed to be perfect as we rode in the red dawn to O'Hare Airport. I talked and laughed excitedly until I was at the point of going through the gate to the planes and turned to say goodbye to Mother. We had never been affectionate, but I felt more warmth and gratitude for her at that moment than I ever had. She was a good woman and had worked hard to get me here. The producer had been determined and she had evidently done well for me. In the days since his visit she'd seemed very happy.

But now as I looked at her with affection, all my sophistication gone for the moment, I didn't know what to say.

"Goodbye, Mother . . . and thank you."

She looked uncomfortable. She'd never been at ease with emotional moments, so I didn't think anything about her uneasiness.

"Goodbye, Hedy, you do what they say and you'll make good."

I turned and walked up the stairs into my first airplane.

Suddenly I was very nervous about flying, and sat down in an aisle seat as far away from the windows as possible. I must have looked fairly cool and collected, though, because it wasn't long before the hostess asked if I wanted a cocktail. "Yes, a martini, please" (it was my first one)—"oh, and a pack of Winstons." I knew you had to be very sophisticated to drink martinis—especially in the morning, and a cigarette would complete the picture.

As I sipped my drink, I thought about my family getting further away each second. Loretta was on her own now, and little Sam was at the boys' home school. And now my time had come.

What had held us together as a family? I guessed it was just the fact that we were mother and children, and mothers and children lived together. But I couldn't help wondering if there weren't families somewhere in which people told each other every day about the love they felt and hugged and kissed each other—where people shared their hopes and dreams, their difficulties and fears at the dining room table. I tried to imagine our doing that, but couldn't. As long as I could remember, I'd wanted to express my feelings of love and affection to people close to me. But the greater fear of being rejected always kept me from it. Maybe that kind of family communication didn't exist at all. It hadn't at school or in modeling, that was for sure. But maybe I'd find it in Hollywood.

My thoughts jumped to the movies, and then to all I'd be able to do for my family. The first extra money I made was going to go for a new car for my mother. I'd decided about that at the airport. Tears welled up as I imagined how surprised she'd be. Maybe I could even move my family to Hollywood and take care of them. They'd never have to worry again. My brother would brag about me to his friends, and I could imagine sending my father a movie magazine with my autographed picture on the cover. I felt all warm and satisfied as I thought about this new chapter in my life.

After a meal and two stops, I picked up the airline magazine and flipped through it, but scenes of future glory kept taking me on to Hollywood. Some time later my fantasies were interrupted by the landing announcement. The moment was actually here. I knew it would be hard. I'd never had any doubt about the work it took to be good at something. But it would be worth it. I was going to be a lovely princess in the movies, and the life of the princess was about to begin.

I checked my makeup and looked once more to be sure I still had the producer's name: Tom Heinman. He'd been very nice to me during his visit to our home, and had promised to meet my plane and help me get settled.

As I came through the gate, I was looking at a sea of unfamiliar faces. Then I recognized him—short, stocky, with black curly hair and a slight beer belly, about forty. He elbowed his way through the crowd and practically ran to meet me, smiling a big welcome. I held out my hand but he went right past it as he picked me up and swung me around.

"Oh Hedy, I couldn't wait for you to get here! You're going to *love* it!"

I couldn't get over his enthusiasm, but I laughed and hugged him back, with real affection and thankfulness, very relieved that he'd shown up and that he still seemed glad he'd made the contract.

After what seemed like a wild ride over freeways crammed with cars, he took me to a beautiful place for dinner high up in the hills with a breathtaking view of the sparkling lights of Los Angeles. The food tasted wonderful and all the wine made me a little lightheaded. But my mind was clear and totally present in the marvel of what was happening.

"I'll take you to a motel tonight," Tom was saying, "and tomorrow we'll look for an apartment. I've got some places lined up for you to see."

"Oh that's nice, Tom. Thank you so much. You're being so sweet to me."

He shrugged it off as he signaled for the check.

At the motel he checked me in and carried my bag to the room. "Hey," he said, "let's have a drink and talk about Hollywood," and he got a bottle from his car.

Tom could really tell a funny story, and we both laughed as he told about some of the dumb things movie stars had done when they were drunk or mad. He had a second drink and a third. But I didn't want another one. I was very tired and kept wondering if he was ever going to leave so I could go to bed. Finally, he ran out of stories and was quiet. Kind of an awkward quiet.

"Why don't you get ready for bed, Hedy?" An alarm bell went off somewhere very deep within me. Tom started loosening his tie. For a minute I thought I was going to be sick, as I remembered the man with the scar. It wasn't just fear I felt—more like shock or terror.

I went in the bathroom and tried to think. Should I run to the motel office and ask them to call the police? But then where would I go? How would I get home? There was no one within two thousand miles who would help me—and I couldn't even pay for the motel. No, I had to be calm and talk him out of it. I'd come out laughing and tell him to go home, I was exhausted, and besides, I didn't even know him. That was it.

But when I came out, Tom was in bed with the sheets pulled up to his chest, apparently naked. "Come on, honey," he said gently, "let's go to bed."

I stood in the bathroom door shaking my head. Panic surged in me and the room started to spin. This was my boss, my only contact. What could I say or do to make him go away? There was no way I was going to bed with him even if he killed me.

Trying to smile and take the whole thing as a joke, I told him, forcing my voice to stay steady, "Put your clothes on, Tom. This is ridiculous."

"O.K.," Tom laughed, "hand me my pants." I pulled them off the chair to give him, but he reached out with a quick movement and caught me by the wrist, pulling me onto the bed, laughing in a playful sort of way.

"Hedy, you're really cute when you're playing hard to get."

That only made me more frantic—he wasn't hearing me. All the fears and memories of the past exploded into one mass of raw terror. Frantically I twisted and turned trying to get away. But he was strong and drunk and having a good time. He started pulling open the top of my blouse with one hand while holding me with the other. My mind wouldn't function and I began to scream. By the time he got to my panties I was kicking and writhing, but he was on top of me, holding me and trying to get his shorts all the way off at the same time.

I turned my head toward the pillow, still screaming at the top of my lungs, and tried to avoid his frantic probing. The whole thing was like a Fellini movie. I heard his laughter rise and my voice begin one long scream. Just then he stopped laughing as his whole body went rigid and his warm dampness spread across my stomach.

"Damn, you're something else, Hedy!" he laughed as he fell back beside me on the bed.

But my mind was frozen, locked. I could only hear as if I were sealed in another world, and my scream continued for what seemed an eternity. Black spots came to my eyes. I wanted to crawl down my own throat and hide. Then I was choking, still screaming, not able to stop the strange noises coming from my throat, gurglings that sounded as if I were drowning, as I felt I was.

"Hey, you all right, Hedy?" Tom was serious now, realizing something was terribly wrong. "What's the matter?"

It was over an hour before I could stop sobbing. All that time

Tom tried his best to comfort me. No longer playing a game, he was obviously confused by the violence of my reaction.

"Listen, Hedy, I thought it was clear . . . I mean, . . . For God's sake!" He shook his head unbelievingly. "You mean you didn't know you were going to stay with me? That's why I put all those extra things in the contract." He looked at me with a dawning understanding, "Why, you really *didn't* know!"

At first my mind couldn't grasp his meaning. Then I realized what he was implying, and I was overwhelmed by the horror of feeling totally betrayed by my own mother. Deserted. *Sold!* Later, I could see how Mother, as naïve as I in many ways, could possibly have misunderstood this subtle and sophisticated man. But not then.

As Tom had been talking, I could sense that here was a nice man who felt that I had been tricked. But he was also beginning to feel that *he* had been conned. And it was obvious that he didn't like the idea. His pride was on the line, and he looked at me skeptically. Now he had this damned girl scout on his hands.

While he put on his clothes, he became very professional. He kept looking at me as if I were from the smallest town in Illinois. But when he tried to make a joke about it, neither of us laughed.

Actually I was still in shock, huddled on the bed, staring at him like a terrified and wounded animal.

When he left, he promised to pick me up the following day.

The rest of the night I lay and stared at the ceiling. How could I stay, face Tom? Everyone would know that I was a naïve child. All my worst fears had come true—someone had seen through my sophisticated veneer. And now I was really alone and helpless. Then the tears came again, great shaking sobs, and I thought of what people would say when he told them. And my mother! No— he hadn't really said that! I knew mother was amazingly naïve. Yet down deep I knew she could repress things she didn't want to see.

As I finally sank into the bottomless pit of sleep, I kept asking myself, "Is this really true? Of course it isn't. But how will I know?

"Oh, dear God, can I trust *anyone?*" There was no answer.

9. Finding a Family

As MY EYES OPENED, I was conscious of a bright shaft of light coming through a crack between the draperies in a strange room. Then I realized where I was and remembered what had happened. I could hear the early morning traffic going by outside—the rush of cars, the roar of trucks, as they shifted gears to make the grade on the freeway. It sounded like a cheerful, optimistic, busy world, thousands of people doing important things, going to see important people who expected them, knew them.

And I didn't know a soul in the noisy city. In fact, I didn't have any idea where in L.A. the motel was.

My feelings about the night before fluctuated from shock to tears to shame and embarrassment. And there was a rising fury against Tom for being so insensitive that he couldn't hear my desperation. In my pride and mortification I hated and resented him. How could I hold my head up? I knew he must be laughing at me for being so naïve. Now, I knew how young girls had to pay their dues to make it in Hollywood. And I was embarrassed that that fact hadn't occurred to me either. But why did things like this keep happening to me? Again no answer.

I took a deep breath to stop the new tears that were threatening.

How could I have tested so high on the IQ tests and be such a dummy about life? Tom would be amazed if he knew I was still too embarrassed to buy a pair of hose in front of a man. I'd learned all kinds of very subtle moves, looks and gestures from the older models, but nothing about how men decoded them. So life was a frightening mystery.

As I sat there on the side of the bed, I wondered how I could find out what was going on without sacrificing my standards for myself. If I didn't find out about close relationships and love, I'd be condemned to live in this bewildering and trackless jungle of fear forever. I was saving my love for the special someone I'd always seen as the "prince on the white horse"—if I could ever find the courage to let him know me now. But maybe that was an unreal dream too. Maybe there wasn't any honorable, beautiful, strong man who was gentle and understanding. I dismissed the thought. Of course there would be. And I was going to save myself for him.

Of one thing I was certain, I was not going to have sex with Tom Heinman or anybody else, even to become a movie star.

I got up and walked into the bathroom. The determined mouth in the mirror told me I was little Scrap Iron again. "O.K. Hedy," I told my reflection, "Let's get busy and *do* something about this. You can make it on your own or not at all!"

As I was bathing and washing my hair, all sorts of thoughts came across my mind. "I'll go home." But then I saw my mother's face. I couldn't risk finding out that my fears about her might be true. And call my father? Never. I'd have to admit that I'd only lasted one day and failed. No, I couldn't go home, that was certain.

"O.K.," I thought, "I'll get on the phone and call producers, telling them where I am and asking them to come pick me up and talk to me about working for them." But of course that was stupid. I was thinking like a fifteen-year-old. I suddenly felt very much the little girl that I was, and I was frightened. But I steadied myself at once—no more feelings, Hedy. Think!

First I had to find a place to live, and money to live there. Then

I could go to the studios for interviews where I'd meet people who could help me become a star. But how? How?

The only answer was to go with Tom that morning and see what happened, hoping for some chance, determined to take the first opportunity to get away.

When Tom came, he acted as if nothing had happened. Obviously his plans still included me, but I was more determined than ever that I wasn't going to stay with him. He put my suitcase in the back seat of his car, and we drove off to meet some of his friends for lunch at the Brown Derby, near Hollywood and Vine.

As we were being seated at a round table for six in the center of the restaurant, Tom introduced me to the other men. One of them had a son about my age named Billy, who sat next to me. It wasn't long before the men ignored us and began talking about a new project in which they were involved. Billy turned to me and winked and then went into a very funny silent imitation of his father for my benefit. He reminded me of my "movie family" back in Chicago —natural and fun to be with.

Inside, behind my smile, I was frantic! I wanted to tell Billy what had happened and ask him to help me get away. But I'd never shared anything personal with someone else. My mind went over and over my situation like a spider going over a tennis ball looking for a crack, a way into the problem. But there was no opening. My hands were damp and I felt slightly sick at my stomach. Finally, knowing it might be my only chance and having no idea what would happen, I whispered my story to Billy as the other men kept talking.

Billy was a really cool kid, and he didn't hesitate. "I'll offer to show you around Hollywood for a while, and get you out of here," he whispered. "Then we'll think of something." Tom thought the drive with Billy was a good idea.

We left immediately, trying to act casual. After getting my suitcase out of Tom's car, Billy threw it in the back of his convertible and we screeched out of the Brown Derby parking lot onto Vine Street.

"Listen, Hedy, I've got this friend who travels for a sewing machine company—you know, goes to fairs and demonstrates. He's taking off for San Francisco this afternoon. Want me to see if you can ride up with him?"

He caught my uncertain look.

"Sam's really a nice guy. He wouldn't bug you."

What was I doing? Getting in a car with a man I'd never met to go several hundred miles with no one to meet when I got there. I hesitated, feeling like a frightened little rabbit I'd once seen, cornered by some little boys in our neighborhood when I was a little girl. I couldn't do this. But then a picture of the night before flashed into my mind. "O.K. Billy," I said, "and . . . thank you."

Sam Estes *was* a nice guy. Checked suit with striped tie and white shoes—the whole works. He was all laughs and a regular party boy.

It seemed like only a few minutes until we were headed up the coast highway north of Santa Monica. Sam spent most of the first hour bragging on himself, looking to see if I believed he was the best salesman and the best card player in California. When I seemed to accept that, he got more confident and began to talk about how he could help me get a job.

I'd told him I had to get away from a bad situation in L.A. for a few weeks. I didn't say any more and he didn't ask.

"I've got a buddy who sells furniture at fairs—those expensive vibrating easy chairs—I'll bet anything he'll give you a job. He's going to be at the fair in San Francisco."

It sounded good to me. I had no idea what selling furniture at a fair would be like, but it would give me some money and a place to be until I could get over my fear of Tom and Hollywood. I felt reasonably sure I could head back south in a couple of weeks, get myself an apartment and start out on my own toward becoming a movie star. After all, that shouldn't be too hard, I told myself, since I'd already been a star in one picture.

As we drove along the coast past Ventura and Santa Barbara, I began to relax. The brisk salt air smelled good and the ocean was beautiful and blue under the unclouded September skies. Near

Pismo Beach we stopped at a roadside park overlooking the ocean.
I got out and sat on the stone retaining wall, dangling my feet. I
felt the soft breeze beginning slowly to blow away the black cloud
that had been hovering over me. The sunshine seemed to warm me
clear through, and I could sense hope and healing welling up in
my body. For months, no for three years, I had been living under
the enormous pressure to be something I wasn't. Now, as I sat on
the wall looking out over the blue, blue Pacific, I was just Hedy—
a fifteen-year-old girl who didn't have to prove anything to anybody. With a start I realized that it was my sixteenth birthday, and
I'd forgotten . . .

"Come on Hedy, we can't stay here forever!" Sam gave a good-
natured honk from the car where he'd been waiting for me.

I took one last look. Somewhere, someday, I'd love to be able to
just be myself, like I was at that moment—except with another person—and feel the peace of not having to be super. Could people
share that kind of experience? I tried to drink in the whole scene
with my eyes so I'd never forget.

"Hedy!! Come *on!*"

The ride to San Francisco was totally refreshing to me. Now
that my job was settled, in Sam's mind at least, he began to set me
straight about my appearance. He told me my dress was too conservative, that he could tell that I was wearing the wrong kind of
bra, that I should let my hair grow out a little more. He was
like a big brother who'd gone off to college and was trying to help
a younger sister get with the way people looked in the big world.
The subtle way of dressing which the fashion world considered
right for me Sam thought was really out of it.

Then he began to confide in me about his personal life, and I
couldn't believe what I was hearing. No man had ever shared with
me the intimate side of his feelings about life and especially about
women. Sam had been married five times, and he went into great
detail about his relations and what it was about each wife that
turned him on and off. I'd never even heard some of the things
he mentioned, so I asked questions calculated to find out what he
was talking about without letting him know how dumb I was. On

that four-hundred-mile trip, I got answers to things I had wondered about all my life but had never dared to ask about men and their feelings and what intimacy might mean to them. It was obvious that Sam, too, thought I knew much more than I did about life.

Throughout the ride, because of my intense suspicion of all men, I kept waiting for Sam to make some sort of advance, with all our discussion about sexiness and close relationships between men and women. But he just talked and joked and laughed like an old friend. Later, I realized that Sam was probably just as afraid of getting close to me as I was that he might try.

As we drove along, I began to get some inkling of everyone's fear of really being known, even men. People like Sam knew just about everything there was to know about sex, but he wasn't happy, and kept hoping the next woman would fulfill his dreams. Maybe there were thousands, even millions, of people who try to look knowing and sophisticated about sex, but who are really crying out for someone to see through their masks and love them anyway. How could someone get the courage to show such things to another person. I couldn't imagine. But my Prince Charming ought to have that kind of perception.

In any case I soon felt that I had nothing to fear from Sam.

As the green fields rolled by, I became thoughtful. It was as if someone very powerful and knowing had sent safe Sam to give me the education about life I knew I needed to be able to cope in Hollywood. It was an eerie feeling, as if a mysterious someone were looking after me. Maybe a genie *had* come out of the fountain in Grant Park to help me become successful.

The highway signs indicated we were getting close to San Francisco, and I began to get butterflies in my stomach. What if Sam's friend didn't hire me? I had twenty-six dollars and seventy-six cents in my purse. Sensing my anxiety Sam looked at me and laughed, reaching over and patting me on the shoulder. "Don't worry, I got contacts. We'll get you a job." But knowing how much of Sam was talk by now, I wasn't at all sure about his "contacts."

Sam's friend, Mort Gresham, couldn't have been nicer. A big ex-wrestler about fifty-eight or sixty, he accepted me like a member of his family. Sam told him I was a real lady and to keep the "crud balls" away from me.

"Don't you worry, honey. You'll be fine," Mort said.

I was in! I had a job. In some ways it was as exciting as getting the offers to come to Hollywood. And this time I'd done it all on my own. No deals, no mother, no Tom Heinmans.

Mort told me to look around the fair for an hour and come back. "Then I'll tell you the pitch and you'll be a real 'carnie.'"

I was taken totally by surprise at my feelings of excitement and belonging as I walked through the carnival. My early childhood came back in a rush of sounds and sights and smells—the merry-go-round music and the funny bright-colored horses I used to sketch at Lincoln Park, the strange mingled sounds and smells of hotdog stands with mustard and onions and chili, popcorn, cotton candy and root beer. My feet spattered little clouds of fine dust in the air which mingled with small paper sample bags swirling off between the concession booths. Empty snow cone cups lay crushed flat in cherry red and purple puddles.

I smiled at a boy about my age wearing a flat straw hat who held out two baseballs toward me. "Here's a lady who can knock down the milk bottles—give you an extra try, honey."

He was one of dozens of different kinds of "pitch men" who were making their sales pitches for the carnival goer's dimes and dollars. There were men with microphones attached to their collars demonstrating dozens of ways to use household items like blenders and choppers. "Tired of having raw meat in your salads? Come on over, lady, show you how to chop your salads in half the time and save your fingers!"

It all seemed strangely familiar and good to me somehow. As a little girl I had read a story about a child who had run away and joined the circus. And now I was living out the same kind of adventure. I expected these people to become the same kind of family the circus people in the story were. "Of course," I told myself, "you're only going to be in their lives for a few days—two weeks—and then back to becoming a movie star." After all, I had big plans for my future.

But while I was here I was going to give this life everything I had and be the best employee Mort Gresham had ever hired.

Our booth was one of the largest. We sold huge massaging lounge chairs that had heating pads built into the backs, with rollers going up and down to massage the sitter's body. It was the most expensive item sold at the fair. And working for Mort Gresham was, I discovered, high class employment.

My job was to walk up and down the thirty feet in front of the booth and try to draw people in and seat them in the chairs. "Wouldn't you like to rest a moment? No charge. Just put your packages down and rest those tired feet. Your back will feel *so* good!"

When I'd guide them gently into their seats, a salesman would take over and sell them on the good points of the chairs. We always tried to get a couple to sit in two chairs facing each other. The salesman, or demonstrator, sat on a stool between them so they wouldn't even have to raise their heads to see him.

I soon learned that the best people to approach were those whose arms were loaded with packages. They were "buyers." The "be-backs" were the ones who liked the chairs but would be back after they thought it over.

I learned a lot about life during those first two weeks. Walking back and forth on concrete in three-inch heels from nine in the morning until ten at night, seven days a week, was the most tiring thing I'd ever done. After work I'd just fall into bed at the motel and die for a few hours each night.

In order to stand the pace the salesmen took pills to keep their energy flowing. The hot sunshine and dust made us continually thirsty. I noticed that the salesmen drank milk out of cartons all day long. But it wasn't long before I learned that the cartons were filled with half milk and half scotch.

Toward the end of the day, I would take a drink of their "milk" now and then or accept a pill. I found myself eating less and less and losing weight I really couldn't afford to lose. But I was feeling more and more at home.

I was amazed to find out that men and women in carnivals were very much like anyone else. Except they accepted each other just as they were. Though the carnies came and went, often dropping out unexpectedly, I learned that they were accepted back without any judgment when they showed up again months or even years later. I began to let myself feel some real affection for these people.

After work I'd join some of them in the cheap restaurant-bars where we'd drink beer, laugh and sing songs until two or three in the morning. The human warmth we had for each other was part of what I'd been searching for all my life. When a family got in financial trouble or someone got sick, the money was gathered in a few minutes to bail them out. It was like a benevolent poker game with emergency money changing hands every week or month. It felt good to be a part of this kind of family.

In many ways it was a hard life. And I was grateful for my strong legs and the stamina I'd developed growing up. Carnies worked in all kinds of weather, without heat or air conditioning, lived in cheap motels or pulled trailers behind their cars. Many looked fifteen or twenty years older than they were.

But this life, exposed as it was to the raw emotional elements, seemed to give some of them a kindness and understanding, a gentleness about people who hurt. And most of these qualities had been missing, or at least carefully hidden, behind the sophisticated faces of the society of Lake Forest and the competitive jungle of fashion modeling.

What caused the sense of brotherhood and sisterhood that was apparent in this world of people considered to be misfits and outcasts? I didn't know. But all the money and glamour in America couldn't seem to buy the sense of belonging they felt. When my two weeks were up, I decided to stay two more—and then two more . . .

10. Life's a Carnival—
But Who Are the Clowns?

IF I HAVE IMPLIED that carnies were morally upright and honest, that's not true. They weren't. Many of the men would sleep with every woman they could talk into it. And for some of the pitch men it was open season on conning customers.

But because of Mort, at first, and then later my three friends, Ben, Will and Sandy, no one ever approached me twice in a suggestive way. Before long the word was out that I was a lady. And since no one wanted to answer to Mort, I was actually much safer and better chaperoned than I'd been in Chicago.

As the weeks passed, my depression lifted. I felt mentally up, excited about life again. But I knew my past insecurities were still with me when I panicked as I thought I saw one of my mother's friends coming toward me out of the crowd.

What in the world should I say? I was supposed to be a successful movie star, not a carnival barker. But, of course! I could say I was doing this for a studio to research a part I was going to play. That was a believable story.

Smiling graciously as if I were at a tea in Lake Forest, I walked up to her.

"Hello, Mrs. Compton. How've you been?"

The woman looked at me like I was crazy and moved quickly away into the crowd. Obviously, it wasn't Mrs. Compton.

Whew! My eyes were playing tricks on me. I must be more tired than I'd realized. Anyway, now I had a story to tell anyone I might run into from Chicago.

This experience made me realize that I was frantically trying to hold my dreams together in my mind just long enough to make them come true.

But as I got to know my new friends better, I became afraid in a different way. I sensed that this life with its warmth and caring was actually a colony of the condemned, a place where people who had given up on "making it" in the outside world came to let their dreams of success and fame die unnoticed by the world.

When I talked about my future, they seemed to believe that I was going to make it in Hollywood. They wanted to believe me. But one afternoon when I was too tired to walk any more and was resting in one of the chairs, I noticed Sandy, looking at me. I saw pity mingled with the love of a father whose child was facing an impossible world, dreaming impossible dreams.

Sandy had come and gone so many times no one could count them. He had spent forty years of his life with the carnivals as his only home. When he disappeared everyone knew he was either in jail for being drunk or was sick. He had a bad drinking problem but could still work hard when he was sober.

Everyone loved Sandy. They took care of him and offered him rides to and from work. He was one of those nondescript people you couldn't remember well enough to describe—brown hair, average height, average build, average face, but always looking hung-over. He would try to make me laugh when I was sad, sometimes by making a ridiculous face or breaking spontaneously into a wild softshoe dance wherever we might be and regardless of who might be watching. In fact he'd do anything to make something funny happen for people. He seemed to be saying to the world, "Hey, I know I don't have anything to give you, but I'm going to make you happy. Look at me!"

And he *was* funny! Sometimes we'd laugh till we almost cried, but one time when no one was around, he began to cry. While he sobbed his heart out, I just hugged him like a mother would hug a little boy. And I wondered how many of the bright shiny people in Lake Forest or Hollywood wanted to cry when they couldn't hold up the mask which said, "I'm neat, I'm rich, I'm beautiful—I'm a clown!"

And there was Will. He was at least six feet four and wouldn't have weighed 150 pounds soaking wet. His veins seemed to stick out like swollen roots under his loose skin. You could see the edges of the bones in his face, neck and hands.

I loved Will. At first he seemed calm, steady and dependable in his work. We used to sit by the hour while he talked about his wife and children at home and his eyes got teary. When he was unguarded, he seemed haunted by the fear that he was already a has-been. He, as they all did, talked about the past as the good old days. He worked harder than anyone else. But when I got to know him, he seemed so lonely and broken down I wanted to cry and tell him he'd make it and that he'd be O.K. soon. But we both knew it wasn't so.

Ben was different. A banty rooster. Cocky, flashy clothes. And never negative. Always "just having a hard time now." But *tomorrow* he'd be sailing again and in the chips. As time went on, Ben shared his whole life with me over beer or while taking breaks. He'd say in his cocky voice, "Hedy, let's take a little walk." But when we were out of sight of the others he'd change completely, acting like a lonesome younger brother, though he was thirty-five years older than I. He talked to me endlessly about his wife, Jeanie, telling the same stories over and over, how he regretted the sorry deal in life he'd given her and how he wished he could buy her nice things and make it up to her for being such a "failure and an S.O.B."

I loved these men and found myself not wanting to leave a place where the people had made me feel cared for. I was amazed one morning when I woke up and realized how much I looked forward to going to work every day—with these men and women the world called "has-beens." But they had let me see at least the front edges of their real feelings and hopes and regrets. There were daughters and sons they were worried about and wives they missed. They were alone, so alone, inside. And because I listened, I became daughter, mother, sister and in some ways almost a priest, as they confessed their failures and disappointments and shared their secret dreams of making it big one day. I began to see that the closeness I'd always yearned for involved this listening to people share their secret lives.

After they knew I accepted them, they dropped the attitude I had thought was part of just being a man: always trying to prove themselves by making sexual advances. I was gradually, and without knowing it, discovering that between men and women there can be a relating which is warm and real and which does not hinge on a demand for performance as a hero, a heroine, or a sex object. I was finding out how to simply let men be with me. And through this listening-without-judging I discovered that I was really feeling loved and a part of a family.

As I talked to these dear older men—some of whom were my father's age—who felt that their lives had not turned out at all as they'd dreamed they would, I wondered if my father felt that way. That thought had never occurred to me before. He hadn't made the million dollars my mother said his heart was set on either. Could it be that he felt disappointed in life? Would he say these things if he could? But of course he could never reveal such feelings to me. And as I thought about it, I began to feel that I was much like him. For I was still lonely inside myself. These men loved me, but I didn't *believe* that love, somehow—because they really didn't know me. I had never revealed my inner self to them. Would they love me if they knew how aware I was of my looks, how hopeful and ambitious, how determined I was, and thus how unlike them?

They had given me a taste of three things my life was bent on finding—the love of a father, a family who loved me as I was, and a touch of personalness that had to be a part of the closeness I longed for. But as the weeks stretched into months, I realized this was just a sort of wax museum. The actors in this carnival of life had already accepted defeat, had given up the future, and were longing for past glories—which I had come to realize were only fantasies.

Like the clowns who came and went, they masked their age and despair with the make-up of the midway, the smile and bravado of the pitch men, the pill and the milk carton.

As I thought about these carnival friends, I was surprised to see a great similarity to the beautiful, successful people in Lake Forest and at modeling school, which I hadn't noticed at the time—the same pretense and fantasy, and the same unwillingness to face the truth about their own lives. It was as if they were all hiding behind their make-up, like the clowns. I realized I was learning a lot about life. "Maybe all of life is a carnival," I thought. "And maybe not all the clowns stay on the midway when the crowds go home."

II. A Carnie or a Star ?

SOME OF THE MEN I knew at the carnival were definitely *not* interested in my being their sister or daughter.

There was Joe. He was a broadshouldered twenty-four-year-old with narrow hips and muscular-looking biceps. Behind his square face and hard eyes he was a mass of hair-triggered violence. It was as though he only felt alive when he was fighting or challenging someone to fight—any size, any place, any excuse. I had seen him fight. He struck like an electric shock, often totally unexpected. And he really tried to hurt people. Almost everyone was afraid of Joe, except Mort of course, who according to stories, wasn't even afraid of God.

I began to notice that Joe was walking by our booth a lot during his breaks. As he came into view, his whole way of walking would change very subtly. He would slow down and almost sway in a kind of a strut—totally male—like a wild stallion—seemingly oblivious of me. Soon I kept seeing him everywhere I went. I'd be talking with Will or Ben or Sandy in different places—and there he'd be.

One day he actually looked at me. "Hi, Joe," I said, and smiled. He nodded.

After that his eyes softened when he saw me and he began to

look directly into my eyes in a knowing way. A look which was a whole conversation—a conversation I was no longer naïve about. I knew Joe wanted me, that he was wooing me without a word. But I knew also that Joe was afraid to make an open approach. And in fact I heard that Joe had never had to. But the experiences of hearing Sam, Ben, Will and Sandy had taught me that inside of some men is a deep fear of failing with women. At first I wasn't sure that this was true of Joe because he seemed so totally unafraid of anything. But when I didn't flirt back, I saw the uncertainty in Joe's eyes and began to realize that he couldn't risk approaching me directly. What if I rejected him and everyone knew? His fearful secret would be revealed—that he didn't feel as masculine on the inside as his behavior said he did. I knew the other side of this coin perfectly: the fear of being revealed as an unsophisticated woman.

Since Joe couldn't get my attention directly, he tried showing off. One night Ben, Sandy and I were sitting around a piano bar talking to the piano player. Joe walked by and sauntered over to the crowded bar across the room, where he pushed a big man aside and made a place for himself.

"What's your problem, Mack?" the big guy practically shouted with a surprised belligerent frown.

Just as I turned, I saw and heard Joe's fist crack into the man's lower jaw.

My first thought was that I was sixteen with a false I.D. and I'd go to jail with all these people, because by now there were several men fighting.

I scooted toward the door and once safely outside sat down in the back seat of the first car I came to. I felt my stomach cramp and thought it was from the excitement. Through the open door I could hear chairs flying, tables falling, glasses—ice—everything—splattering on the floor along with much shouting and swearing. Carnival men on Saturday night could work off an amazing amount of pent-up hostility in a short time. Joe really whipped the big man, and I was relieved that all our people got away before the police got there.

Secretly, I knew that Joe had started the fight to get my attention. But that knowledge gave me very mixed feelings. I had known for a long time that my appearance gave me some kind of power over men. Now I'd found that when I also listened and simply understood their feelings, the feelings went deeper and my influence with them was multiplied. Perhaps this listening and acceptance was what men hungered for almost as much as for sex—maybe at some level more. It was certainly true for me, since I was looking for acceptance. Except somehow I still hadn't found anyone *I* could talk to. In these relationships I was the listener and kept my deepest feelings to myself. I hadn't found anyone I could trust that much, since I was terrified of being known and rejected. I saw that being an understanding listener can make one seem to be open when in fact listening in my case was another way to hide.

One day as I walked back and forth and watched the everchanging conveyor belt of faces moving endlessly by the booth, I wondered how many of these people were terrified of sharing their secrets, their hopes for personal fulfillment, their dreams of success, their fantasies—shy, afraid of being exposed and then taken lightly or rejected. But when people broke down and told *me* who *they* really were—even if what they told me involved failures—I loved them *more*.

"How crazy!" I thought. "No one does it to us! We *keep ourselves* from being loved by our fear of being vulnerable. *That's* why we're so lonely!" Yes, but where did one get the courage to risk it. Because for me it was almost impossible to share my past which seemed so shameful. I had no idea how to share myself, but I knew that life would never be complete unless I found out.

My two weeks with the carnival had now stretched into three months. We had moved from one fair to another on the West Coast every week or two, five of us driving together in Mort's Chevy. The inexpensive motels, the greasy fried foods, never enough rest—it was all beginning to get to me. My stomach felt queasy a good deal of the time. Maybe the time had come for me to leave. Anyway, I'd have to go back and face the realities of Hollywood if I ever wanted to fulfill my dreams of success.

Suddenly I was very tired. My legs had begun to ache a lot.

One morning I walked through the midway with a heavy heart. An early December chill was in the air, but the sunshine was warm through my heavy sweater. It was going to be a nice day, but I couldn't shake the feelings I'd waked up with. I smiled and spoke to everyone getting set up as I always did. But I felt sad. Why did life put such a burden on me to succeed? Why couldn't I just stay here and be sort of a princess in residence with a special place? But something deep within me kept prodding me on, reminding me that the love I was out to win was more important than all of this.

Will and Ben were having a cup of coffee at the hot dog stand and kidding each other as I passed. Sandy was washing his face at a hydrant, trying to sober up enough to work. The lady who ran the snow cone place was chewing him out and telling him to "hurry it up," she needed some water.

Beneath their gruff exteriors, these warm and responsive people had a way of clinging together, of holding on to each other to protect themselves from the harsh coldness and emptiness of the world over which they had so little control. Their future was just the hope of getting by in a hopeless situation. With jokes and pills and whiskey they would try to forget and not be haunted by their inability to fulfill their dreams of wealth and fame.

I would leave soon, I told myself, and get on with my career. But when the time came to move on to the next place, I couldn't leave. I jumped all over myself, "Hedy, don't you have the guts to go it alone? What's the matter with you? Is being accepted by a few people who are going nowhere more important to you than all your dreams?" Suddenly I didn't know. I'd never even questioned the rightness, the inevitable nature of my drive to succeed. But things were familiar here. And somehow it was easier to accept a familiar dead end with these people than to risk looking for a glorious alternative in Hollywood.

I had learned so much with these good-hearted, earthy people— even if they weren't beautiful or educated or "socially acceptable." The love they gave me had made me different somehow, more able to listen and understand them. And I worked better, even when I felt empty on the inside—because I didn't want to disappoint them.

One morning I woke up with bad stomach cramps and could hardly get out of bed. That day I had a hard time walking, and by four o'clock in the afternoon I noticed perspiration on my forehead. Then I felt a sharp pain go down my right leg. Mort saw me almost stumble. "Hedy, for god's sake, what's the matter. Here, sit down." I tried to shrug it off with a Scrap-Iron smile.

"It's nothing. I'll be O.K., Mort."

But within a week I could hardly use my right leg, and my stomach cramps were almost constant. I tried to keep the tears back when I was working. The salesmen kept telling me to sit in their chairs, thinking that would make the pain go away. I assured them it helped, but it didn't. The circles under my eyes were getting darker from pain and lack of sleep.

One day the leg got so bad I couldn't stand it. A woman was sitting in one of Will's chairs.

"Pardon me," I said through the pain, "but could you possibly help me?"

She took one look at my face and led me to the telephone booth where she called her doctor in San Mateo.

12. Christmas at the Crossroads

THE OLD DOCTOR took off his glasses and looked at me seriously. I was still groggy from the anesthetic.

"You're a lucky young lady," he said, nodding his head.

I had taken a taxi from the fairgrounds to his office. After a quick but very painful examination, he had rushed me to the hospital and into surgery. A cyst on my right ovary had ruptured and peritonitis had set in. But the surgery was successful.

"You'll have to stay in the hospital with complete bed rest," he said. "I don't want you trying to walk for two weeks. How you stayed on your feet I'll never know."

I was tired, bone tired. For a few days I must have been sedated, because I hardly remember anything except the feel of clean sheets, the antiseptic hospital smell, the doctor's kind voice in the distance, and the nurses gently waking me up to give me pills or to urge me to eat something. I felt safe, and relaxed into the deepest sleep of my life. It was a wonderful feeling. I dreamed that my white knight, my ideal man, had come to get me, I'd told him all about my past, and I was secure in his care.

Several days later, I'm not sure how many, I rejoined the conscious world. The carnival was getting ready to move on. Mort brought Will and Sandy to my hospital room to say goodbye. And then they were all gone.

As I gained strength among the friendly people in that small-town hospital, I began to try to pull the pieces of my life together, to regroup for whatever lay ahead. By the time I could get on my feet again all the fairs would be over for the Christmas season and everyone would be heading home in a hundred different directions.

The damp December greyness was already closing in around the little hospital one evening as I walked across from my bed to the window. I looked out into the cold, wet, December world and saw the car lights sliding across the parking lot toward the entrance, taking people home, home to warm fireplaces and caring families. Loneliness like the damp fog started to close in around me.

Turning away from the window, I pushed the loneliness out of sight into my unconscious like a large black beach ball and began sorting out my options. Again, I had it to do by myself. This time, however, I wasn't afraid, at least not as afraid. I knew more about getting around in the world than I had. And I'd found out a lot more about what made people tick—all different kinds of people. But really, I had only one choice, since going home was out of the question. All I'd had in mind since I was fourteen was to be a movie star. And I was so close to the only place it could happen, I had to go back and try.

After asking some questions, I discovered that the easiest way to get from San Mateo to L.A. was to fly from San Francisco. But there was no sense in arriving in Hollywood at Christmas time. When I went to pay my hospital bill, I found that Mort and the others had already paid part of it. It would take most of the money I'd saved to pay the rest. But I had enough to take the bus to San Francisco, stay at a cheap place until the 26th, and then get to L.A. and begin my new search for work. The kind, balding doctor walked me to the door of his office.

"Why don't you stay at the YWCA in San Francisco a few days, Hedy? At least it's clean and safe."

I hugged him and felt the tears in my throat as I saw him blink his back. But mine never made it to my eyes.

I stepped out of the hospital into a cold, driving rain and hailed a taxi. After checking my bag at the bus station, I had an hour to kill before bus time. Restless, I wandered out into the street in the midst of the holiday crowd. People looked happy in spite of the rain. There by the door was the Salvation Army bell, the frayed, wet-looking Santa with the umbrella. The Christmas carols from the record store across the street mingled with gusts of wind and fine, cold rain.

I pulled up my coat collar, retied my scarf around my face and dove into the river of holiday shoppers swimming past the brightly lighted store windows like fish in a giant aquarium. Suddenly I was in front of an art gallery, caught and held by a beautiful oil seascape. Oh how I longed for my paints! Suddenly I couldn't wait to have a place to start painting again. That seemed secure and warm compared to the cold tinsel all around me.

Christimas music had always made me sad for some reason. It sounded happy, yet it made me want to cry. But everyone else seemed to be laughing as they heard it. What made all these people so happy? They couldn't be doing it all by themselves. I had tried and worked as hard as anyone I knew, and I wasn't happy at all. What was it all about? Was I the only one in the world who always felt out of step? Would I ever find my own place to belong?

In front of a Catholic church I stopped with a group to look through the iron fence at a manger scene. There they were! The shepherds, the wise men, and the animals. And in the middle, Mary and Joseph and the baby Jesus. Very unexpectedly, as I stood there wondering what Mary must have felt with the little baby in her arms, I was crying. I moved quickly on in the crowd but the warm tears kept coming faster than I could wipe them away. "Dear Jesus," I found myself saying, "please, help me."

13. Hollywood: Scene II — Take 1...2...3

In calling up all these memories of California, I realized something that I hadn't seen at the time—something that was hard for me to admit about myself. The memories I'd had so far were of the inside of my life—how I felt about me and the people around me. And these memories describe someone who seems grim and very serious. But outwardly there was a completely different Hedy. I was a radiant person and people told me I brought life into a room when I came in. Many times people stopped talking and paid attention to me. And when I visited with them, I could almost feel them responding to a kind of shine that came out of me toward them as I looked into their eyes and really cared about hearing what they were saying. As I remembered these things, I wondered how many people always look radiant and happy who are as grim and serious as I was on the inside where the world could not see?

THIS TIME I WAS a different girl when the seat belt sign came on as we circled Los Angeles. The clouds swallowed the plane. I felt much older now. I'd learned some things about people and clowns, including myself, which would change my whole life. Something was missing this time: excitement, that was it. I was calm about

Hollywood—calm and very cautious. But my determination was cold steel.

Within a few days I had my own apartment and seemed to be making all the right phone calls. I had dropped off photographs and resumes at several of the studios.

Before long Tom knew I was in town. He was to be apologetic and a perfect gentleman during the rest of the time I knew him. And I'm sure he began to work behind the scenes to see that I got a lot of the chances that came almost at once.

Three weeks later I found myself in Hawaii. The beautiful tanned bodies on the beach, the clear blue sky and blue-green waves with white frothy caps and the clean air from the sea—all these things made me feel alive and new. Hawaii was to be taken in as the 49th State and I was to cover the celebration on national TV. There were all kinds of booths with different arts and crafts and island products. My job was to wander around interviewing people and introducing Hawaii and Hawaiians to their new brothers and sisters on the mainland.

I felt very much at home. The carnival had made me totally at ease talking to strangers. I think my sponsors were surprised that I was so natural. And I was feeling good. In fact I was more secure than I had ever been.

When I got back to Los Angeles, I was on nighttime talk shows discussing the Fair in Hawaii and my new career. People everywhere told me I radiated a kind of life and confidence I'd never thought of myself as having. I'd found a place for myself, and I felt very much at ease talking to all the different kinds of people I was thrown with publicly.

But I didn't let anyone get close. And my private life, which was totally hidden from anyone I knew in my work, was very isolated. In fact, it was almost nonexistent, I was working so much.

I got to know people at almost every level of the business and was always interested in them. But I had no real friends or relationships. I told myself that was all right because I'd made up my mind for sure that I couldn't depend on anyone but myself. As I watched the successful people in Hollywood, I decided that the ones who made it had to develop a very tough shell. They seemed to be only out for themselves and to be loyal and faithful to no one else.

The contrast with the carnival people was stark. The warmth, trust and caring was replaced by an intense competition, a back-stabbing game of making and grabbing opportunities however one could get them. One day, waiting in a casting line, I could almost see the feelings of loneliness and discouragement rising like a black cloud above people's heads. A young woman I'd never seen, with a sick child in tow, came late and began to cry when she saw the long line which had already formed. She seemed so hopeless as she turned to leave. Just as she got to the door I called to her, "*There* you are. I thought you'd *never* come back." And I let her in line ahead of me.

There was among some of the big stars—those who had made it to the top and been there for years—a kind of knowing friendship. But it wasn't so much because they had worked together and supported each other like the carnies. It seemed to be more from a common understanding and appreciation of what it cost to pay one's dues to get to the top.

But would there, I wondered, be any warmth and fulfillment for the little girl who sat in the apple tree wanting closeness with another human being? Suppose I did make it to the top, which didn't seem too impossible given the right breaks and superhuman effort. What would I have then?

That thought kept coming and ballooned my feelings of emptiness between assignments. Because even after I was working regularly, there were occasionally two or three weeks or even a month between studio calls. At times it seemed as if there were so many people all wanting the same assignment that I was awed and felt extremely lucky when I got the job. At other times I felt insignificant and rejected when I didn't get a part or a job I'd wanted. The fact that established stars went through the same cycle didn't seem to help.

One of the first things I'd bought after returning to L.A. were some paints. I began to make an emotional home where I'd always found it—with my canvases. When I painted, I wasn't alone somehow. It was as if the genie or whoever had been watching over me were there, encouraging me to paint and paint and paint. I would begin a painting between calls, and a strange thing would happen—the painting would take on an identity, and I would find myself somehow "falling in love" with it. Perhaps it was a compensation for the emptiness in my life, but every painting called something out of me and became a love affair. I was deeply involved with each one and felt a strong relationship to it in my heart.

I painted carnival scenes. One was of a man looking up at the balloons he was selling which were shaped like animals. I painted kites and flowers. The smell of paint and turpentine would settle my anxious feelings. Here, with a brush or palette knife in my hand, I could be myself, Hedy. Ponytail, no make-up—it didn't matter what I looked like, what I wore. It was the only place I'd found where I could be totally comfortable just being myself.

I remember once sitting and looking at a finished painting. I was a mess, covered with paint, but the painting was good. It was a carnie with Will's face standing in a crowd. And I felt a kind of peace and at-homeness with myself I couldn't describe as I looked at what I'd created. "Why, dear God," I asked, "isn't there an experience like this somewhere with another person?"

When I worked, I got paid very well, but the life was erratic, and the assignments often came at the last minute, allowing for very little in the way of an organized life. By the time I got a check, I either owed the money already or spent it at once, or sometimes both. The rule was: "Always look good and successful." This fit right in with my needs. From the first grade on I had paid the price to look good. But regardless of how good I might look, or how well I might do on an assignment, the only personal security I had was my paintings. My art gave me love, structure—a home from which I could dress up and go out to win a place among the stars. Down deep I knew I needed someone to share my life and my dreams. I didn't want "men." But I wanted one particular man who was out there somewhere.

As my career developed I began to be invited to parties at a different level of Hollywood society. I wore beautiful clothes. My agent encouraged me to be seen in glamorous places. And there was nothing unusual about sitting at a dinner table with Dinah Shore, Sal Mineo, Glenn Ford, and having John Wayne drop by the table to say "hello."

I remember sitting at dinner in an exclusive club one night, looking ever so calm and natural—or hoping I did—supposedly listening, and wondering what in the world I was doing with these people. But with them I did learn a lot about the Hollywood myth —which the press has sold the nation.

Gossip was one of the primary sources of conversation material. Everyone knew what everyone else did, what they had done the night before, who they were with, when they got in, if ever. There was a lot of joking and laughing about it all. And the actors and actresses were like high school kids, exaggerating everything they did for the press. Every party where some drunk took off his or her clothes and led the way to the swimming pool was reported as an orgy—but it wasn't true. As a matter of fact I found that the more "sophisticated" the people were publicly, the lonelier they seemed to be "off camera." There was sex of course, but not much of the kind of close relating in which people can relax and feel safe. At least I never heard about anything like that.

But all of my partying was strictly a superficial and professional "appearing." I was so uptight about physical intimacy after the evening with Tom Heinman that I never even let myself get in a situation where something out of my control might happen. I simply did not trust men. To make things worse I can't remember meeting a man during that period who was loyal or faithful to his commitments. And I can't remember meeting a married man socially who didn't have a girl friend or mistress (according to the grapevine) or who wasn't ready to take me out.

Even though the thought of sexual intimacy was still frightening, I was beginning to be conscious of warm, loving feelings—but what on earth was I going to do with them?

About this time I met a wonderful group of young people who were stand-ins and minor stars at Atlantic Studios. Three of the men I met were stand-ins for western stars. All were excellent riders and loved to go to rodeos and eat hamburgers and hotdogs. Young and mischievous, they joked a lot and made me feel like a kid again.

One of them in particular fascinated me. Buzzy was Glenn Ford's stand-in. I met him in the studio coffee shop during a lunch break. He was sitting with some friends when I came in. The girl I was with steered us toward their booth as they whistled at us and laughed, waving for us to come sit down.

Buzzy seemed very much at ease with himself—"self-contained strength" was the phrase that came to mind. As the others talked, I noticed that he was toying with a beer can. I was surprised to see him unconsciously crush it between his thumb and two fingers.

Glancing up suddenly he caught me looking at him and smiled. I hadn't quite been able to get my wall up in time to hide my feelings. Those penetrating eyes seemed to see clear into the cellar of my soul—and I felt instinctively that they weren't shocked or turned off by what was there.

When he got up to leave, I was surprised at how tall and straight he was. I loved his dark hair and tall lean body. And as he moved away, there was an easy confidence and grace about his movements which stirred subtle feelings in me I'd never known.

As we met more often, Buzzy started asking me out. Almost casually, like a friend. He seemed to have no need to hustle me. In a world of aggressive, demanding males, Buzzy just liked to be around and accepted me as I was with no questions, as if that were the natural thing to do. He didn't have much to say, and I found myself almost chattering before I realized it. He felt safe to me. But fear was mounting with my loving feelings—which I didn't understand.

When I saw him ride during the filming of a movie, I was amazed at how good he was. He was full of talents, but the need to show off seemed to be completely missing from his make-up.

One night we were eating in a restaurant with several of his friends and their dates. His two buddies who were also western riders got the M.C. to call Buzzy up to the stage to sing. I hadn't known he could sing and was caught completely by surprise. This quiet man! He started with a western ballad, and before he'd sung two lines all conversation stopped. Without any self-consciousness he held the audience for two hours. It seemed that he sang every one of his songs directly to me. My protective wall began to crack, and before he came and sat down, it had totally crumbled. Here was my man, and I wanted him to love me forever.

But we had a strange relationship. Although we were together much of the time when we weren't working, he didn't press me to sleep with him. And I wouldn't have, even though I longed to. I was afraid he would think I was cheap.

We would be together constantly for several days. But then he'd disappear for a day or two, sometimes three—with no explanation. This kept me longing for him and aware of how much I loved him and missed him. I was in agony because I could never tell when he'd leave saying, "I'll see you in the morning," and then not contact me for three days.

I became afraid to leave the house for fear of missing his call. So I'd stay at home, wash my hair, take care of my clothes, paint and even polish furniture.

Buzzy was thirty, and everyone I knew in Hollywood thought I was twenty-two. I was, of course, only seventeen, but now I was really feeling like a woman. During this time I fell in love with my kitchen. Buzzy liked homemade pies and buttermilk biscuits. The smell of hot apple pie was a tangible way I could express my love. I imagined being his wife and the mother of the strong handsome little boys we'd have. To complete the picture I started growing flowers in a little garden outside my kitchen window. Flowers on the table were the finishing touch which made my place seem like a home. Everything, was for Buzzy.

He was always a gentleman, and treated me like a lady—doing things like holding my chair, opening my car door, walking on the street side of the sidewalk. He was always kind and gentle, and his lack of aggressive demands and possessiveness completely won my heart.

Although Buzzy had never mentioned marriage, I knew I was beginning to long for it. Maybe he'd get the picture and ask me soon. Here was a man at last who gave me secure enough feelings that I could trust him with my life, my love, and maybe even someday, my past. One day I painted a strong male figure. With an array of colors I gave the impression that he was a knight without being dressed in armor. My heart, my whole being was singing. I felt like a picture I'd seen of a happy young woman running through a field of daisies into the arms of her man.

Buzzy had just been through a divorce about the time I'd met him. His ex-wife was a ballet dancer, and I knew he still had to see her to take care of property settlement details when she was in town. Probably that was the reason he hadn't been able to think about the future with me or mention marriage. I realized he'd need some time to get over his pain and fear of commitment. After all, it had taken me seventeen years.

I was deeply in love and couldn't wait for the time to come when we would plan a home, share our dreams, and love each other completely.

One night he was especially tender with me. Everything he did told me that he was getting up the courage to ask me to be his wife. And I was ready.

14. Death of a Dream

ALL THE NEXT DAY I was in a strange mood—dreamy, excited, impatient, and blissfully happy. I couldn't wait for Buzzy to come that evening. I cleaned and cooked and baked, and changed my mind a dozen times about what I'd wear.

But Buzzy didn't come. And he didn't call. "He must be deciding about proposing to me," was my reaction, and I was very excited. But he didn't call the next day either, or the next. After five days I was hurt, and then furious. I knew this was his way. But he could have called.

On the seventh day Buzzy rang the doorbell at about 1:00 A.M. When I saw him, my skin tingled all over. I forgot about being mad at him and started to throw myself into his arms. But something stopped me. Buzzy gave me a little kiss and came on into the living room. He sat down on the couch and I waited and waited. He didn't say anything for twenty minutes. I began to talk to fill the void, which somehow frightened me. I felt like a babbling idiot and laughed and joked about things that had happened while he was gone, on and on about nothing. Inside, my stomach was in a knot and I was tight down the middle of my back. My whole body was screaming that something horrible was coming. But I didn't want to know what it was. Maybe it would go away if I just kept talking, and we could get on with my dream. Any minute he would look up, come over and take me in his arms.

Finally I ran out of words. The silence was excruciating.

"Hedy," Buzzy said flatly, without looking up, "I've gone back to Ginny." It was the nearest to an emotional statement I'd ever heard him make.

I felt my head shaking slowly. Suddenly I knew why he'd been such a gentleman, had not pushed me sexually, and hadn't been possessive. All his reserve that I'd cherished—he'd only had it because he'd been seeing Ginny. I didn't say a thing. But inside I saw myself crouched in the bottom corner of my soul screaming silently, "Oh my god! Oh my god! I can't stand it! I can't stand it!"

I don't remember his leaving, but I knew he'd never be back.

I don't know what I did the next few days—except drink. I didn't answer the phone or leave the house. All I can remember are the waves of feelings and thoughts which came over me, threatening to sweep me over some cliff into a unknown bottomless cave. Certain phrases came out over and over again in screams, whispers and sobs, "You stupid fool, Hedy. You stupid, *stupid* fool!"

My thoughts were jumbled, but I knew I was a total misfit as a woman. "That proves it!" I remember thinking. *"Why* did you think anyone could really love *you??* You knew it all the time! How many times do you want *proof,* Hedy??"

I was mortified. Buzzy had seen my secret, my unlovableness. I *showed* it to him! And he'd walked away. I hated him for knowing.

I wanted to ball up like an unborn baby and stay inside my soul. I wanted to withdraw my membership in the human family. *"Family!* Ha!"

I knew now beyond a shadow of a doubt that my daddy had been right, but I couldn't bear for anyone else to know that his daughter wasn't lovable.

Some time during that nightmare there was a calm period. I remember lying on the floor with my hands behind my head staring endlessly at the ceiling, thinking, listening to the telephone ring in another world. "This doesn't make sense," I thought. "Everyone *treats* me as if I were lovable. I listen, I'm kind. I don't brag or push myself ahead of people. They invite me places and talk to me endlessly. And I do things for people—even strangers."

Men and women both responded to me as if I were someone nice to know. They told me I was beautiful. And the women weren't threatened by my being after their men. *Why* then did Buzzy walk away when other people everywhere I went seemed to love me?

But, I reminded myself, they didn't know me well enough to see that I wasn't at all lovable basically. That's why I didn't let them know me that well. And now NOBODY ELSE EVER WOULD!!

I vowed it, swore it, and promised myself never to forget the lonely heartache of that moment which had been caused by opening myself to a loving relationship. To hell with closeness!

The pent-up misery and feelings of rejection I'd been sitting on all my life flowed out and swept through me like a fever. I ached in every bone. I was angry at Buzzy, at the whole world, but most of all at myself. Several times I thought, "I'm going to die. I *can't* go on!" I remember staring at the walls for hours, taking another sleeping pill and then another, then a drink, trying to sleep. But sleep wouldn't come. Only the empty future and the empty past pressed into my mind like a poison gas, threatening to destroy me with the horror of being nothing, nobody with no future.

During those few days alone in the midst of my helpless frustration, my life was changed. Piece by piece I was bolting in place a protective suit of armor. It was already cold and lonely inside; but at least it would be safe.

Finally, I cried out in utter desperation, "Please help me, God!" And I fell asleep.

I don't have any idea how long I slept, but when I woke, the sun was streaming across the bed where I was sprawled with my head at the foot, in the same robe I'd had on the night Buzzy had left.

Slowly I looked around without moving. My head ached. I walked through the jumbled house, half remembering how some things got that way, but mostly just filled with a quiet exhaustion: "It's finished—period!" something seemed to say to me. I knew it

wasn't only Buzzy. It was something else. But it was several weeks
before I realized what it was that had died when Buzzy left.

The telephone was ringing. And I remembered having heard it
in the background for several days.

"Hedy, where the hell have you *been?*" It was my agent. "I've
got three fantastic jobs for you. Get down to Atlantic as fast as
you can."

In the weeks that followed, my career exploded. National television shows: "77 Sunset Strip," three full pages in a national
magazine, and several national television interviews.

But things weren't the same. *I* was different. And people in
Hollywood seemed childish all of a sudden, like little kids playing
dress-up and show-and-tell on someone's back porch. Only the stage
was national television and world wide movie distribution, and
their costumes and jewelry (at least some of them) were real.

Whereas at parties before Buzzy I had seen sophistication and
successful stars who were "loved by millions," now I saw the same
people frantically hiding their fears of exposure or failure. The
same people—but my eyes were different. I realized then what had
died with Buzzy: my dream that beauty and success were going to
replace the love of a father and the natural sharing with another
human being. I'd been chasing the fairy princess fantasy like a
phantom through my dreams, my nights and days.

I found my thoughts more and more drifting back to Chicago, to
Lake Forest. I imagined that many of the girls I'd grown up with
who'd seen my pictures or watched me on television had thought
I was successful, the girl with everything. But now I'd have traded
places with any of them. Their world, which I'd scoffed at in my
jealousy, now seemed solid and warm, loving and secure. Hollywood was phony to the core, promising love and intimacy to everyone and delivering slippery success to a few and broken hearts to
thousands.

My world had become a kaleidoscope of bits and pieces of life,
of relationships, ever changing, without overall design or connection. The mirror of publicity made us think there was a blueprint,
a plan for success, but it was all an illusion.

Yet I had a growing conviction from my painting that whoever created the world, whoever created life, had some kind of overall design for living it. But what I'd found in Hollywood was like the movie sets, only a façade, a thin painted front wall which said: "Life inside! Free! Glamorous! For *you!*" But inside was nothing, no merchandise, not even a proprietor—only fantasy.

Chicago. From two thousand miles away, life there seemed almost cozy. There was some form and regularity to life. I pictured women getting up, getting their families off to work and school, having coffee, going to meetings, luncheons, coming home and greeting their husbands with a listening ear, tender loving care, and dinner. Following dinner might be reading or television and perhaps talking about the day's happenings. And after the children were in bed, the sharing of intimate thoughts . . . and love. Life seemed so simple and uncomplicated. So neatly structured in an understandable package. My imagination said to me that there might be a place to belong, a rock, a nest, a home.

But then I thought about the wives in Lake Forest, "How naïve can they be? They think their husbands are so good and faithful." I smiled cynically to myself. From what I'd seen in Hollywood, I thought I knew what every single one of their husbands was like behind their wives' backs. And I felt very sorry for them.

Yet, even though I believed men were totally selfish and untrustworthy, I wished one of them cared enough about me to come home every night and take care of me, to call when I didn't feel well—just to see how I was. But no one did.

The Lake Forest I dreamed about seemed to be a million miles away. In the meantime I had made some very hard decisions about my relationships with men: No man was ever going to get control of my life again. *I* would make all the choices in any situation involving a man who was interested in me. I was no longer worried about hurting them. Men, it seemed to me, had the deck stacked in their favor anyway. And from now on they could look out for themselves.

Before I knew it, I found myself engaged to three men at once from three different parts of the country, all of whom spent time in California. I had no intention of marrying any of them. One was a male model in New York, thirty-two, very tall and handsome; his face appeared on billboards across the country advertising a popular cigarette. The second was from a financially and socially prominent family in Illinois. He had a good personality and was fun. The third was a successful Hollywood producer. But I didn't love any of them.

Although I'm ashamed now of this outright manipulation, just knowing they wanted me gave me a much needed confidence after the rejection by Buzzy. But I knew this way of relating to men wasn't the answer to life—I wasn't happy and felt guilty about hurting people. But I'd been so crushed that my own natural desire to be gentle lost control. The bit was in my teeth.

I had all my men in order, rank order. But I had no real closeness with any of them. And part of my power and appeal was that I was not available to them sexually "until we're married."

My only real moments of peace and honesty, and of closeness to my feelings were still wrapped up in my painting. One day I found myself painting a Madonna and child. Since I didn't attend church and had no religious training, I was surprised. But the mother and child spoke to me of love and caring and gentleness as well as the mystery of life. I couldn't put my thoughts or feelings into words but somehow that painting said everything for me.

Then one day I realized my birthday was coming up. I remembered when I was a child how I'd always longed for my daddy to come see me on my birthday. But after my parents divorced, I was lucky to see him for a few hours on Christmas. Over the years I filled in with my imagination what I couldn't remember about Daddy to keep him close to me. So I really knew very little about what my father was like, or what he thought about me, or for that matter anything else.

And yet I had in one sense played my whole life to him as the audience. All my studying, practice, discipline, work to succeed— was done, at one level, in order to become important so he would pay attention to me and realize that I was worth his time and above all his love and approval.

I sat in front of the painting of Mary and Jesus and thought over what I'd done since I'd seen my father. I had become well known as a model and starlet, was making a good living—a great living if one considered I'd done it before I was eighteen—and I had done some very acceptable paintings. My status and prestige as a model should be enough to allow me to go back and at least meet my father. At every step along the way, every success or failure, I had wondered: Would he be proud of me now? Ashamed now? Would he want to tell me he was sorry he hadn't paid any attention to me? Would he think I was interesting now that my name could possibly become nationally known or even a household word? I didn't know. But I *had* to find out. Maybe he *would* be proud now.

His approval would make up for all the bad feelings I had about men. Then I'd be secure when I met my man and settled into "the good life."

But what if he wasn't proud of me? That was ridiculous. How could he not be? Besides that thought was too scary even to think about. I wired him and told him I was coming from Hollywood.

PART FOUR

LAKE FOREST

15. Daddy, Will You Love Me Now?

THE PLANE WAS leaving at midnight for Chicago. My date was going to take me to dinner and then to the airport.

After packing, I spent two hours dressing myself to the hilt. I
wanted my daddy to think I was as bright as Eleanor Roosevelt but
as beautiful as Elizabeth Taylor. Smart, sexy, but pure as Queen
Victoria. I fixed my long hair, put on a black silk cocktail dress,
slightly low cut, and high heels—for my date—and for Daddy. I
thought I was so sophisticated. But looking back I probably appeared to have everything but a red rose stuck between my breasts.

My heart was singing. I was so excited I felt high enough to fly
home by myself. And especially after the cocktails and wine with
dinner. But I'd have several hours to get sober before meeting
Daddy.

On the plane just as I sat down, I saw a Hollywood friend coming on board. Everyone seemed to know who he was, especially the
hostesses. He had obviously been drinking and sort of greeted
everyone in the first class section with a wave. Elizabeth Taylor
was with him in a full length sable coat—escorting him onto the
plane. In front of everyone, she planted a big kiss on his lips and
made a dramatic exit.

Then he saw me, let out a big "Hi, Hedy!" and sat down in the empty seat beside me. It seemed a good way to start this trip home. I really had made it in Hollywood. My daddy would be impressed. Over drinks, we visited and told stories, ordering several more scotch and waters until we were giggling like two teenagers.

Suddenly the seat belt announcement came on—we were approaching Chicago. By 6:00 A.M. my eyes seemed to be in two different control panels, and I tried to squint to line them up. At the airport, after telling my friend goodbye, I washed my face in the ladies' room and tried to do something about my hair and makeup. But it wasn't much of an improvement.

In the cab on the way to my father's house, I let the cool morning air blow on my face. The thought of actually meeting him in a few minutes jarred me into a very sober, nervous state.

What would he be thinking about my coming? Would he be anxious to see me? The same thoughts and questions I'd been through a hundred times crowded in on me.

At three places I started to have the cab stop so I could have breakfast or at least a cup of coffee—and put off arriving. Then, although it was miles out of the way, I had the driver take me along the North Shore through Lake Forest. All the way I kept telling myself that any daddy would be interested to see his own daughter —especially if she were a successful model in Hollywood.

When we passed North Shore Country Day in Winnetka, some very strong feelings came over me. I was young again, a very scared girl, as I'd been when I'd gone to school the first day. The past with its blankets of feelings began to get thicker and heavier as we turned west and finally were going down the familiar streets in Libertyville. Everything looked smaller, yet the same.

As the cab pulled up in front of our old home, I caught a glimpse of the backyard. It was full of apple trees.

With each step toward the front door I seemed to get smaller, like Alice in Wonderland. By the time I rang the doorbell I was seven years old again and terrified that he wouldn't let me in— feelings I hadn't had since he left us.

After several rings the door opened. It was his wife, Lucy. What a relief! She seemed very pleasant and was obviously expecting me. More relief. Just then my father came out of the bedroom door beyond the dining table.

He looked me up and down. I suddenly felt ashamed and cheap. I wanted to turn and run. What was I doing on my father's doorstep at 6:45 in the morning wearing a wrinkled, black, low-cut cocktail dress, after drinking all night?

I didn't know what his expression meant, but I interpreted it as disgust. This wasn't at all what I'd planned.

I said in as steady and mature-sounding voice as I could manage, "Hello, Paul."

"Hi, Hedy," he said coming through the dining room in his shirtsleeves. "I didn't know you'd left Chicago. I thought you were still in school someplace around here. What in the world were you doing in Long Beach?"

"Hollywood, Daddy," I managed to mumble, and I felt the blood rushing to my face in mortification. *He didn't even know I'd left Chicago!* I was getting dizzy and had to blink and take a deep breath to keep from bursting into tears. This was the one reaction I hadn't even considered. All my work, loneliness and sacrifice to succeed as a model and as an actress to please him. All my efforts to win his attention and love meant absolutely nothing. *He didn't even know!*

The three of us stood there awkwardly. Lucy excused herself, saying she had to fix breakfast.

"Hedy," Daddy paused and then looked at me a little uneasily. "How long are you staying?"

I thought I was going to faint. "About—just about a week," I finally blurted out. "Just a few days."

What I expected from that week I don't know. But it was something very important to me. For some irrational reason I needed to have some sign of my daddy's love. Life seemed meaningless without his blessing, or at least his approval.

Both my father and Lucy worked until about 5:30 in the evening. So I was alone much of the time. The days were a blur. I wandered around the house and yard, walked my old haunts in the neighborhood, and waited. Waited for something, some sign from him that I was all right, that I deserved to live and love and enjoy life like other people, that I was forgiven for not being— what? I didn't know.

"How about a drink?" These were his opening words when he hit the house in the evening. And so we began. After two drinks, conversation got a little easier. We talked about his garden, the horse races, his friends, the family. Always safe. Always "out there" somewhere, away from the room we were sitting in. He was kind even though he couldn't seem to be personal about the reality of me. A couple of times when he looked at me I felt he was about to talk about our relationship. But he just couldn't.

I heard myself every evening screaming silently in my mind, "Hedy, *ask* him if he likes you! Ask him why he didn't call you on your birthdays! Ask him how you can get to know what he's really like as a person!" Finally, as he would stretch and say he was turn-ing in, the urgency rose in me to say, "Please don't leave yet. Answer my question, Do you love me? Love me? Love me?" But it echoed down the corridor of my mind into the silence as I sat alone after they had gone to bed.

Often during the day I thought about Mother and wondered how she was doing. So many things reminded me of her, the old neighborhood, our house, and being with my father. And I re-membered a lot of good things about her I'd forgotten. But she'd moved to Waukegan. One weekend I got a friend to take me to visit her. I never mentioned Tom Heinman and neither did she. We just stepped back into our old relationship as if I'd gone away to school for a year. As I started back to Daddy's place that after-noon, I realized that in raising us Mother had done all she could with a hard situation, given her needs and frustrations.

A week later my father said, "Hedy, you're interfering with our life. We go to bed early and need a lot of sleep. When are you leaving? Besides, you need to be doing something. Sitting around like this'll only make you depressed."

When was I leaving? I was crushed. I couldn't answer for a few seconds. Then I mumbled that I'd do something and let him know my plans right away.

The next day I called a friend who had a modeling agency. There was an opening for modeling expensive clothes at Marshall Fields. So I had a job for two weeks. I asked Daddy if I could stay for two more weeks. I'd be modeling late and wouldn't be home until about 10:00 P.M. I wouldn't bother them unless they wanted to stay up. That way I could spend two more weeks with some hope. After that I simply had no idea what I'd do. But I wouldn't go back to Hollywood. I'd proved what I wanted to there, and it didn't even count.

Now I was beginning to be afraid that my father wouldn't, or maybe couldn't love me as I imagined he might. Maybe no one could love me the way I wanted him to. And why was I so desperate for some sign of my father's approval? Even if he didn't think I was so great, surely he could give me *something*.

I was getting very tired of this search for something I couldn't find, tired of seeing my dreams dissolve in the glaring light of reality. Maybe there was no love in the world. Maybe all our training and talk about love were lies told to us as children to keep us from despair.

On the way to work the first day, in my father's car, the traffic was bad, as it always was in Chicago. I stopped at a traffic light on Dearborn Street trying to get myself together to turn on my enthusiasm for another new job, more new people. But my mind would not turn loose of the hope that something would happen about Daddy. A knocking on the closed car window startled me out of my thoughts. A cracked voice said, "Woman!"

It was a white-haired old man with a long bushy white beard and an armload of pamphlets, signaling me to open the car window. He obviously wanted to give me a pamphlet. In spite of the wild way he looked and his grim frown, he seemed harmless.

His eyes burned into me as he asked directly, "Woman, have you gotten to know your father? He's waiting to love you!" His words shocked me since I'd just been with my father. As the light changed, he asked again, "Do you know your father?" I was embarrassed. The man behind me honked and I started moving. "I'm trying to get to know him," I said, laughing a little nervously. And the traffic swallowed the man behind me. Glancing at the pamphlet on the seat beside me, I was sorry I'd been so flippant. It was about God. After staring at it for a moment, I wadded it up and threw it on the car floor.

16. A False Ending — A New Beginning

THE ASSIGNMENT AT Marshall Fields was a designer style show, and we modeled three times a day, always for a large number of people.

Most days I would come to town very early and stop by Lincoln Park, enjoying the carnival feel and the sound of the music. Something about just being there, comfortable and happy, made everything brighter, like the fall sunshine. As I walked toward the merry-go-round, I found myself looking for familiar faces from my carnival days. But of course there were none two thousand miles from San Francisco. I missed that strange caring family very much. But often just hearing the music and walking through the park made me feel content to be alive. And now I wasn't selling chairs but was one of the queens in beautiful clothes. Will and Sandy would be so proud of me, and Mort.

The atmosphere at Marshall Fields was sophisticated, the people were beautiful, and I was proud to be a part of the style shows. One day as I was modeling, I looked out and saw a familiar face, Findley Robinson, III, a man I'd met two years ago, just before I'd moved from Lake Forest to California. When my eyes met his, I felt a warm feeling go through me and almost smiled. His smile,

which always looked something like a little boy's who'd just stolen
a cooky, was infectious. And I hoped he would stay so I could say
hello to him after the show.

I had really liked Findley when we'd met. And now he looked
wonderful, standing there in the crowd grinning and shaking his
head, pretending that he couldn't believe how I looked. His hair
was dark red and thick. His suit was stylish and there was something solid and secure about him, which spoke of maturity and
sophistication. He was one of those rare men who look respectable
but have just a hint of the forbidden, the playboy about them.

Findley did wait for me. "Where in the world have you been?"
he asked as I walked up to him. "I've been thinking about you for
two years." Over coffee he told me he had graduated from Northwestern and had been working in the trust department of a very
large bank in Chicago for seven years. Having gone back to gradu-
ate school in finance, he was just finishing the work for his M.S.
degree.

We laughed a lot that evening, and I felt at ease with him. It
was obvious he loved to have a good time. When it was time for
me to go, I found myself asking him to come out and meet my
father and Lucy.

Since I'd started working, my father hadn't said anything more
about my leaving. And the pattern of life at their house had
changed a lot. Not getting off work until late, I often found that
they had already gone to sleep when I got home. But other nights,
they would be up having cocktails and seemed to be waiting for
me, which always thrilled me. That night as Findley and I
walked up the front walk, I hoped they would be up. They were,
and Findley and my father seemed to take to each other right away.
"At last I've done something right," I thought, smiling at the two
of them drinking together.

After the Marshall Fields assignment, I had all the modeling
jobs I needed for several months. Findley would often pick me up
at 10:00 at work and we'd go out to dinner. He was attending
school at night, so it worked out very well. When we'd get to my
father's house, he and Lucy were often still up. And frequently

they invited Findley and me to have dinner with them. I couldn't have been more pleased, having a family to bring someone home to.

Looking back, I realize that Findley and I never actually got around to talking personally. The fact that I was modeling during the day and he was working meant we only had late evening dates for dinner or coffee. We had a good time together but we didn't really know each other on a feeling level. I kept thinking we would, but talking about personal feelings was just not his style. As a matter of fact, we were almost completely unaware of the intimate details about each other's lives. For instance, one night at the table after dinner, my father leaned over and said, "Findley, can you believe that my daughter came two thousand miles to meet me on her eighteenth birthday?

Findley's mouth almost dropped open as he looked at me. When I'd met him two years before, he'd thought I was twenty-one—even though I was actually sixteen. Since Findley was twenty-nine, that meant there was a much larger difference in our ages than he'd known. I was so private about my life it just never occurred to me to tell him.

The more I was with Findley, the more I appreciated him. He was attractive, fun to be with, and bright. His maturity was complemented by a certain special charm, and he was sophisticated about getting around in Chicago. Everything he was represented security and respectability to me, and before long I realized that I loved him. As the days went on Findley talked to me about marriage. I wanted to say yes, but I was still very wary of men. But even though I had come to love Findley very much, I couldn't seem to make up my mind about putting my whole future in any man's hands.

One evening we got in very late and found my father sitting in the living room alone. Just the night before he had asked again when I was leaving. I'd told him Findley had asked me to marry him, and that I was considering it. But I was still surprised that he was waiting for us alone this evening. He stood up when we came in and looked at us.

"Findley," he said quietly, "my daughter tells me you want to

marry her. I think she's lying, because if you wanted to marry her,
I know you'd speak to me about it, wouldn't you?"

I was furious! A twenty-nine year-old bachelor would certainly
be turned off by an aggressive parent trying to trap him into marriage. Besides, even though I wanted to be Findley's wife, I had
just made up my mind I was not going to marry anyone. I had already walked away from three men I'd been engaged to. And I
had made it clear to both Findley and Daddy that I didn't think I
could trust anyone to be faithful. I loved Findley, yes, and had
wanted him to ask me to marry him, but *no man* was going to hurt
me again. And I said so.

But to my surprise, Findley looked at me, then turned to my
father and said,

"I certainly do want to marry Hedy."

Daddy smiled and looked at me.

"Hedy," he said, "you're eighteen years old. It's a girl's job to get
married and you're certainly old enough to. It's what you ought to
do."

Findley just stood there smiling, as my father stared me down
and made his pronouncement. But I stared back and held my
ground. Daddy might be the most important person in my life,
but I had had some very painful experiences of rejection from men.
I wasn't going to be a fool. I told them both I wouldn't live
through infidelity and rejection, pretending that everything was all
right. No man had ever come through on his responsibility to me
or really kept his promises, including my father. And I certainly
didn't want to have my heart broken again. The pain of Buzzy's
rejection was still too real. But it was obvious that my father didn't
understand. And it was also obvious that he wanted me to marry
Findley.

Arguing with these two men I loved, but who I couldn't believe loved me, was like butting up against a thick stone wall.
Somehow they couldn't hear me, or didn't believe me, or something.

Finally, through the haze of my fears and confusion I heard my
father saying, "Damn it, Hedy, don't you want my blessing?"

His *blessing!* I knew he meant on the marriage, but something in me heard him offering me his *acceptance.* And something in me *did* want to marry Findley, though I was afraid of what might happen if I did. I loved him and wanted to be his wife. As far as I could tell, we had the ingredients for a good marriage.

So as the clock struck 6 A.M., I said "yes" to Findley and to my father. Daddy shook Findley's hand, smiled at me and poured us all a drink.

Finally I was going to have a home to live in and to love in. And at last I had done something to please my father.

17. Marriage, Side One: Homemaker of the Year

FINDLEY, HIS FAMILY, and married life in Lake Forest gave me a whole new audience. Now I was on the inside of those homes I'd walked by and felt so "outside" of as a child.

But inside this antique-gold society where I had wanted to fit, to belong, I wasn't sure what to do. As a model I had learned to wear clothes with as much style as any of them. And I had certainly learned to look cool and hide my unacceptable or insecure feelings. But I wasn't sure how I was supposed to act, feel, or think as a part of this group, or what was proper to discuss? And most of all I was unsure of how to do things "right" socially—those subtle touches in entertaining, which let people who are really "aware" know whether or not a newcomer is acceptable. Even though I had already picked up a lot from Findley, I was still insecure.

I soon discovered this was another game, like modeling, only much more subtle and intricate. But it too could be learned and absorbed. So I watched Findley's friends and his mother and her friends. I was young enough to ask discreet questions about social rules and duties in such a way as not to reveal the enormity of my feelings of ignorance. Before many months I knew more than a lot of the women my age who had lived in that world all their lives. But I also knew that a sense of belonging in that society is much deeper than knowing the rules. And I was always secretly afraid of making some colossal blunder which would reveal my lack of social experience.

Besides being in the banking business, Findley had other investments and often worked seven days a week, and sometimes on holidays. When he wasn't working, he was trying to finish his master's degree at night. That meant he had to study in his "spare time."

I had waited all my life to love my man and to be loved by him. My dream of intimacy included hours spent together doing and saying—I wasn't sure what, but certainly doing loving things which would make me feel loved and desirable at last.

But the day we got back from our honeymoon Findley practically disappeared back into his already full life of work and school. It was almost as if I weren't there. At first I thought he had just gotten behind and was catching up. We had moved into a furnished apartment, so it didn't take long to get settled. Then I found myself with nothing to do all day except wait for Findley to come home. I'd fix dinner with flowers and candlelight. Sometimes he came home and we were close. But he often skipped dinner and didn't get home until very late. Other times he even forgot to call. And all my insecurities and bad feelings about myself started rearing their ugly heads. This wouldn't do at all. While Findley was getting through this busy time, I could not just sit on my hands.

This was when I began in earnest to tackle the task of trying to be the most outstanding homemaker in Chicago. During the next seven years, I learned the Chicago social and civic worlds as I had learned painting, acting and modeling—with every ounce of energy in me.

I started out by joining one small club and within a few years was president of five social or civic clubs at the same time. I became active in local politics and city betterment efforts. I learned to play bridge and tennis. I worked with handicapped and underprivileged children. And we began taking teenage children into our home, primarily young girls or boys who had been judged delinquent by the juvenile courts in Cook County.

Findley did join me in forming the Teenage Republican Club of Chicago which eventually included at least fifty active members in most of the white collar high schools. We took representatives to statewide and then national conventions.

In the evenings we were regular in attending the North Shore Little Theater, the Lyric Opera and the Chicago Symphony. We had season tickets to the Chicago Bears football games from the first year we were married. And of course there were the Shore Acres Country Club and the Onwentsia. Because Findley and Daddy got along so well, we stopped by to see him and Lucy every now and then. We didn't see Mother much. She had moved back to the North Shore, and occasionally I went by or called.

In my efforts to weave myself into the social and civic fabric of Chicago, I supported all the major charities and benefits and found myself on the city board of goals for Chicago. Ironically, I was also teaching family communication at College of Lake County at night.

And finally, for two years in a row, I was on the Chicago Home-maker Panel, having been named a "Homemaker of the Year."

It was incredible: Homemaker of the Year—and teaching family communications—and Findley and I only seemed to pass each other in the halls of our home. By this time there was even less intimacy than there had been.

Sometimes, driving to or from a committee or board meeting, I would be conscious of a dull pain or ache in my heart. The need for a father's love had somehow blended with the need for intimacy and focused now on Findley. I longed for him to hold me, to assure me, to share with me and to love me passionately. But he could not—or would not—do these things except on rare occasions or when he'd been drinking. I began to feel an awful dread some-where just outside my consciousness. And I would try to reassure myself, as millions of women must have, that my man was true and loving. It was just that he was so busy. Then I'd quickly get back to work at doing the only thing I was trained to do: trying to earn approval and love from the people "out there."

Eventually my living portrait of the "perfect wife" was almost completed. But along the way I had realized that there were several things missing—children for one. It was time to start our family.

Our first child Susan was born when I was twenty. Maybe children would bring us together or at least make me more desirable as a woman. When we brought Susan home from the hospital, I decided we needed to pick a church (another missing credential) because I had no idea where to have her christened. We didn't actually join until Janie was born; but we had both children baptized in the church Findley's family belonged to. After their baptisms we attended church every Easter.

Looking back over this period I felt good about the place I had made for myself. From an outward view I did belong in Chicago and Lake Forest. I had wanted Findley to be proud of his wife. And I had succeeded.

But there was another side to my life, one the world did not see at all.

18. Marriage, Side Two: The Truth Behind the Mask

"REMARKABLE! HEDY'S a radiant and *remarkable* young woman! A real life force in Chicago." I overheard a white-haired dowager-queen saying this as I was in a buffet line at Shore Acres one day. We were on the same committee.

Inside I smiled grimly, "Yes, Hedy, you *are* remarkable!" I told myself. "You're a life-force and you're not even *alive*."

The press had been very kind to me. And the fact that at such an early age I was so involved with helping other people gave me a special kind of notoriety and public acceptance. But the truth was that my loneliness was getting to be almost unbearable.

I really did want to make things better for people, to reach out and see that those who couldn't do anything for themselves got help. I felt as if I had a lot of love to give. But my world was filled with society matrons twice my age, and I wouldn't dream of sharing anything personal with them. They evidently saw me as a wonderful, loving, giving young person, who had everything she needed. I dressed like these women, ate the same foods at luncheon every day, and maintained an amazing enthusiasm—amazing since I was sometimes bored and increasingly discouraged. After a lifetime of practice, I had become an absolute expert in making sure life looked good.

One day I stood on the Onwentsia terrace looking out across the golf course. What was life about anyway? At that moment I realized an amazing thing. Life in Lake Forest was like life at the carnival and in Hollywood. Some of the wives were huddled together for security, in exercise classes, beauty shops, women's clubs, and at Onwentsia. Many of them, like the carnies, had seen their youthful dreams crumble. On the other hand, I saw that some of those wives who seemed to have it made as they laughed gaily over their luncheon martinis were terrified, lonely and insecure like the Hollywood stars. No one really listened to anyone else.

People who were in the top spots—like those who had it made in Hollywood—respected each other in a knowing way but were very careful about being too personal. It was the Hollywood star system through and through. There were the social glamour queens who had arrived, and those on their way up, some of them going almost to the point of having publicity agents. And then there were those who, regardless of money and background, would never make it—who didn't even understand the game.

Findley had in some way taken over the role of my father in withholding his love. So often I had waited for him to come home with candles burned down and fancy dishes I'd prepared so lovingly turned cold and soggy. I knew he was busy with his work and was teaching classes at night. But I soon became aware of the great gap between the end of classes each night and the time he actually got home. He had to be seeing someone else. But I couldn't think about that.

I began to change in my feelings toward him. Whereas at first I'd been trying to make him proud of me, now I was trying to be more successful than he—just to show him I was somebody.

But finally one night, I couldn't stand it any longer. I not only felt desperate for intimacy but simply couldn't understand why we didn't have it. I'd never told him the story of my life so he couldn't have known how terribly lonely I was. And I put on such a good show of intimacy. Maybe Findley thought I already had it. Maybe he was more terrified of closeness than I was. I wondered what went on behind closed doors in other people's marriages. Were they all like ours?

All I wanted was Findley, and all I was trying to do consciously was love him.

I remembered how the black cloud of hiding our feelings had dropped from the sky right after our honeymoon and had never drifted away. I had started trying to be the perfect wife, and Findley had almost disappeared emotionally and physically.

Now several years later, I was admitting to myself that I was lonely and utterly miserable. Finally I got up the courage to take an enormous risk and find out if I were really lovable. Three other men besides Findley had wanted to marry me. I *must* be desirable. But after our honeymoon, I'd had only my waiting and my self-doubts to fill the days and nights.

On that particular night, Findley came home late again. I heard him stomp in and drop his books on the dining room table. I was in a honeymoon gown, listening for his every sound, waiting for him to come up and—I hoped—love me. He had missed dinner again, but suddenly I didn't care. He was home. The minutes passed. I started to turn out the light and surprise him. But then I turned it back on and sat up in bed in what I hoped would be a very sexy pose.

But he didn't come up the stairs. What had I done wrong? I thought back over everything that had happened the past few days, but couldn't see anything that he'd be hurt or angry about—certainly not enough to despise me. I'd cooked, cleaned house, dressed up for him when he came home, received him with open arms and parted lips. I'd done everything except seduce him. I stopped. Could I do it? I didn't know. I got out of bed and stood in the middle of the room, trying to figure out what to do. I was very aroused at the idea I had in mind. But could I bring myself to do it?

I slipped out of my nightgown, walked over to the full-length mirror and looked at my body. I knew enough about men to know that I was not unattractive physically.

"Okay, Hedy," I said to myself, *"This is it!"* And with all the courage I had ever gotten together, I didn't even give myself a second to think it over.

Without putting my gown back on, I went down the stairs slowly. Findley was sitting in a chair at the table, engrossed in one of his books. I walked over, stood beside him and put my hand on his shoulder.

My heart was beating rapidly and I had very warm feelings for him. "Findley," I whispered in his ear, "I love you. I've missed you so much, and I'm glad you're home." He shook my hand off his shoulder.

"Damn it, Hedy, I'm busy. Can't you tell I'm studying?" And he went on reading, never having even looked up.

I can still see myself cringing inside with shame and humiliation as I pulled myself together and almost crawled up the stairs.

Not a word was ever said about that night. But at some deep level I knew I could never risk myself with Findley again. My embarrassment was beyond description. Another bolt had been locked in place in the suit of armor. The young girl with her dreams of finding acceptance and love had almost shriveled away. I would never make the mistake of being vulnerable with Findley again. I was convinced, or thought I was, that whatever intimacy was, if anyone really had it, I knew it would not be with me.

19. Home, the Place for Love and Security

Now THE MEANINGLESSNESS of my life began seeping into my conscious thoughts like a poison, threatening to kill every hopeful impulse.

In the beginning I had thought we had the ingredients for love and closeness in our marriage. We'd had our good moments, and I replayed them again and again in my mind. But as the months and years went by, I was bewildered by the increasing distance I felt from Findley. Since I had no place to turn, no one to talk to about such personal things, I fought back waves of panic when I thought of my apparently hopeless marriage.

As I made beds, cleaned the house, bathed Susan and played with her, I would calm down a little. When I'd dress her up in pretty dresses to take her out with me, I felt alive and proud. But everything seemed to be for "show" in that there was no continuing center to my life, no one who could hear me and receive me as a person and a woman. I filled my life with safe things to love—we had dogs, cats, and even a rabbit. And Susan and I loved them all as we fed them and played with them. One dog in particular, Penny, almost seemed to understand me and was a great comfort.

It was at this time in my loneliness that I began to take in foster children from the juvenile court. By the time our second child, Janie, was born, we had three teenaged foster children living with us in a two bedroom home. It seems incredible. Everyone was impressed that we would do this. But my motives were not all that unselfish. Working with those kids in trouble represented the only close personal relationships in my life. The teenagers were young enough to be safe and yet, unlike my babies, old enough to fill some of the vacuum for a family kind of love and for the sharing of thoughts and feelings. Findley didn't object, since their presence took the pressure for closeness off him.

Mother helped out by babysitting Susan some, and Lucy had always loved it when I brought the baby to see her and my father. He never said anything, but I thought I could see signs that he liked Susan from the beginning.

But suddenly, with Janie's arrival we realized how jammed together we were in our small house. Since something had to be done, we began looking for a larger home. Just at that time Findley's father died. His mother was going to move out of their large well-built house on Westminster in Lake Forest and offered it to us. We decided to move. This was what had been missing—a home of our own—one which we could plan and furnish together, a place where we could feel secure. That must have been what we had been wanting, lacking. It certainly seemed to be what everyone else was working toward.

When I first stood in front of the large four bedroom, four bath, high-ceilinged home, I knew this was what I had been dreaming of to complete our lives. I loved the old heavy solid doors, the casement windows, the shining wide plank hardwood floors. Working with the lighting engineer and the landscape architect was a breath of new life . . . and miracle of miracles, Findley and I were together. We were talking, planning and dreaming about the details of our home. My heart was singing.

And Findley was sparing no expense. Everything I'd ever wanted went into my kitchen. The furniture was all custom made. We even had our mantle carved in Italy, which took six months.

The quality of workmanship and materials which went into our dream home spoke to me in a tangible way of love and security from Findley. When something was finished which pleased us both, we'd look at each other and laugh like two kids in a candy store, something we had almost quit doing. Those eight months of working on that house were the happiest and most exciting months I'd ever known. I was even afraid to smoke during the construction for fear I'd burn down my dream. That should have told me how much I had riding on that house. But I didn't realize that until it was finally finished.

The house was beautiful and we were both proud of it. It felt good to say *"our* home." We went out to dinner much less often. And since we loved showing off our new house, we began to entertain more.

One of the nicest things which had happened in our marriage was the coming of Helen into our lives. This wonderful black woman was our maid. In one sense she almost created an atmosphere of home and family by her presence.

"No, no, Susan," she'd say firmly, "That's not the way we do it in this family." She knew how to be a mother. And the children loved her as she entered every aspect of their lives. She was a fantastic housekeeper. When we needed something like floor wax for the new floors she knew just what kind was best and went in my car to get it. She knew how to clean silk lampshades and do a dozen things I'd never heard of doing to maintain our new house and furniture. Also she talked and listened to me by the hour.

And mysteriously, through the process of building and getting settled in our home, a new hope—just a hope—was born for a more loving relationship with Findley.

I knew that when he was at home for parties there would be some time for the two of us after the dinner guests left or before they came. I felt all warm and loving toward Findley again. But when the last guest would go home, a pattern began to develop in our behavior. I would check things out in the kitchen and give instructions to Helen. When I came upstairs toward the bedroom I'd see that the light was still on. The first time, I smiled and felt a warm shiver, knowing that Findley was waiting up. But when I came in, he was in our bed with the children, having gotten them up to play with them. This became his habit, which I felt was another way to avoid loving me.

It was bewildering and very frustrating. I had everything, almost literally, that I'd ever wanted. I wondered how many other women in America had nice-looking husbands, friends, attractive homes, enough food, clothing, cars and "things," and yet felt unloved by the one person who mattered. During the day I roamed the house from one end to the other like a caged panther. Strangely, the beautifully furnished home seemed empty. I kept looking for missing things to add and bought them. The house seemed so big and vacant, not even warm. There had to be more to life, but for god's sake, what could it be?

On one hand I felt settled at last, but on the other I began to experience a new restlessness which I should have paid attention to, but ignored. All I could do was wonder silently, "What's the matter with me anyway?" What did I want? It wasn't sex, although that was certainly involved. I'd have settled for touch, presence, listening, sharing. Other people seemed to have these things. But the more I listened to my friends at the beauty parlor and over coffee, the more I began to suspect that not too many people had them. And some of the ones who *said* they did couldn't seem to look me in the eye. Since *I* was pretending things were great at our house, I couldn't tell if *they* were being honest or not. I decided that maybe no one had the kind of love I dreamed of. And that real intimacy was a fantasy sold to the American people by television producers.

But the morning after I'd reached that conclusion, I was standing in the check-out line of the supermarket. Alone, I was absently watching and listening to the couple ahead of me. Suddenly I was spellbound by what I was seeing and hearing. The woman was overweight, about twenty-five years old, no make-up, small tight lips, thick bifocal glasses. Her clothes were out of style and lacked class. Her hair was stringy and needed shampooing. Everything about her seemed disorderly. But the man with her was nice-looking, well groomed in a clean sport shirt and slacks—the exact opposite of her sloppiness. He looked responsible and seemed to be genuinely interested in her and everything she said. The way he laughed and casually touched her spoke of the very sensitivity and caring I had just decided didn't exist. It was obvious that this man adored his woman. He stood there with his arm around her waist, as if she were a beautiful lady, then effortlessly picked up their packages and went out with her.

What on *earth* did he see in her? What did she have? What did she do? How did she do it? But in that brief encounter I knew once more that there might be some way that two people could relate which would meet the haunting need in my own life.

During the next month I noticed several couples who obviously weren't as well-off or as nice-looking as Findley and I—yet they acted as though they possessed a wonderful and mysterious secret. I wondered if what I saw in these couples was what intimacy looked like from the outside. But as in so many areas of my life, I seemed to be an outsider wondering what it would be like to *know* the inside truth.

About this time I discovered for sure that Findley was conducting his own search for intimacy—outside our marriage. The ache of that knowledge simply added to the mountain of discouragement, lack of worth, and anger which I was beginning to feel. Even my full seven-day-a-week, social-heroine schedule couldn't handle this news. At times I was so lonely I'd say to myself, "I wouldn't even mind his looking somewhere else if he would just look at me too. I'd settle just to be included!" My self-esteem was at its lowest ebb. And I knew that our new home, by completing the outside picture of the perfect life, only made the inner emptiness more hollow and barren.

One morning I sat in front of our living room window looking out into a cold, rainy November day, feeling sad clear into my bones. Yet somehow that day I became resigned to life. I would accept my lot. At that moment something welled up from the basement of my soul—a stark realization that came to me full blown: no *thing*, no home, no clothes, no husband, no city, not even the prestige and social position that went with money—nothing *outside*

myself was ever going to fulfill my basic need and search! It seemed
so obvious. I couldn't imagine why I hadn't seen it sooner.

In that moment I turned a page and stepped into a new chapter
of my life. All day I let the message sink in—that I must look
within to find out about love and life. If this was true, then there
was hope! Because whatever I might find there could not be taken
away from me by anyone.

With that insight came a strong urge to wake up the artist self
I'd stored away when I moved to Lake Forest and began to get involved with people and projects there. I wanted to let the dreamer-
artist out of her cell to express herself through what had happened.
With my hands almost trembling, I got out my paints. And I disappeared into the magic world of my canvases, as I had done so
often when my dreams of completion turned out to be only shattered fantasies.

The inner world I had denied again and again while I was trying
to win love competitively in the outer world—that inner world now
opened its arms to me. The closer I got to the creative "otherwhere,"
inside, that world beyond the reach of social games and selfish demands, the nearer to the warm center of life I seemed to be.

I began to paint all day. Paint and see that the children had their
needs met. I bought them a double easel and spent hours teaching
them to draw and splash colors. The pain and loneliness started to
drop off like scales. I began to feel like a butterfly stirring within its
cocoon. Instead of longing for Findley to come home, I found myself painting all night long, hoping he wouldn't come in and inter-
fere with my work. Even on Sunday mornings if he were at home,
I would paint.

There were big pictures as well as small ones. There were paintings of dreamy landscapes which were haunting and soft, sometimes with a child in them. There were faces again—some were
portraits—and many happy scenes with flowers in them.

Emotionally I felt the blood of life begin to flow through my
veins again. The breath of a creative spring brought its young
green shoots and earthiness into the barren center of my life. There

was no way to understand what was happening. I was alone, yet I had never been less alone. Maybe I loved painting because I could commit myself totally to it and be totally received somehow—feel acceptable, accepted.

One day, I brushed a wisp of hair out of my eye and looked into the face I'd just painted. It was a happy, loving face. Although I'd stopped hoping I'd find intimacy, it was alive somewhere in the dark recesses of my life. And it was nearer than it had ever been as I looked into the honest, vulnerable face which had been brought by my hand from the hidden part of my soul.

The bedroom converted into my studio was the most personal room in the house for me now. But when I hung my paintings on our walls, the whole house was more personal. One night someone asked about one of my portraits, "Hedy, where did you get that painting? It would go perfectly in my house." I began selling paintings off my walls. In buying my works, I felt people were saying that the inner Hedy that was most truly me, the Hedy I had to protect and hide from them, was real and was worth taking into their lives.

What a difference from scoring in the social competition! When people I respected loved my paintings, they were really loving the unlovable child in me—without their even knowing it. I began selling everything I painted and getting several commissions a month. Now my large sunny studio room had become a fountain for a stream of happy faces and scenes which were flowing out of my life into other people's homes.

But leaving that room only made me more aware of what was absent in the other parts of the house. The dinners alone with two tiny children were grim, with Findley's empty place staring at me like a missing front tooth as I chatted with the children and heard about their day. I am amazed at the enormous capacity I had for repressing my anger and all of my feelings as a woman, as I pretended that somehow this charade of a marriage was all right.

But as I began to get in touch with my real self and as the spirit of life began to quicken my blood, some other feelings which I had repressed began to move in me. I wondered how it would feel to be fully a woman. People had looked in the windows of my soul through my paintings and seemed to like what they saw. Maybe some man might find me lovable as a woman. I quickly dismissed the thought. But it came back more and more often.

At parties I began noticing nice-looking men and secretly wondered if one of them might want me if I signaled that I was interested. I knew that adultery was hardly unusual in our circles, though everyone pretended it never happened. And it didn't take a fortuneteller to know which men were interested. These men had kidded me about being so straight for years. But I simply could not take the step. From my childhood I remembered vividly that "nice girls don't—and you'll be rejected if 'they' find out you did." But there was the even more terrifying prospect that a man might make love to me and not find me desirable after all. I shuddered and cringed at that thought.

Then one evening I saw a small ad in the evening paper. It read, "Tried everything else? Why not try God?" "Why not?" I thought, in my private desperation, never dreaming of the nightmare that it might lead to.

20. Into the Hands of God

THE THOUGHT OF going to a minister—or anyone else—for personal help had never entered my head. I had always controlled my feelings and handled them myself, but neither had I ever been in quite such a desperate dilemma. The powerful woman feelings which had surfaced were crying out to be expressed. And I knew men who wanted to talk to me, to be personal and to make love to me. Would I die without knowing what it felt like to really be wanted and loved as a woman? I felt guilt even having such feelings as a married woman. The conflict was excruciating. This whole idea made me rush back to Findley to get our marriage healed.

So in the middle of a Tuesday afternoon I got dressed up and went to the church we belonged to. Rev. Cowell, about ten years older than I, seemed glad to see me. Having decided to trust him, I asked him to help me make our marriage whole. He listened with great understanding. I felt better just having someone I could trust know our awful secret struggle.

By the time I got home from the church he had called and left his number. When I returned the call, he wanted to know how I was and assured me that he would be praying for me. He suggested I see him the next day. The following day he called twice and the day after, we had lunch together. I was overwhelmed and

very relieved. At last here was someone who accepted me, seemed
to understand and could assure me God loved me.

After that we met often. I could discuss my marital problems
with him without fear of rejection, of being misunderstood or revealed to anyone else. I asked questions about life and religion I'd
always wanted to ask. I didn't have to be afraid of this man as a
male because he was a minister. So I could let down my defensive
walls a little and be myself, as I'd never been able to do. Rev.
Cowell insisted that I call him Bert. Since I had him to talk to, the
intimacy needs I'd been afraid would lead me to try a sexual adventure appeared to have subsided. I had my art and a fine, bright
sensitive minister and friend.

After several months, I was sitting in Bert's office one day, trying
to thank him for all the time and concern he'd given me. "I
don't understand how the church can be so good to me and you
can give me so much time when I've done so little ever for the
church."

"Hedy," he looked at me, shaking his head slightly, "do you
really believe this is the church? I've loved you since the first day
you walked in that door." He stopped and looked with real yearning
into my eyes. "Listen, honey, God wants you to be loved, Jesus
wants you to be loved. And I need love too. I can give it to you."

Listening to his rush of words, I felt myself go into shock—the
same fear I'd had when men got unexpectedly close ever since that
long ride home at fifteen. A minister!

I had sensed a real closeness with this man. He had given me his
attention, his interest, as no man in my life had. I could accept it
because it had been without a physical price tag. I had thought Bert
was genuinely interested in me and my problems, and because of
this I'd shared things I hadn't planned to at all. Over the months he
had begun to tell me some of his problems, marital and vocational.
It was more exciting than he could know, because after a session
with him I came away almost content, as if we'd gotten close to
the heart of intimacy. This was what closeness was about—
sharing problems as well as ideas. And I was actually experiencing
it. He had no way of knowing that I had never shared at this level

before—that in fact I knew almost nothing about being personal with anyone except to listen to their problems, trying to be helpful. But until this time I'd always stayed in the superior position of the helper.

Now that he had declared himself, we were in a different emotional world. He was suddenly all male, and he wanted me. How could I have been so naïve about ministers? I'd always thought that for "men of God" there were extremely strict rules about women, particularly married women. I couldn't have conceived of a legitimate minister in a respectable church thinking of and acting out sexual thoughts with a counselee. And I'd been totally open about my lack of sex with Findley and my agonizing need for love and affirmation as a woman.

I left his office in a state of great agitation. Whether Bert was a minister or not, he was an attractive man; he had looked inside me and evidently liked what he saw. I was afraid and yet fascinated. After a lifetime of being suspicious and very controlled physically, I wasn't about to let this go too far. But I was flattered that he wanted me. I tried to cut off the relationship, yet I put off any decisive action. Even though I knew it was wrong, I simply could not shut the only personal doorway in my life.

Bert began appearing at our house in the evening after jogging several miles. He'd ask for a glass of water and want me to drive him home. Other times he'd call in the mornings just to say hello and talk. I was being courted as I imagined girls who had stayed in Lake Forest had been courted. And though everything in me was screaming, "Look out, Hedy! break it off! This is not right," I kept thinking, "Just a little bit longer," and "We're not actually *doing* anything wrong"—meaning adultery. But I was troubled about our relationship in spite of my rationalizations.

We played the game of seducing each other with our eyes. And I felt an exciting intensity building in me. But I kept it from getting beyond words or looks and glances. I was keenly aware of his ministry, his beautiful wife and young child. His ministerial position was the safeguard—*mine,* so that he would never find out that I was really undesirable and afraid. I played a game of seduction and keep away, which gave me a lot of pleasure and fed my fantasies without doing any harm—or so I thought.

Then a really strange turn of events took place. Knowing all about our marriage, Bert began to get nervous on those rare occasions when Findley and I would spend an evening together at home. Or he'd become sullen when Findley and I had been out socially and I'd tell him about it the next day. I realized with a shock that Bert was jealous of Findley and afraid we would start loving each other again, physically.

Suddenly Bert seemed to be everywhere. He'd drive by at all hours as I was leaving the house. And when we were together he questioned me about everything I was doing.

But, one day, the inevitable happened. He came by when Helen was gone with the children, and he and I were all alone. We were sitting on the couch talking about our marriages when he stopped and looked at me with open longing.

"Hedy, I can't stand it. I've got to have you. I've loved you for months and never have wanted anyone the way I want you!"

He took me into his arms and kissed me. I pushed him back, feeling very uncomfortable—and not knowing quite what to do. I wanted him to love me, but all I could do was think about the fact that he was a minister—and married. And I was afraid—afraid of the situation and afraid of being rejected. I tried to be gentle and sensitive in telling him to let me alone. He began to weep. My compassion and understanding only made his frustration greater. I knew I had to either quit putting him off or end the relationship. But in my heart I didn't want to end it. Why couldn't it stay as it had been? Why were men either totally distant or totally demanding physically?

Now I realize that on that day I probably gave him just enough hope to keep the relationship going. Having a man who said he couldn't live without me, who "had to have me," felt good—for about three days.

Finally I realized that Bert was not going to be put off much longer. And I began a hasty withdrawal. But the more distant and inaccessible I was, the more frantic and drawn to me he seemed to become. He began to be irrational and I got very frightened.

One evening he called to say he thought he was having a nervous breakdown. He was leaving his wife and was coming to get me in about an hour. The way he talked I knew he meant what he was saying—that he was ready to walk away from everything he'd worked for all his life.

In a panic I called Findley at his office, but found out that he was on the way home. Just as I hung up I heard him coming in the back door. Throwing myself into his arms, I said almost hysterically, "Help me, honey! I've gotten myself in a horrible mess!" And I told him about going to the church for help and what had happened. I think underneath I was very relieved—now Findley would realize that an attractive man could want me and care that much about me. And besides, my lifelong fantasy-view still held that a woman's husband was the white knight who, whatever differences there were in the marriage, would ride out in a great rage to defend his woman's honor. Since I'd never needed my honor defended in our marriage, I had kept this dream intact. And now I was sure Findley would stand up for me, look after me, and maybe appreciate me at last. He held me silently as I poured out my story.

The doorbell rang. I was frightened about the confrontation of two angry men. But when Findley opened the door, he said, "Hello, Bert, come in and have a drink." With a friendly smile he led Bert right past me and into the living room to the bar. "Scotch and water, isn't it?" Bert nodded, never taking his eyes off me.

I couldn't believe what was happening. For a few minutes I thought he was setting Bert up to smash him in the face. But then they sat down and began to talk about pro football and hunting season.

I stood watching them, trying to grasp what was going on. It was like the sickening feeling of being lost and deserted in a bad dream. I was horrified, yet in a strange way, fascinated at the unreality of

these two men talking to each other as if nothing were wrong—
when all three of our lives and futures were hanging in the balance.
I sat down across the room, watching them.

After about forty-five minutes, Findley asked Bert to stay for
dinner. Almost without being conscious of what I was doing, I
walked into the kitchen and started getting a meal together. As I
went into the dining room to set the table, the truth of what was
happening hit me. I closed my eyes and shook my head trying to
clear my thinking. I could see only two options at the time: Findley
either didn't care that Bert wanted to take me off, or he felt he was
too sophisticated and too "civilized" to get upset over a little thing
like someone wanting to steal his wife. In either case it was the
most painful nightmare of any I'd had. I kept saying over and over
to myself as I automatically put the napkins and water glasses in
place, "This can't really be happening to me. This is some crazy
kind of dream. It cannot be! It is *not* so!"

I didn't want to know if it was true. I was dizzy, sick at my
stomach, and my mind was numb almost to the point of not being
able to function. I didn't say a word during dinner as the two of
them, a little tight now on the Scotch, laughed and talked. All I
could think of was, "Surely Bert will leave after supper!"

But what would I do then? I couldn't even look at Findley. I
felt completely irrational and completely detached from both of
them.

When dinner was over, I watched them get up and move to the
floor in front of the fireplace, talking like two old friends with their
after-dinner drinks.

Finally I stumbled back into the kitchen. I'd just stay there
until they both left. But then what would I do? Where would I
go? No, Findley would finally get drunk and tell Bert to get the hell
out of our house. I forced that hope to be reborn. The minutes
dragged into hours. My god, what could they be talking about?
Maybe they were getting serious at last. Then I heard them both
laugh uproariously.

Some time later I heard Bert's drunken voice calling, "Hedy,
baby, where are you?" He was stumbling through the various rooms

looking for me. And his slurred voice was getting louder and more desperate.

"Hedy, tell me where you are!"

Then I could see him careening into the breakfast room toward me. I felt myself tighten all over with my old fear. I backed up against the refrigerator in the corner as he came across the kitchen with both arms outstretched. He was lurching sideways, obviously very drunk, tears streaming down his face. Then I saw that he had a scared, desperate look in his eyes. He caught my shoulders and leaned against me, pressing my body into the refrigerator door.

I tried to push the dead weight of him away from me as he spoke in a jerky unreal voice, his face soaking wet with his own tears, "Hedy, I can't live without you any longer, I love you, honey. I can make you happy, I promise. Nothing else matters."

I shook my head violently. This was my *minister,* the man I went to for help and revealed my soul to. A sudden revulsion swept over me. I just looked at him. "Oh, no!" I thought, "You selfish little man." Why wasn't he at home taking care of his own woman? This man represented the whole church to me: faith, Christianity, God, my last hope for a moral decent solution to an impossible marriage. And here he was trying to meet his own needs at the expense of two families, not seeming to care about his own or about saving mine. All this flashed through my mind in the instant his hands caught me by the shoulders.

I was filled with such a rage that the shove I gave him almost threw him on the floor. I remember looking at him, unable to believe the condition he was in, and feeling total disgust at his sloppiness, his weakness and his denial of all he was supposed to stand for.

I ran into the living room. Findley was asleep in front of the fireplace. I grabbed a coat and ran out the front door. Where could I go? Whom could I tell? *I* couldn't understand what had happened. How could I expect anyone else to? All I could feel were waves of rejection and betrayal sweeping over me from my whole lifetime. I looked up at the stars, "God, are you there? *Please* help me! Please send someone who will love me just for myself!"

I don't know how long I stood there staring at the night, watching the sky through the dark shadows of the oak trees, and trying to pray. But evidently no one was up there. I shivered. But I couldn't go back in. I was the rejected little girl again. So, as I had when I was a child, I went around to the garage, crawled into the back seat of the car and curled up in a ball, wishing I could stay there forever. Finally the tears subsided and I fell asleep until daylight.

21. The Beginning of the End

THE CHILL OF DAWN woke me. I was shivering and could see my breath as I opened my eyes in the car and realized where I was and what had happened. The windows were gray-white crystals. I had the same fear I'd had when I'd run off as a child: fear that my family would find me—and a greater fear that they wouldn't even know I'd gone—that they wouldn't realize I'd felt rejected enough to run away.

The house was very quiet. Findley had evidently made it up-stairs to bed and Bert was gone. I bathed and put on clean clothes, aware of a childish impulse to burn the clothes I'd had on, as a symbol of the end of an era of my life.

As much as he'd drunk, I knew Findley would be asleep till noon. The children slept late when everything was quiet. So as I came downstairs, I pretended my husband and children didn't exist. That way I didn't have to face what I had seen the night before about my relationship with Findley.

I am continually amazed at the strength of habit and training and how one can live through the most amazing crises, doing all sorts of routine things as if controlled by an automatic pilot. I watched myself making coffee and cleaning up the kitchen like a zombie. But when I walked through the dining room, I felt the

146

deep hostility I was repressing beginning to stir. And then as I stepped into the living room and saw the empty drink glasses and the cigarette butts in front of the fire place, a rush of anger flooded through my body. While I picked things up, I got angrier and angrier. I wanted to go up and throw Findley out of bed, tell him what I thought of him and beat him in the face with a high heeled shoe.

But there was no way to reach across the chasm between his emotional world and mine. I knew that now. That part of my life was over.

As I fluffed the pillows on the couch, I thought of Bert. And then I felt the full heat of my anger. Findley couldn't help the way he was. But Bert's behavior was different. He was preying on the flock God had entrusted him with. I had never felt such hatred.

I walked into the breakfast room and dialed the church number for the last time. As I was listening to the telephone ring on the other end of the line, I glanced up and saw myself in the dining room mirror. I was standing very straight and proud.

All the numbness and fuzziness of the night before were gone. My mind was clear now, clear as a bell. I could hear the secretary ringing the pastor's office. With each ring I felt my anger swelling like a boil about to burst—once, twice, the third time—only now I had complete control, and my hatred was focused like the blue cutting flame on an acetylene torch. Then I heard his smooth, cultured voice:

"Hello, Pastor Cowell speaking."

"Good morning, Bert," I said with a quiet, silky voice. "How do you feel?" He started to tell me, but I broke in very sweetly and said, "I know how busy you are, so I don't want to keep you. But I just had to call and thank you for what's happened."

"What?" He was puzzled.

"Well," I continued, "after you left last night Findley and I went upstairs and made love in a way I couldn't ever have even imagined. It was almost more than I could stand or have hoped for. I think everything will be fine with us now, and I just wanted you to know."

There was a long pause on the other end of the line. I could almost see his face, see him slump. Finally he said in the weakest voice I'd ever heard, "You mean you *slept* with him?"

"Yes, Bert, and I never knew what it could be like to really give myself to a man in every way. It was fantastic!"

Another pause. Then much louder and in a voice filled with agony and almost panic, "Hedy, you really *slept* with that bastard?"

"Yes, Bert, and my heart's singing for the first time. Please thank your wife for all the time you've given me. I only hope I can repay the church some day for all your trouble and unselfishness."

I could hear him begin to say "Hedy—"when I cut him off with "Goodbye" and hung up. I knew what I'd done was cruel and terribly wrong, but I couldn't help myself. Life seemed to be a confusing mixture of cruelty, rejection and pain.

I stood in the breakfast room with my hand still on the telephone and chalked up another fact of life never to forget: "If God's anything like his representative on the North Shore, don't ever get in the trap of trusting him either."

Now that my last fantasy about Findley as a sweetheart-lover was dead, I had to decide what to do. I couldn't leave yet. Because of my pride and my conversation with Bert Cowell, I was determined to have the best-looking marriage and family life in Lake Forest—for a respectable time.

I couldn't plan beyond that. Like Scarlett O'Hara, I'd think about that tomorrow.

22. Homemaker of the Year... Gets Divorce

COMMUNICATION WITH Findley had been difficult before, when I'd been trying so hard. Now it was impossible. The taste of relationship and personal communication I'd had with Bert made talking with Findley seem like a scorched wasteland. Bert may have had bad motives, but he'd given me something I'd never had from a man: his total interest and the sharing of his own hopes and dreams. Though he had never leveled with me about his inadequacies, and I hadn't admitted much about mine either, yet we did talk about our lives. And I knew we'd at least been in the kind of atmosphere in which true intimacy might take place.

Although I hated Bert now, I had a disturbing feeling about my own part in what had happened. I was afraid to look at it too closely, but I had encouraged Bert to come closer and closer, as I had always known how to do. And I'd felt very warm about it. But when he'd gotten *too* close, I was suddenly turned off, frightened, and found a perfect excuse to run away.

I wondered during those next few days if I wasn't really terrified of the very things my whole life seemed bent on finding: intimacy and unconditional love.

I spent almost all my energy appearing lovable and keeping this outer shell as perfectly in place as possible. But when *anyone* got close enough to see that inside me was a cancer of loneliness and lack of worth, I *had* to drive them back. Good Lord, was this why I seemed to pick men to pursue who would not or could not relate to me intimately? If they "didn't love me," I might not be happy, but my secret was safe. And I could cry and complain about their not loving me—as I always had done. Or if they did love me, I had righteous grounds on which to push them away. Maybe it was *my own fault!* No, I refused to believe it. Anyway I couldn't handle that in the midst of all the chaos going on inside me. For the time being just keeping myself together was a full-time job.

Whatever the truth might be, I was miserable. I tried to get back to my social and civic duties! But my world was like a giant Humpty-Dumpty. It had cracked and was threatening to fall apart at any moment.

As I sat in familiar meetings in the same clubs with women whose every opinion on the subjects we discussed I'd learned, I felt as if they were total strangers. It frightened me when my mind began to wander in these sessions which dealt with things I'd always kept right on top of. I'd break out in a cold sweat for no reason, and become frightened and very anxious, because I couldn't understand what was happening to me. There was something changing, something ominous, a black cloud of some kind on the horizon moving toward me. I had the terrifying feeling that things were getting out of my control and I might be losing my mind.

The world of women and civic duties was the only structure where I had a place in which people told me I was O.K. Now that was all slipping away from my grasp—like sand through my fingers. Nothing I did seemed to stop the process. I'd told Bert about the problems between Findley and me, but I had never told anyone my inner feelings about my father and about feeling unlovable. I'd tried the church, seeking help for my outer relationships, but found only despair, instead of hope. So I wasn't about to trust another minister now with these even deeper problems.

I'd heard some friends talk about a local psychiatrist who was supposed to be really good. Two things had kept me from going to see him. First, I'd always handled my own problems, and second, I had been raised with the notion that people who go to psychiatrists are crazy and are just about ready to go to a mental hospital. But both objections melted in the intense anxiety which, like a scary night fog, blotted out everything except the terror I felt about the future. I told no one that I was going. But I went.

After the first session I came out with hope. This man could really "hear" me, and it was obvious that he was a good counselor. I was clinging to the hope that my time with him would provide the answer, that I could learn how to make the pieces of our marriage fit together at last.

But as the weeks moved on, the hours with the analyst uncovered the fact that our marriage was hopeless. Still I could not bring myself to dissolve it.

So the next few months were spent building up my courage for the future. The doctor said that my life was crazy. I had gotten an idea somewhere that there were certain elements which would make me a good wife and insure us a happy marriage. I had learned the social game, the civic game, had become the hostess and public relations woman for my husband, I kept a beautiful home, and tried to look nice at all times.

"Doctor, how can all this lead to a bad marriage?" I asked one day.

He studied his gold Cross pen a moment.

"Hedy, your life and your views of marriage have almost no contact with the realities of human relationships. You have no *real* contact with people, even though your life is filled with them. Your life and marriage are completely phony, a pretense you and Findley are sharing."

A "pretense"? If that was true maybe my whole life was built on sand. As this thought sunk in, I almost panicked. What was real life like? Was there any reality for lonely driven people like me? But the thought that there might *not* be drove my attention back to what the doctor was saying.

He tried to explain that there had to be more to a marriage than two people going their separate ways in separate worlds in the same house. People had to have some intense personal sharing, some touch of intimacy somewhere in their marriage—even if it was mostly open hostility. We hadn't even had that . . .

I knew in my heart that everything he said was true. And I also knew that Findley wasn't going to change. But as the fog lifted, uncovering these facts in my mind, an intense agony came with them. When a woman *knows* she'll never have closeness in her marriage and her heart cries out for it, how can she take the step of actually breaking up her home? What would happen to our two lovely little girls without a daddy? I knew what it was like to grow up without a father. What would I do and where would I go with two little girls? Who would have me? And what about my home? That represented security and stability to me. And if I were on my own, would every relationship with a man lead to a traumatic revelation of my lack of desirability as a woman? I wouldn't have even the protection of a bad marriage.

Those days were like an emotional roller-coaster ride.

One day I would know I *had* to leave and I could imagine a life in the future free from the frustration of our marriage and the indecision I felt. But by bedtime of the same day, I was afraid again, and could imagine only guilt and feelings of selfishness in the future. I cringed at the shame of my failure as a woman being made known and my public failure as a homemaker of the year—getting a divorce. I went back and forth as the bowstring of indecision tightened to the breaking point.

Another thing which brought things to a head was that Findley was talking as if he might sell our beautiful home. After seeing so many of my various security involvements slip away one by one, I found the prospect of losing my house horrifying. That place was the only tangible symbol of hope that my dreams might come true. My anxiety was intensified a hundred times. I suppose the straw that broke the camel's back was that for Findley selling the house seemed to be strictly an economic decision. If he felt that way, I knew that we really weren't in the same world emotionally.

The next two weeks were unbelievable. My nights were filled with frightening dreams and restless stirrings—imagining the loneliness of growing old with no one to care about me, while experiencing the frightening prospect of endless aloneness in the nights to come. Every day I went to the psychiatrist. And through his steady kindness and understanding, the scales began to tip toward the courage to live.

I was expecting a dramatic explosion to blow me into the orbit of a decision to leave. But instead, one day I simply stepped across a line somewhere in my mind and I knew it was going to happen.

The strangest thing took place that night. Instead of elation or anger, I began to weep, as if I had just gotten news that a dear family member had died. All of the sense of failure, loneliness, and the terror of the unknown I had held inside since I was a child flowed out of the basement of my soul and rolled over me in waves, leaving me surrounded by a steaming cloud of grief. Then the grief stopped.

I hadn't slept all night. But just before dawn I fell into a restless sleep. I was dreaming of myself as a little girl looking down out of an apple tree reaching for my father who was about to fall in a chasm and be lost to me forever. I could see the bottomless pit because I had dug it. But he couldn't see it and I couldn't talk or shout to him. I realized that if he did fall, I could never win his love. There was something he had asked me to do which could save him. But I couldn't remember what it was, and I was frantic. Just as he stepped over the edge, I realized he'd asked me never to dig that pit. I woke up in a cold sweat. It was morning.

I got up, bathed, dressed and was sitting on the couch in the den by the telephone sobbing when Helen came to work. I'd poured out my heart to Helen for months, and she had seen this moment coming long before I had. She loved me, and I'd learned more about her than about anyone I knew in Lake Forest. Her whole family had become my friends. Helen had the wisdom of the ages about her. She seemed to be at peace. And I was amazed at the wonderful relationship she had with her family, particularly her father. They were friends and actually seemed to have fun together. Helen and her husband loved each other, too, and their kids. I had decided that one of the requirements for being able to love your husband intimately must have something to do with having your father's love. But maybe only blacks had that, I didn't know.

For all her concern for me Helen had also been able to see Findley's side to the marriage too and defended him to me. "Honey, you gotta make allowances for his *nature*." But also she had always protected me when Findley was unreasonable.

This morning she was standing in the kitchen door looking at me. Then she pretended she was mopping the kitchen floor as she sang, laughingly, "Stand by Your Man."

I felt rage rush to my face. In that instant I realized that I was jealous of Helen for her understanding of life, for the love she had from her father and the intimacy she had in her family. I hated her for the advantage she had over me in life. All I had was everything —she had love.

"Shut up, Helen! You don't even know what you're talking about!" But the trouble was I knew she did. I was just past the point of no return and realized there was no going back. I looked at her with tears in my eyes. My heart hurt, ached—I couldn't know then that I'd even lose Helen, but I sensed it somehow. My life was over.

As I sat there, scenes of life in Lake Forest formed in my mind— I could see the chic ones at the country club smiling and saying "Homemaker of the year . . ." Then I saw my father's face. I knew he would think I was stupid, but I shook my head and took a deep breath.

Picking up the phone, I called a lawyer.

23. Lancelot ... At Last

"HELLO HEDY?" The voice on the telephone was that of my friend Shirley. The phone had waked me. She was one of my few younger friends and had understood about our marital troubles without my ever having to tell her. Shirley had been divorced six months earlier. Today she sounded cheery and warm.

"Hi, Shirley," I answered sleepily.

"Listen, Hedy, why don't you come on by for a drink a little later? I haven't seen you in weeks."

I looked at my watch. I had slept till 1:30 in the afternoon. Then I remembered. I'd filed for divorce the day before and had sat by myself and drunk a quart of good wine that night. Findley had moved out. I'd reviewed my life in our big house and our marriage. The truth had sunk in that I was losing not just a husband but everything that I had learned to depend on—even my way of life. The house had belonged to his parents, so I'd lose that too. But Findley and I hadn't really been together as man and wife for most of the past three years. Still I didn't want to face anyone I'd worked with or known socially. But Shirley was an exception.

"That'd be nice, Shirley, I'd love to."

I saw him the minute I walked past Shirley into her living room. He was sitting very relaxed in a big chair by the fireplace and looked up at me through the clearest light blue eyes I'd ever seen. They jolted me and I felt a trembling go through my body—just for a second. Without being self-conscious or aggressive, his eyes captured mine and drew me gently into the room.

Before I had time to react, Shirley had me in tow, introducing me to the several other people who were having cocktails. They were all my own age or younger, many of whom I'd never met. But all I could think about was the handsome clear-eyed man by the fireplace.

When we were finally introduced, he stood up in a very relaxed way. Everything about Danny Baker appealed to me instantly, except his hair and sideburns, which were a little longer than I'd been used to. He was dressed very casually in faded jeans and a blue work shirt with rolled up sleeves—but all fresh and immaculate. He was very calm, nothing of the "What can I get you to drink?" or "Where did you go to school?" or "What do you do?" kind of glib, tip-of-the-tongue questions.

His eyes crinkled when he smiled and hinted at gentleness. He had that strange combination of a strong, lithe, masculine body and yet a sensitivity and firmness which seemed to promise security.

We sat beside each other and began to talk. I noticed a hundred little things. His hand raising his drink was large and strong. When he laughed, a vein in his neck stood out. His fine blond hair tended to stray down on his forehead, and he'd absently sweep it back in place with his hand. His fair skin seemed alive to me and his light blue eyes, which kept reaching out and pulling me gently to him, were devastating with his pale blue work shirt.

Here was a combination of my junior high sweetheart with the athletic form and my cowboy sweetheart, Buzzy, from Hollywood. Yet Danny was from a very fine and socially prominent family in Lake Forest. And most of all, I felt immediately that he was sensitive to me as a person and as a woman. Although I knew I was vulnerable and susceptible to a rebound relationship, I also knew that all my dreams seemed to be combined in this man, whom fate had me sitting next to in Shirley's living room. It seemed incredible that this was only the day after I'd filed for divorce. It was only in the severing of that dead relationship with Findley that I could have seen this man. Surely my magic genie was taking care of me.

In the back of my mind I recalled a recent conversation with my therapist. "Your relationships with men are not based on reality." But I also knew that my intuition had been right in almost every other area of my life. I pushed the thought away.

As we visited quietly with the people sitting near Danny, I was almost physically soothed by his voice. Although we were the same age, he seemed younger. His appearance was almost boyish. I listened to the conversation and realized that these people were in a very different world from the one I'd just left. They used slang I'd never heard in ordinary conversation. It was the language of the hippie subculture. I kept hearing terms like "heads," "uppers," "syringes," "reds," "coke," "acid." And the conversation was about the psychedelic rock stars and concerts they had been in touch with recently.

Danny turned to me.

"Hedy, we're all going to dinner together. Can you come?"

I hesitated a second. He looked into me. Then I nodded my head, "yes."

I went home, bathed and made myself as beautiful as I knew how for an evening on the town, complete with a Pucci print dress. I was excited as a sixteen-year-old on her first date. But when Danny arrived in his blue jeans, I went back upstairs and came down in a pair of black slacks.

The night club we went to was different from any I'd ever been in. It was almost calculated to be unsophisticated—everything but sawdust on the concrete floors. The music was acid rock, screeching, loud and crude. Mantovani was my kind of musician for dining. A waiter walked up to our table with a tray. His hair was long and tied back in a ponytail. "Who the hell wanted the pizza?" he shouted above the music. I couldn't help thinking about the clean, respectful waiters and waitresses at Shore Acres. Still it was exciting, being with Danny.

In my usual way of failing to recognize unpleasant truths about myself and the people I loved, I assumed that Danny and his friends had come here out of curiosity or just for kicks. But I soon realized that everyone in the place seemed to know them. The flashing strobe light twisted their faces, and their laughter became piercing and wild in the midst of all the unfamiliar whining and grating of rock noises. I found myself laughing stupidly, trying to act like I knew what they were talking about, feeling like a naïve fool and realizing how insulated and out of touch with real life my existence had been—that is, if this *were* life.

I knew with everything in me that this couldn't be the real Danny, because I'd gotten a glimpse of someone very sensitive who knew the people I knew. But he did seem to love this music—and these people certainly knew and liked him. I listened to his friends and was really interested in trying to get to know them. As the evening went on, they seemed to accept me and include me more and more.

A couple of hours later, I found myself thinking that these were a bunch of strange wild kids. Their conversation indicated that they were very familiar with the people whose names were always on the front page of the society section of the *Tribune*. It began to dawn on me that this was a social subculture made up largely of drop-out children of the wealthiest and most powerful people in the area. But everyone here seemed totally irresponsible.

I was amazed at how much of the conversation was made up of jokes and slang. No one talked about their jobs, their business deals, their children, clothes, shops, the balls and parties, or football games. The gap between them and me was enormous.

In my world competition was a part of everyone's life, and somehow subtly behind almost every communication—with men or women. But not here. We had rules about ignoring indiscretions and certainly they were not joked about openly, as they were with these restless young people. In my world nothing had been taken lightly. Here nothing was taken seriously—or so it seemed.

But soon I realized there was one serious theme which absorbed all these people. They were trying "to find themselves." From what I could determine, however, most of them were doing nothing constructive. The rules seemed to be that one was justified in doing or trying anything, however wild, which might help him find himself.

It was obvious, though, that this was a very expensive experiment. Their pleasures cost a lot. They drove fine cars, went all over the country to rock concerts, were avid record and tape collectors, bought good whiskey, took girls out to dinner. And their parents paid the bills.

It all seemed bizarre and unreal. Some of them were thirty-year-old men and women! Even though Danny didn't look like he really belonged, it was obvious that everyone thought he did. I was anxious to leave and get to know Danny without these people. But he seemed in no hurry to go.

It was late when we got into his car. I was very sad and my heart seemed heavy. Over the years I'd learned, I thought, what I was looking for in a man. And I knew I really wanted Danny. I'd felt things for him immediately I'd never felt for anyone. But his world—if this were his world—seemed so shallow. And as hard as I tried, I couldn't picture myself ever being part of it. The old fears that I would never find fulfillment crept into my mind, and I withdrew as Danny drove me home.

But things didn't make sense. Danny didn't use the slang expressions the others used. He was articulate and his voice was clear. He seemed to be very sincere and deep like a river. I wanted to get into that river and go with the current of his life, though from the surface I couldn't see the current or where it was going. I knew I couldn't ever live the life style I'd seen that night. And yet what was this strange attraction? I seemed to have known him since I was a little girl. And then a familiar childhood image flashed into my mind, and I smiled. Why . . . why he was my "white knight"!

Then we were in front of my house. I suggested a night cap, and Danny accepted.

Danny built a fire in the fireplace, and we sat on the couch and talked. Now, in the stillness, I began to see beneath the surface of the river. He began to tell me about his life. He'd married his high school sweetheart at North Shore Country Day and gone off to the army, very much in love. He looked at me, deciding whether to go on. Then he continued, "When I came back six months later on leave, my wife was three months pregnant."

He looked into the fire in the fireplace and put his hand on mine beside him. "I was shot in the arm in combat and was in the hospital in California for six months. When I got home, I really tried to pull the family together. And I loved the baby from the first, but I kept remembering whose it was."

It was obvious that Danny had been heartbroken. He'd gone on to get a good education. Now he was divorced. My heart reached out toward him. All my past hurt and rejection came to the surface and was transformed into a warm love for Danny. As he talked, I was fitting him into my world, placing him in familiar places—the homes of my friends, the clubs, dressed in the sharp suits I knew he would look great in with his strong shoulders and slender hips.

I realized that this man who had seemed so silent and self-reliant might really need me—and no one knew how much I needed someone to need me. When I told him about my filing for divorce, he put his arm around my shoulder. And I felt the tenderness and understanding I'd known would be there. When we had talked ourselves into silence, it was almost dawn. We sat gazing into the glowing embers in the fireplace. Although I knew it was incredibly impulsive, I also knew that I loved Danny Baker.

He turned to me and kissed me gently on the lips.

"Hedy, I've never wanted to make love with anyone as much as I want to love you right now. But I'd like for our relationship to be special, so I'm going home."

He kissed me again, very softly and lovingly, and then left.

24. The Tender Trap — He Needed Me

AFTER DANNY had gone, I turned the hi-fi up and danced around the whole house with a pillow, as the pink lights of dawn seeped in the windows. The children appeared at their door, rubbing the sleep out of their eyes and wondering what in the world their mother was doing. When I saw them, I threw the pillow aside and swept them up in my arms, hugging them tightly, singing "I love you girls, I *love* you!" They giggled and hugged me back, not knowing what had happened. But I knew.

Danny came over the next night and the next. He said he'd been sick and discouraged for the last few months but that he had an interview the following week for a management position in a factory. My heart stirred with hope. He'd have to wear a suit every day, maybe a first step toward reentry into Lake Forest. I was ecstatic. Why shouldn't we live in a world where we both belonged?

My children thought he was wonderful. He would bring wine and we'd cook special meals together, or he'd grill steaks. We were really more like two teenagers in love than two thirty-year-olds.

When dinner was over, we'd sit on the couch by the fire and talk by the hour—about nothing, about everything. I did notice that after the first night—when Danny told me about his tragic marriage—he never again got personal about himself, what was going on currently in his feelings and in his life when he was away from

161

me. But some day I wanted to share my whole life—even my past —with him. One night I almost told him about having been raped. But as I thought about telling him, I imagined his look of disgust. My stomach knotted, and I realized I couldn't risk it. So I tried to draw him out instead.

But it didn't matter that we couldn't share everything yet. Nothing mattered. I was in love, totally, idealistically, blindly in love. And one of Danny's greatest charms those first nights was that he seemed to respect me as a lady. We necked like two sixteen-year-olds. But he wasn't aggressive and didn't push me.

So much of my romantic life had always been fantasy, lived out in my mind. Now I spent my days at home floating through the beautiful bright canvases I was painting and thinking about Danny. I began painting seascapes and did a lot of pictures with little girls in them. I was working with a palette knife too and did some dramatic animal pictures—all kinds of leopards, jaguars and other exotic jungle cats. Since I'd filed for divorce, I didn't want to see anyone I'd known. So I lived in a world filled with painting and romance. I had found my Lancelot.

Our love grew more and more intense until my whole being was silently crying out for it to be consummated.

Finally, one evening when the children were spending the night out, Danny and I had finished a beautiful dinner with linen and crystal and candles. The candlelight and wine made his eyes sparkle softly across the table. We moved to the couch and sat watching the fire as we had so often those past three months. We talked and kissed and held each other. But our talk got less and less, and there was an urgency in our kissing. Finally I stood up and took Danny's hand. He had never been upstairs in my bedroom. Neither of us said a word as I closed the door behind us. And all of the hurt and disappointment of my lifetime dissolved and flowed into Danny's eyes as he took me gently, but with great strength, into his arms and out of the world of the unloved.

The next few weeks were the happiest I'd ever known. Danny seemed absolutely perfect to me. I couldn't see any fault in him.

It was true that he began not coming over some nights, sometimes with excuses, often with none. But I forgave him and believed him completely when he said he was exhausted or working. Then people began telling me they had heard he was taking hard drugs and even stealing to support his habit—that he was worthless. I was furious and withdrew from anyone who said anything bad about Danny. He was too wonderful to be those things. In my desperation not to lose the dream I'd been waiting for all my life, I shut myself off with my paintings and fantasies more and more, refusing to face anything that might hurt me or destroy my dreams. If this relationship was unreal, then I believed beyond a shadow of a doubt that there wasn't any reality in the whole universe.

Sometimes Danny was tired when he came to be with me. I yearned for him, but he was often very passive. At first I had felt that his lack of aggressiveness was an expression of tenderness and concern. Here was a man, I thought, who wanted me as a person and not just to use me as a thing.

But it got so he would go to sleep as we sat and talked. And his thinking sometimes seemed to be vague and disconnected. It's amazing to me now how long I kept myself from realizing it, but one day I just knew the rumors were true. He was on hard drugs. Still I couldn't give him up. I wanted to marry him. I loved him, and the tender trap was that he needed me. He had said so, and now it was apparent. So I forgave him and encouraged him when he seemed to be clear-headed and working. But often he went out with his friends and didn't ask me to go—and I never asked, so I never went with him when they were together.

There was a while that I was tempted to join him in his world just to be with him. But I couldn't. It was such a self-destructive life. And I was very proud. Besides, I had to paint to support my children. And for that, I needed a clear mind. So I waited and painted and painted.

I wouldn't have believed that communication for Findley and me could be as difficult as it had become during the eighteen months between my filing and the final divorce decree. I don't know what I had expected, but certainly not that it would take almost two years to get a divorce. We went to court three times.

Through his connections Findley knew almost every judge in our area. And they were such good friends of his that they disqualified themselves, saying they knew one of the parties in our case too well. Finally we got a judge to take our case. Findley fought the divorce every step of the way, and the court was very sympathetic to his wanting to keep the marriage together "at all costs." I found myself feeling sorry for him too. But then I remembered the complete emotional block we had reached over the years. I had to fight hard just to get out. And in the process I became exhausted.

At the end of it all I said, "I just want out. I don't want anything from Findley, just my freedom." So I walked out of the courtroom the last day with custody of our two small children and a few thousands of dollars. I'd lost the house, and I'd even lost Helen, since I couldn't afford to keep her.

Then I stood on the courthouse steps in the late afternoon sunshine and realized it was the beginning of fall. It had just rained, and I inhaled the smell of the wet earth and leaves. I breathed deeply and looked around. It was as if I had never seen those long gray courthouse steps and the huge maple and oak trees in the park across the street.

It was evidently 4:30, because people began streaming by me on both sides. Everyone seemed to be happy and to be with friends. From scraps of conversation I realized it was Friday.

Slowly I walked down the steps. I kept saying to myself over and over: "It's finished Hedy, you finally did it." I had no sense of time passing as I walked the two blocks to the parking lot by myself. Driving home, I don't know what I expected to feel, but I was only conscious of what I didn't feel. I didn't feel free. I didn't feel elated or excited about the future. And most of all I didn't feel as if I belonged anywhere.

I had a sudden urge to go see my father. But then I remembered how he had looked shaking hands with Findley the night of our engagement. And I just felt numb, realizing I'd blown the one thing he'd ever wanted me to do.

Now I was on my own. I was living in a duplex with my two little girls. And since my only income was Findley's child support,

I decided I'd better take my art very seriously and learn to survive alone in the world. Because I'd finally realized things might not work out with Danny and me.

Danny hadn't held a job in some time and didn't seem to be planning to get one. He was back living in his parents' large house, and kept talking about a scheme to move to a wilderness cabin and farm. But I finally realized he was planning to grow and sell marijuana for a living.

So I kept painting. And eventually by pouring myself into my work, I had enough canvases for a one-man show.

Danny volunteered to help me get ready for the show by making frames and doing a few minor things I asked him to do. I was shocked to realize that even small responsibilities were almost shattering to him, although he really tried.

As time for the show approached, I was very nervous, actually frightened. The night it opened I had butterflies in my stomach and my mouth was dry. But I was poised and smiling—Scrap Iron was in charge again.

Everyone said my work was good, and the paintings sold better than I could have dreamed. People I hadn't seen for years came to the show. Danny stood next to me at the door, but was strangely silent. When I introduced him, he seemed ill at ease, and I realized he had nothing in common to talk about with my friends. It was the first time we had been out together in the midst of my world, the world I had built our dream life in. As I smiled and greeted old friends above the laughter in the background, I realized that Danny could never change. My paintings were going to be the sole support of me, my kids, Danny—and his habit.

When the show was over, I knew I would have to give Danny up. We had lived between our worlds. I had walked to the brink of the valley of the shadowy world of drug addiction with him. But I couldn't enter that world, and he wouldn't, or couldn't, come out and enter mine. I'd tried to leave him before, but always when he came to me with color in his cheeks and clear eyes and promised to get himself straightened out, I'd taken him back.

Now I knew it was the end. But it was like cutting off my own legs and burying my lifelong dream. I still loved him. Every night for a week after the art show, I tried to end the relationship. But I kept putting it off. Finally one evening after supper, I turned to him.

"Danny," and I began to cry. "It's all over! And . . . this time it's forever. I've got to take care of my girls—and you live in another world." Through my tears I could see Danny looking at me with a sort of dazed, panicky look.

This time there were no "but if you ever . . ." or "let me know how you . . ." or "call me if you need me . . ." This time it was over! Finished! Dead!

Danny shook his head. He couldn't get his words together. But he knew I meant it. I finally had to push him gently toward the door. When he left, I fell on the couch and sobbed myself to sleep.

The next few days I walked a lot through the trees in the park, as their changing colors and falling leaves marked the death of another year's growth. I picked up a dying yellow leaf and studied its lines, feeling the smoothness on the waxed front side. Looking up at the tree it had fallen from, I wondered how many cycles of hope and the death of hope I could stand. I grieved about my dying love for Danny and felt my girlhood dying too. I saw that I had always tried to force reality to fit the shape of my fantasies, and had always been surprised when it hadn't. Maybe I was growing up. But facing the real world without the security of my dazzling dreams was frightening. What would be out there if I really began to face the truth about my relationships? I pulled my coat closer around me. The end of October was approaching.

One day I began to feel better. Something changed. I looked up at the lead-gray sky through the bare branches and felt ancient and cynical, but glad to be alive. Gone was the young girl with the dreams of winning a father's love and finding true intimacy. Even in the mad romantic adoration I'd felt for Danny, the closeness I'd hoped for had been missing—or only hinted at. I knew now that real intimacy was far more than physical closeness and more than romantic love, or even talking endlessly. Danny had been hiding his real self from me through it all and I from him. Whatever true intimacy might be, if it existed at all, it *had* to include something about openness between two people concerning who they really were.

But I couldn't think about that. The idealistic young girl was dying, like the fall leaves. What would I be, or what would replace the search for my father's love and for intimacy? I had no idea. But I knew I could never make my dreams happen by myself. I shivered with the cold but more with the knowledge that the life I'd tried so hard to carve out of the jungle of feelings and relationships was over. I couldn't beat the jungle by myself. But I could go on for my kids. I tried to arouse Scrap Iron. I *had* to go on.

As I turned and started back to my apartment, I realized I'd been a pretty selfish mother—thinking about Danny and my own needs most of the time. Maybe now I could start again and let my kids know how much I really loved them. I realized with a great wave of feeling just how much they did mean to me. How could I have been so blind and selfish? Suddenly I was grateful that I still had a chance to be the mother I should have been all along.

It was October 31st—Halloween! I had arranged for the children to go trick-or-treating and spend the night with their daddy; so I had this night free to celebrate my new freedom.

I was moving back toward life. I'd planned a lovely intimate dinner for some of my long-time friends from out of town—whom I'd avoided since my divorce. It felt good to have my crystal and china out, to be cooking an elegant dinner for dear friends—two couples who talked my language and accepted me as I was. I was anxious to hear how they'd been, how their children were—a thousand questions.

When they came that night, I hugged them all and wept. It was good to be alive. Something new and wonderful was coming into my life. Maybe I was going to grow up and live in the real world at last. Everything seemed so good. I felt clean and even slightly confident about the future. After all, I was a recognized competent, professional artist now. All my paintings had sold.

I'd bought the best champagne I could find to toast the new chapter in my life and getting together with my friends again. It was a warm and wonderful evening. We laughed about old times—more than I'd laughed in four years. It was late when they finally left—I kept begging them to stay and hated to see them go. They had walked with me out of the valley of the shadows into a new beginning.

When the last couple left, I stood with my back leaning against the front door, savoring the peace of the evening in my mind. Finally I took a deep breath and sighed with happiness. Life wasn't going to be half bad. Maybe I'd even be happy without my compulsive drive to find the impossible love and intimacy I'd chased through my long, long adolescence. I walked back into the dining room.

I hadn't been stacking the dishes for two minutes when the doorbell rang. Who in the world could it be at this time on Halloween night?

I opened the door. There stood Danny.

PART FIVE

DEATH AND LIFE

25. Meanwhile, Back in Wesley Memorial

As I LAY ALMOST totally paralyzed in the intensive care ward at Wesley Memorial Hospital thinking back through my life, I could hear the strange rasping noise of my breathing from the hole in my throat.

Through the jungle of tubes, all ending in me, I could only see the faded green ceiling and a small area of space on either side of the bed, if I cut my eyes to the right or left. That was my world.

At first in the hospital as an unresponsive paralytic, I had almost no sense of love or caring for me as a person—I was a case, a center of pain, a repository for tubes and life-saving equipment. The light, no matter how soft and low, was hard, the sounds noisy and impersonal, the walls bare, empty even with the plastic pictures—or so it all seemed—even though Findley was faithful in coming and I received excellent care and attention. But since I couldn't communicate, I felt more and more an isolated object.

The heavy body cast, the casts on my legs and feet, and the metal halo bolted to my skull held everything rigid with metal rods running down my sides under the cast. I was sealed in the cold paralyzed wax of my own dead skin and wrapped like a mummy for burial—BUT I WAS STILL ALIVE! Concentrating every bit of strength and effort I could muster, I strained to move a hand, a foot, a toe. Nothing. Silence, except for the steady rasping of my throat. The quiet nurse reading beside my bed wasn't even aware of my life-and-death efforts, these all-out thrusts toward the land of the living. I felt hot anger rising toward my face. Tears. Despair.

Why? Why *now*? just as I had committed myself to my children and my new career as an artist. Inside I screamed at God, "It isn't fair!" But no sound came. I felt very grim, as if my death mask was already intact.

Everyone had begun to seem distant as if on another planet. My father was only a memory. Suddenly for no reason at all as I thought of him, I felt unworthy. I wondered if anyone else agonized so through feeling unloved by a parent that they considered themselves unworthy of love from anyone. But these questions didn't matter any more, at least for me, since I'd never be able to do anything about them.

The only conversation I ever had now was an inner conversation, as if with some unknown but knowing presence. I told him that after thinking through my life I was in complete agreement with what he was doing to me. In spite of all the people I'd helped and the genuine feelings of love I had for them, there was a core of total selfishness in me that I'd avoided facing before. It was as if I'd tried to be the center of everyone's life around me. This basic bent toward self-centeredness seemed incurable by any amount of effort and had caused so much havoc in the lives which had touched mine. I only wished God would get on with my execution. But I couldn't even seem to end my life right. And by now time seemed suspended and unending.

While I was waiting to die, I remember one day in particular when Findley came to visit me.

He was standing beside my bed. Through the window behind him I could see the high white clouds against the cold blue winter sky. Under his ruddy complexion he seemed pale, and I noticed his dark red hair was just beginning to be salted with white.

"Hedy," Findley began tentatively, as if not quite sure I could hear him, "I know I've told you some of this, but I want to tell you everything that's happened since you went out with Danny on Halloween night.

"I got a call about 2:30 in the morning from the hospital to come to the emergency room at once. When I got here, they told me that your body was like a crumpled beer can after they got you untangled from the floor under the dashboard. You were brought here and listed as 'Mrs. Findley Robinson, Dead on Arrival.'

"As soon as I arrived," he continued, "they took me directly to the emergency room and introduced me to the doctor who was on duty. He just happened to be the trachea specialist. When your body arrived and was examined, you were pronounced dead. But a young intern was allowed to do a tracheotomy—which was a hopeless gesture, but would give the intern some valuable experience. The guy almost fainted when you began to breathe.

"The specialist told me frankly that he could hardly believe that you could have lived in any case. Your neck was broken, there were compound fractures in both legs, in seven places altogether. And following x-rays and complete tests they knew your throat was crushed and the vocal chords had been severed. The impact also crushed and destroyed your voice box. There was simply no breathing space left. 'Only a miracle will work,' the doctor told me. 'But we'll do what we can, Mr. Robinson!' "

Findley told me that Wesley Memorial was connected with Northwestern Medical School and that by 4:00 in the morning the doctor on duty had assembled a team of nine surgeons who agreed on a schedule of surgical procedures and began a series of operations to save my life. When the neurosurgeon completed his work, the orthopedic man began. Then several members of the eye, ear, nose and throat department took over. They were amazed that my body took the shock of the multiple surgeries. But there was no alternative except to operate. Without intending to, the medical school faculty had taken me on as a joint project. And some of the top medical men in the country were together on my case. If I had been taken to any of the exclusive private hospitals in the suburbs instead of Wesley, I wouldn't have had a chance.

As Findley told me about one miraculous chance circumstance after another, I was becoming awed. "Why?" I wondered. Maybe God wasn't trying to get me. If He were, He was either very cruel or very stupid to allow all of these amazingly gifted people to be on hand just when I needed them.

Findley continued, "When all the operations were over, the doctors called me in. I'd been waiting for hours, and was sure you'd died. They looked plenty worried. I started asking questions when I hit the room. The head surgeon calmed me down by saying, 'Mr. Robinson, your wife has about one or two chances out of a hundred to live at all.' They didn't know we were divorced. 'If she does live she will be—virtually—a vegetable. She may have severe brain damage, the extent of which we can't even tell because of the lack of oxygen when she was "dead." Having virtually no throat, she'll have to have a permanent tracheotomy. And of course she'll never be able to talk. Her spinal cord is in such bad shape that she'll never move. Just saving her life last night was our first priority.' He looked at me and shook his head slightly, as if to say, 'I'm not sure we've done you or her any favors if she does live.'"

Late in the afternoon the day following the accident, they'd let Findley in the intensive care ward for a five-minute look at me. As he said, he could never have gotten ready for what he saw. I was laid out on two levels of mattresses that looked like swimming pool floats; an air pump under the bed kept air sections in the mattresses rotating to keep my blood circulating. I was, the nurse told Findley, in immediate danger of kidney and lung congestion, and pneumonia was also a real threat. Since my fever was dangerously high, a fan was operating above my body, which was draped only by a sheet covering my midsection.

"Your legs were raised by pounds of traction weights attached to bars running through your ankles. As a matter of fact, you were in some kind of traction or another from head to toe. I couldn't believe it. Your head had been shaved to accommodate a brace which had been bolted into your skull at various points. And beneath your chin where your larynx had been, your throat lay wide open from one side of your neck to the other. A few inches further down I saw that you were breathing slowly and with strange noises, as if you were drowning. The trachea reminded me of a little garden hose. A plastic throat had been inserted and tubes were going everywhere out of your body—an IV tube attached to a bottle and your right arm, blood going in your left, a 'feeding' tube down your nose into your throat, and a catheter with a rubber bag."

Findley looked white, just remembering how he had almost fainted when he saw me.

"You were in a deep coma, Hedy, and I couldn't help wondering if it might not be better if you never woke up.

"There are two special wards on the West Wing of the ninth floor where nurses are on duty all the time. There are two other patients in the ward they moved you into." Findley began to whisper now as he continued. "A big black guy is in the next bed. He was shot in the neck, and he's paralyzed from the neck down too. His body's in a thing like a basket. Every hour they put a top over the basket and he's rolled over. The nurse said they'd have to do this the rest of his life.

"Across from your bed is something even weirder. A small fellow, about five-four, in his mid-thirties, sat grinning as they brought you in. His head is completely shaved. He looks to me like he's just arrived from Mars—but friendly. Wires about an inch long close together are sticking out of a long S-shaped surgical incision that begins on one side of his lower neck and runs up across his head and down around the other side of his neck. He's had brain surgery.

"The night nurse told me he killed a patrolman. He's chained to his bed most of the time and considered more dangerous than critical. A policeman is standing across the hall, outside the door.

"I came to the ward twice a day for the first few days to see if there was any change. But you were still in a coma. When you woke up, you could only look, but not move. That's when I first blurted out what the doctors had told me about what had happened to you and what your chances were. You didn't answer or anything, of course, and I had the feeling I shouldn't have laid it all on you at once. But I thought you were going to die right then, and so did everyone else. A few days later I thought maybe it would help if you saw the kids. The doctors agreed."

Just then, my private nurse, Henrietta, told him he'd have to go since they had to change my bed. Findley looked at me with real gentleness in his eyes. He'd been so faithful about coming to the hospital and making sure I had anything I needed. I realized that he was a good man in lots of ways, and I was sorry we hadn't been able to make our marriage go.

When he'd gone, I tried to piece together what I could remember from those first days and weeks after the accident, to see if it matched what Findley had told me. Some of my memories were jumbled scenes: Men in green surgical uniforms came at all hours of the day and night, sometimes alone, often in clusters of five to eight. Each group of young doctors had a leader who was teaching them. I was their subject. They talked among themselves but never to me. As a matter of fact, after a week or so of my not responding, almost no one ever really talked to me.

There was one exception. A tall doctor, a few years older than I. I noticed him as soon as I began to be aware of the people coming around my bed. He was tall and handsome in a rugged sort of way. I noticed him first because he was the only one who ever challenged or questioned the leader-doctor. He was very serious about his work and obviously disliked anything phony. He took time to smile and speak to me as the others were leaving. Later, when I was getting better, he'd stick his head in and wave or smile and blow a kiss in a good-natured way, letting another side of his life show for an instant.

I didn't know what his first name was for a long time, but the supervising doctor once called him "Art." Everyone else called him Dr. Parker. I overheard the nurses talking about him and discovered that he was married to his childhood sweetheart and that most of the nurses in the hospital had a crush on him, but he was totally out of reach—not that such things could ever matter to me again. But my woman's curiosity told me that at least I wasn't totally dead.

Before long I became aware of the little man in the bed across from mine. He seemed to be close to me or watching me all the time. He smiled like a crazy little elf, and I had the feeling he never looked away. Even when his back was turned, he'd look over his shoulder. The way he smiled made me very uneasy; and I sensed something was not quite right with him.

In the bed next to me I could vaguely see, when they turned me in his direction, the enormous black body that never moved. He must be going through what I am, I thought. But the little one across the way was different. And since I couldn't tell anyone that he stared at me all the time, all I could do was close my eyes to blot out his wild cunning gaze.

A day or so after Findley had first told me what had happened, the children came to see me for that horrible first visit. I still remember the hot, huge tears pouring down my face. "Oh, my God," I thought, "somebody please wipe these tears away! I can't even see my children." Was I just given this one more time to see my babies? I still thought I was going to die any day—as did many of the doctors. Was this a punishment from God or a favor. I suddenly felt ugly-looking and was ashamed to face them through my tears. They had almost never seen me cry. But I couldn't turn my head. It wouldn't move. I closed my eyes. "Oh, God, why did you do this just when I saw what a poor mother I've been and was starting to change?"

I closed my eyes and screamed silently, "God, are you there? Help me! Let me at least say goodbye to my babies." I opened my eyes, but they were gone.

I could hear them crying, sobbing, but only from a distance, as Henrietta quickly closed the door.

I lay there begging God to end this mistake in letting me live. "Why does it take so much to die? Why is it taking me so long? Please, God, *now!*"

26. Murder in Intensive Care

But God didn't get me out of it, although I literally faced death every day. Every morning I had the opening in my trachea cleaned and the breathing filter changed. I would wake up with a team of five or six doctors standing over me. One doctor would be holding a suction tube attached to the machine beside my bed, and my heart would start pounding in terror over what was about to happen.

One of the chief doctors in the medical school, it seems, had made me a classroom study. Since an unusual amount of fluid accumulated in the opening in my throat, sometimes my tracheotomy had to be cleaned several times a day. Every time they removed the device, my throat would instantly fill with fluid before they could insert a new tube. I would literally feel myself choking or drowning. Being paralyzed, and lying flat on my back, all I could do was experience the horror of the fluid collecting, choking my air passage, cutting off my life. The team of doctors had to make a quick decision every time: could they get the tube inserted in time or should they prolong the procedure by using the suction machine in my throat before inserting the other tube? Either way, for me it was a life-or-death experience. And each time I felt like I wouldn't survive.

Since I couldn't jerk away, hide my face, or even move, I was terrified to open my eyes every morning. I would keep my eyes closed as long as I could, knowing that the moment I showed signs of being awake, they would come and begin the procedure again. When I knew they had arrived and their shadows were hovering over me, I felt as if my breath had already stopped. The agony and the fear, which would ordinarily have some outward physical release in a person not paralyzed, concentrated in my chest.

I can't describe that terror—of not being able to breathe—in words. Only those who have drowned or almost drowned would understand. But the experience was a nightmare that I relived— relived and relived—thinking there would be no ending until one day they wouldn't make it and I'd choke to death. Sometimes in my sleep I can still hear the suction machine with the gurgling noise.

As a rule the doctors didn't talk to me. They were very business-like about what they were doing. Since it was a serious process and since I couldn't communicate with them, I understood. But they didn't know about my terror and the awful loneliness inside the shrinking shell of my body. One morning, as I was about to choke, I realized that one of the things I'd been searching for all my life as a part of intimacy was someone with whom I could share my moments of fear and even terror, and who would love me and respect me anyway. That was a surprise—I had never thought of sharing fears in connection with intimacy. But it made sense.

Dr. Parker began to recognize the fear. He started talking to me and being kind to me, even though I couldn't respond. He would touch my hand as they began the procedure. And after we'd made it through, he'd stay behind and talk to me a moment. Sometimes what he said wasn't particularly comforting—as when he'd tell me, "We almost didn't make it that time, Hedy." But then he'd touch my hand to reassure me. And since no one touched me for any reason except to change a tube or perform a medical service, he could not know how much the kindness of his touch meant to me.

As I watched these doctors work day after day, I wondered if the others realized the amazing power to calm and heal they could transmit to patients through a smile, a personal word or an explanation to calm some of the fears and terrors which lie just out of sight behind the eyes of every patient. At least behind mine.

Every morning I was nothing but two terrified brown eyes as they walked in. And even though that day might be terrible, Dr. Parker's touch and his presence actually seemed to transmit courage and calmness to me. There was so much I'd never gotten to find out in my relationships with people when I'd been "in the world." But somehow this kind doctor's touches of intimacy without any demands, as he tried to communicate across death's doorway, were like cups of spring water from another world into my shriveling soul.

One night, after things had been especially bad, Dr. Parker came and sat beside my bed. It must have been about 3 A.M. Taking my hand, he said gently, "Hedy, you are all brown eyes, and I love your eyes."

For someone to say that under normal conditions, when I was a successful model, would have been a nice gesture. But I was almost a skeleton, a paralyzed skeleton, weighing less than seventy pounds. I was just a hopeless little bag of bones. Yet somehow he saw, or seemed to see, something beautiful in my eyes.

That moment in the middle of the night meant more to me than any compliment I could have ever received. It was like a tiny bird of hope, in a bleak and hopeless winter wasteland. "Maybe," I thought, "just maybe, my condition will change."

Hope is an amazing thing. I went to sleep happy for the first time in months.

The next day I found myself thinking about Danny, wondering where he was. Findley had told me that Danny left the scene of the accident before help came. They found him walking down the road dazed, with a fractured jaw.

I was uneasy about the fact that I hadn't been able to tell anyone that Danny had really tried to kill me the night of the "accident." But I'd pretty well repressed the wreck.

Now that I'd had a spark of hope from Dr. Parker's kindness,

I started to be more philosophical about the mistakes and tragedies in my life. I began to see some of the ways I'd failed to give love and that maybe I'd blocked my own search by not knowing how to receive love.

Henrietta's voice interrupted my thoughts. "I've gotta go down and get your medication. The hall nurse will be right in." She cranked my bed up to more of a sitting position and left the room. I kept thinking. I wondered how much of a chance I'd actually given my mother and father to love me. I saw how often I had waited for other people to be first in expressing love or revealing themselves. Good lord, maybe I had unconsciously set myself up for failure and rejection by being so private and secretive about my personal thoughts and feelings! I wondered if I had demanded a closeness from others I wasn't willing to give myself. These thoughts made me very tired and restless and I lay with my eyes closed and tried to rest.

Then suddenly something in the room caught my attention—a slight secretive noise across from me. I was totally alert, yet somehow afraid to open my eyes.

The little man in the bed opposite me had seemed particularly intense lately. He was almost always staring over his shoulder at me now, his eyes fastened on my face—with virtually no expression in them. I knew something was going on in his head, but couldn't handle thinking about what it might be—since I couldn't communicate with anyone in any case. I opened my eyes.

He was sitting on the edge of his bed looking at me with a kind of wild little smile. I looked toward the nurse's chair but she was gone and I could hear the hall nurse's laugh from down the corridor. There was no one else in the room except the black body in the basket next to my bed. When the little man stood up, my heart began to beat wildly. He wasn't chained! He began to turn very slowly and face me. As I saw his eyes, I had this desperate feeling of dread. Then he began to walk softly but deliberately to the foot of my bed—Oh, god!

He looked at me for a moment. Then suddenly he reached down, grabbed my casts at the ankles and began to bang my legs together wildly. Suddenly, unexpectedly, there was pain. He moved up my legs and began to bang my knees together. Then he moved up the bed to my hips and began to shake me up and down. I didn't know whether he was going to assault me sexually or murder me. Then he moved up to my neck with his hands like claws right above my face and throat. The wild eyes bored right into mine the whole time. "This is it," I thought. "Go ahead God, let him kill me—just let it be fast."

But his hand stopped as it touched the tube in my throat. I looked back into his eyes trying to appear calm, although every fiber in me was raw terror. The seconds seemed to last a thousand years. I could make no signal nor movement at all as I waited to see what he would do. He raised one eyebrow and slowly began to withdraw his hands.

Just then I heard the nurse walk into the room. She stopped. Slowly he turned toward her. She called his name. There was a pause which seemed endless. Then he stood up and walked back to his bed and got in it. The nurse looked at my bed and must have known what had happened, because the man was taken away and I never saw him again.

The pain was real but I had no way of telling anyone. Of course, as it was happening I didn't know that pain might be a good sign.

Since the wreck, life had become my own private chamber of horrors. I didn't have any hope for the future. And my past life would not quit parading by. I was again at the brink of despair. Before I could stop myself, the tears began to flow. Automatically I tried to lift my left hand to wipe them away. And it *moved!* It MOVED! Not much, but I could feel it move. I couldn't believe it. I concentrated everything in me to make it move when anyone was around so they would see it. That afternoon Henrietta saw it and ran to get the doctor.

Findley brought me a big crayola and a pad. I couldn't see much of what I was doing but for weeks I spent hours every day trying to hold that crayola and make letters on the pad. My first sentence was: "Get my father." The second was: "Bring my paints."

The doctor was kind but firm. "Hedy, you have a very slight

movement capability in your left hand, but I don't want you to count on ever being able to do what you could do before. Your right side shows no signs of life at all. I don't want to discourage you, but just take it easy and be grateful for the miracle that's already happened."

The doctors told Findley I was a "very determined woman" and this determination would help, but that my expectations to paint were impossible. During the next few weeks there were faint signs of hope, a little pain in my left hand, an itch I could feel. But then the signs of improvement would disappear. I'd latch on to each new hope or suggestion and imagine health or meaning in the future. I knew the best I could hope for might be a life sort of like the man with no legs who sat on a mat in front of Walgreen's when I was a child.

The doctors decided that it was time I had some visitors. Maybe that would cheer me up. They said people could come for five minutes in the morning and five minutes at night.

By this time I had become accustomed to my wires, casts, tubes, etc. And since I never really could get a good look at myself, I didn't quite realize how much of a change had taken place in the way I looked. But my first two visitors gave me a clue as to what a strange hollow-eyed little skeleton I was. One of my dear Lake Forest friends, Elizabeth, came with her husband. She was dressed for a party and wearing a beautiful mink jacket. She walked in with a bright prepared smile, saw me, stopped and fainted. Her husband caught her before she fell to the floor.

My second visitor was a twelve-year-old neighbor boy named Bennie with whom I'd spent a lot of time talking and listening when he had come over to ask if he could watch me cook or paint. Bennie had sent me an orchid a month before and couldn't wait until I had visitors. When he walked in the hospital room, his face turned to a mask of disbelief, and they had to lead him out.

But there were funny and happy moments too. My dearest friends, Pepper and Bill, came from Milwaukee. I don't know how to describe these wonderful people. When the term "salt of the earth" is used to describe someone fine, I always think of them.

But they're also full of fun, especially Pepper. I hadn't seen them since they left my apartment the night of the accident. Having talked to Findley, Bill didn't want to embarrass me so he waited out in the hall. Pepper came in and filled the whole room with warmth. Her face tensed when she saw me, but then she smiled even though I had tears from seeing her.

I felt I had to get out in the hall to see Bill. I wanted to surprise him and tell him how much I loved him for coming and for his thoughtfulness in not wanting to embarrass me. By this time I could scrawl notes and make directional signs when my left hand was "on." The only way I could be moved was by being lifted out of the bed on a sheet and carried in my casts to a wheelchair.

We told the nurse our plan. After some shakings of heads, the attendants put me in a wheelchair and wheeled me out in the hall. I had on a short black nightgown. But with casts from head to toe, I had forgotten until we reached the door that the only open space between my body cast and my leg casts was covered by a pair of brief leopard skin panties which could be seen. It's hard to describe how ridiculous I must have looked. I could imagine Pepper's laughing when Bill, being the perfect gentleman, refused to notice the panties. But when I actually saw Bill it was a very serious moment. I'll never forget the way he stood there. I could see the pain before he covered it. But he looked at me with such warmth and kindness.

"Hedy," he said seriously, "you've never looked more lovely to me. And I've never been as proud of you as I am right now." With these words he gave me back my dignity.

During the next days and weeks, I was surprised at who came. People I'd known and considered to be nice came—but I hadn't expected to see them. I wouldn't have felt they cared that much for me. They were kind and thoughtful. But in a way their thoughtfulness was very painful, because many people I expected to come never did. My brother, Sam, who had been with me so often—didn't come. Later I found out he'd heard how I looked and couldn't bear to see me. But I didn't know that then. And worst of all, my father never did visit me. I began to withdraw.

Seeing all my happy friends who stopped by on their way to and from Christmas parties or shopping was nice, but it only accentuated the incredible loneliness and lack of contact inside me. I lost interest in using my hand, and felt myself disappearing behind the veil of tears which was always there. Everyone around me began to feel that I was slipping away. They all called to me in their various ways to come back. But I could hardly even hear them and got further and further away. I was drifting toward another world.

There would be brief flickers of hope, but I would soon spiral down through them. The only thing which kept me going at all was the intense toughness and inner control I had learned and practiced since I was a tiny girl. But I could feel that beginning to crack. I began to sense fear and dread as I glimpsed something I'd never even let myself get close to: actual despair.

One day, when I was feeling a little hope, something happened which awakened in me a whole new kind of terror. I was scheduled to have a special surgical procedure on my throat early the next morning. The doctors had prepared me and put me in a private room. Henrietta was with me. It was late in the evening, and there was only a night light on in the room. I was dozing and listening to Henrietta hum some Negro spirituals softly. Suddenly I saw a shadow in the doorway. I was always tense when someone appeared at night because it meant doctors and pain. Then I heard Danny's voice and my heart leaped in a kind of terror.

Henrietta knew about Danny. I had managed to write out for her what had happened the night of the wreck so she wouldn't let Danny in, but I'd sworn her to secrecy and hadn't told anyone else.

Even in the dim light Danny's eyes had that strange vacant Halloween night look I had seen a dozen times in my nightmares. It was not a sane look.

Henrietta saw my eyes and knew exactly who Danny was. She stood up.

"Mrs. Robinson's not allowed any visitors!"

Danny swore, a thing I'd never heard him do, and walked toward her—and me.

"Shut up, you black bitch, and get out of here!" I couldn't ever remember seeing or hearing Danny like this.

Henrietta took off, calling out to get some help. And Danny came over and stood by my bed.

As he stood there, I was amazed at the thought which flashed across my mind. In spite of my fear, I was embarrassed about the way I looked with my head shaved and my frail body with all the tubes and casts. I wondered in that instant whether or not he could ever see us making love again.

But that thought was gone the moment I got a clear look at his face. He was looking at me with utter contempt and disgust.

"You little phony!" he hissed. "There's nothing wrong with you and I know it. You're trying to get everyone's sympathy. But you're not going to put the blame on me."

"Good lord," I thought, "people must have been calling him, and in his guilt his tormented mind had decided I was *faking* an injury." He reached for my halo cast.

"I'm not going to have any phony, gimpy woman on my hands." And with that he grabbed my halo cast and jerked so hard one of the bolts tore out of my forehead. Blood went everywhere. He pulled me forward.

"Goddamn it, Hedy," he grunted, "you're going to stand up straight." And he hit me across the back. He was having a terrible time getting me on my feet to force me to walk. When the tubes got tangled, he threw me across the bed. I was half on and half off the bed sideways.

Somewhere in the background I could hear running footsteps. Danny stood back. I could see only the part of him between his chest and knees because of the position of my body. He had on a black leather jacket and jeans. His hand came out of his jacket pocket hiding an unsheathed dirk knife. Walking toward me very slowly, he spoke gently. "Baby, I'm not going to hurt you. I'm not going to make any more mistakes, Hedy."

Just then Henrietta reached the doorway with two policemen. One of the local police force who had been badly injured was right down the hall. And these two had been visiting him.

Danny turned and faced them, leaning against my bed, knife in hand behind his back.

"Give me your knife," the bigger man said.

"I don't have any knife," Danny said, as he put it in his pocket. Then they must have seen his eyes.

"All right then," the officer said soothingly, "put your hands up and let us search you."

Danny slowly began to raise his hands and suddenly doubled his fist and hit the big man full in the face. The other policeman took out his pistol and whipped Danny's head with it until he was on his knees on the floor. I had clamped my eyes shut, but I can still hear the sickening sound of that pistol hitting Danny's head. Eventually they got him out of the room—I'm not sure how.

I guess I had counted on Danny's love overcoming his feeling that he should kill me. But the reality of the hatred in his eyes had stabbed me more deeply than the physical pain. The unconscious hope that I could overcome Danny's fear and hatred must have symbolized my hope for my own recovery against all odds. Somehow this encounter with the blood, the pain, the sense of total helplessness to protect myself or even to talk to Danny—all these things said to me like a chorus of evil spirits from a darkening sky: "You'll *never* get well, Hedy! You'll never get well!" Those imaginary voices seemed to get louder and louder in a chant as the chilling front of their icy presence moved into my mind. With them came despair.

The proposed surgery had to be postponed because my cast, throat and forehead had to be repaired. And inside something snapped noiselessly—the last thread of spunk and courage. At a very deep level in tears I heard my inner self as a child saying in a way I never had, "I can't do it myself." And I gave up.

After that I was convinced I'd never·be well. I had at last come to the end of myself. Scrap Iron had melted in the heat of life. I thought again of my father. *Why* did I need a father's love so much? Now I knew there was no father's love. Life must be a cruel meaningless game filled with haunted people—tons of pain and fear with a few touches of pleasure—if one had the tools to bend people and situations her way. But I had lost the main outward gifts I'd had to make life work, to make people notice me—my physical appearance and my painting—the things which had made me strong and hopeful and kept me going, even when everyone seemed to be rejecting me.

I couldn't stand it any more. The next day was the last day of December. I knew that I was falling apart and could almost see the melted scrap iron—my pride—being poured into a bottomless crack in the ground. There was nothing I could do to stop it. At last I was totally defenseless and alone.

27. Substitute Angel from Oak Park

HER NAME WAS Doris and she was a substitute nurse from Oak Park. Doris came into my room on New Year's Eve like a breath of fresh air on a sultry night. Somehow she brought with her another world, beyond the pain and loneliness of the intensive care ward. All the regular nurses were out celebrating the end of the year. This bubbling little woman was plain, yet in some way I couldn't put my finger on, she was radiant and happy. The amazing thing to me was that she actually seemed to enjoy being there, even glad to see me.

I learned later that several of the nurses called to work my case that evening had refused to come. My future seemed hopeless, and it was too discouraging to be around a case like mine. But this woman *had* something, something inside that seemed to fill the room with a freshness, like the scent of rain. She was obviously intelligent and moved about efficiently.

Doris evidently didn't know that almost everyone had quit talking to me because of my lack of response. Or if she did, that didn't stop her. After checking my charts and getting accustomed to the room, she came over and asked if I minded if she talked to me. The others were evidently asleep. When I didn't say no, she smiled into my eyes, sat down beside my bed, and began to talk as if we'd known each other before.

"You know, I don't usually take cases on holidays, and never one as serious as yours. But I had the strangest feeling I was *supposed* to come be with you. Can I call you Hedy?"

As she kept talking, I felt a calmness easing into the room, creating an intimate circle in the usually impersonal glare of the night light that was always on. She began to tell me about her life in a matter-of-fact way. She too was divorced and had had all kinds of personal problems, looking for "something" in her life that would stop her frantic running and doing. She'd been an alcoholic, and finally had lost all hope of there being any meaning to life. Her face was very sad as she looked toward the dark wall and into the past.

As she said these things and I saw that she really meant them, I found myself listening with quiet intensity, identifying with her in a way I never had with anyone. But then she began to smile.

"You know, honey, something's happened to me I'd never have believed. I went to this church meeting—and you may not believe this, but I heard that God loved me in spite of all I was. And I gave my life to Jesus Christ that night. For the first time ever I found hope, *real hope!*" Her face seemed to shine as she nodded to emphasize what she'd said.

"Hope!" The word sank in—and the fact that she was really serious. Suddenly I had a strange tingling sensation all over me, and tears came to my eyes. Tears—coming from so deeply within me I was almost shaken physically as the tight ball at the center of my soul cracked and released them. Tears I'd never cried before because they were too locked up in my pride.

I found my left hand, which I had almost ceased using, fumbling for my crayon and pad. Somehow through the blur of hot tears I scrawled as fast as I could, "TELL ME ABOUT JESUS!"

And there, in the middle of the night, in that lonely intensive care ward, this ordinary—yet very special—woman helped me gently and slowly to see Jesus Christ, the Son of God Almighty. I had never known anyone before who seemed to know God personally, almost intimately. There was a dawning sense of awe as I realized she was saying that God, who had been responsible for creating all of life, loved *me*, Hedy Robinson, almost as if I were an only child. And that He had something like a plan or design for my life—if I wanted to find it and learn to live it. She said He could heal me too. Suddenly my sophistication and cynicism about Christianity dissolved. I wanted to find out exactly what she meant, how I might commit myself to this loving, healing Jesus Christ who had so obviously changed her life.

All that night I laboriously wrote out questions on my pad, and Doris patiently answered them, often with the help of the Bible she had in her bag. I remember as if it were an hour ago her reading these words which were like a giant lightning bolt across the whole darkness over my life—but this time the light stayed on as she read: "Therefore, if any man be in Christ, he is a new creature: old things are passed away, all things are become new!" A *new life!* And she said God was offering *me* that life!

But it meant turning loose of everything I'd depended on. I'd clung so tightly to my few supports that I felt a wave of fear rush through me as I thought of turning loose. But I knew, and had known for days, that my life was hanging by a mere thread of pride. And now just as the thread had broken, I reached out and took the life Christ was offering me. Somehow I took it with everything in me—no reservations in my mind or body.

Doris prayed with me, giving me the words to repeat in my mind that would make a beginning commitment of my life to God. Afterwards I lay there in wonder, knowing that I had never been so excited in my entire life. The giant steel coil of guilt in the basement of my soul which had been wound so tightly that it was like a solid ball began to uncoil, and uncoil, and uncoil! The release was unbelievable. Hope soared through my mind and seemed to be flowing into the veins and arteries of my broken body.

Sleep was out of the question. My mind was razor sharp, and my whole life came into a new perspective. As I visualized the panorama of my past, I could see that it was as if a prewritten plot had been unfolding. All the frustration, all the failures and bad things

I'd done, all the vague, undefinable searching, all the longing, made sense suddenly. I had almost *needed* my past to lead me to this moment! I had demanded that my father love me and accept me unconditionally. I had wanted other people, and particularly some one man to accept me so completely that his love would make me whole, complete me in some way I believed passionately to be possible. It was no wonder people had run or felt like failures when I demanded a perfect love.

As the hours went by, a realization came to my mind which was so wonderful that all I could do was cry softly out of sheer joy and amazement. I kept saying over and over to myself, "I can't believe it, Lord. I can't believe it." What I had been demanding and waiting for from my father was the unconditional love of *God*, the Father. And now I could feel that love. A loving Father's presence seemed to be in the room with me, telling me silently, "It's all right, Hedy, you don't have to work, or be a star, or be outstanding to win my love and acceptance. You already have it, all you could ever want. I'm your Father, Hedy, and—you're home, at last."

I *felt* loved. And if God loved me, no one could say that I wasn't lovable! I could see how it could have been God who had been with me all along, my genie in Belmont Harbor, the presence I longed for on that awful night when I was a girl, shamed and knowing no one could ever love me. Now I could see the search for God in the haunted eyes of the people at the carnival, in the hollow laughter of Hollywood, in the busy-ness and chicness of the housewives in Lake Forest. I saw with amazement that everyone must be unconsciously looking for this love of God which had come to me and was filling my life with meaning and love.

I'd almost had to die trying to win love by my own manipulations. I'd gone through the valley of the shadow of death. And then came Doris, this strange, prosiac little angel from Oak Park, Illinois, who had led me to the brink of a new existence.

It's not possible to describe the relief which kept settling into deeper and deeper levels of my mind. To realize that what I had unconsciously known must exist and was a reality somehow verified my whole existence. The problem had been that I'd been looking for it in all the wrong places and the wrong ways. The thought occurred to me that maybe there were millions of people who were also rushing frantically down the wrong paths looking for life.

Silently I laughed and cried and drank in deep breaths of new life.

By morning the angel from Oak Park was gone. But in her wake was a whole new person in the west wing of the intensive care ward.

28. A Broken Body, Lost Career, No Man, No Money — Nothing Except Happiness

THE NEXT FEW DAYS were some of the strangest and most fascinating I have ever lived—or in some ways could have imagined. I could practically feel life moving into my wasted body inside the casts. And if what had happened to me were true, millions of people must need the same experience, the same personal relationship with God. But no one was telling them—at least the people I knew.

I thought about all the lonely, agonized men and women I'd known who had no idea that they might be hunting for a loving God—who was reaching out to them. Who was going to tell them? Maybe I should. Now I had something I *had* to talk about. So I made up my mind that I was going to talk again. The doctors had said I never would, but I got the strong impression God wanted me to.

I began to exercise my left hand and arm endlessly, and eventually got to where I could reach my face. I began experimenting on my own by pressing the trachea device into my throat in different ways and trying with every ounce of concentration to make a sound. Finally and miraculously I began to whisper—like a bullfrog with a sore throat, but I could communicate with my lips.

Henrietta couldn't believe it and called the doctor. He wanted to know what I had done and what had happened to me. It was not only my whispering talk but something had totally reversed the direction of my slide toward death. I told them I was talking because of what Jesus Christ had done in my life. Knowing the sophisticated life I'd come from, they simply couldn't believe what had happened.

I'd never even heard the expression "Christian witnessing," but suddenly I began to tell people about God and the meaning of life and being loved by Christ.

I was happy. My prognosis was still impossible from the doctors' perspective. Nothing had changed medically and yet everything was different. I laughed as I hadn't been able to in months. My throat had gotten so bad that they had to drain my trachea every few minutes, night and day. This experience had become so terrifying I would have done nothing to disturb my trachea. But a couple of weeks after New Year's Day, I was laughing so hard that the trachea popped out of my throat. Instead of panicking, I simply put my hand over the hole and waited until the nurse got it back in. This was a whole new experience.

Even the most cynical of the doctors agreed that a miracle of some sort had taken place which they couldn't attribute to any medical procedure or cause. But *I* certainly didn't need one.

One of the first people to come by after hearing about my conversion was Dr. Art Parker. Much to my surprise, he said he'd had a dramatic conversion experience himself, several years before. He was very active as a layman in a local church, "They're about to kill me," he said, "asking me to teach Sunday school and travel all over with a lay witness team." He laughed, "I'm so busy talking to people at churches that I hardly have time to be a Christian."

What a funny thing to say, I thought. How could anybody be so busy doing God's work that he didn't have time to be a Christian? But I laughed with him.

Art came to see me almost every day. He encouraged me to believe that I might even be able to paint again some day. Shortly after that, he left the staff. He was going to a hospital in Omaha, Nebraska. I felt very sad. He had a kind of strength and

openness as a Christian that I wanted. He gave me his new address, writing it on his old card, and said goodbye. And I didn't
see him for a couple of years.

Inside my mind Spring had come! The signs of death and despair were being replaced by flowering hope. It was an incredible
experience for me. I bathed in the warm sunshine of the father's
love I'd dreamed of. And it was more than I could have hoped for
because it always seemed to be there, regardless of what I did or
didn't do. But the thing which was most surprising to me about
my relationship to God was the *meaning* it gave to my life and to
the drama of life as a whole. But I soon realized that unlike knowledge about beauty and clothes, knowledge about God is often very
strange. For instance, I saw that all my life had been leading me
to the place where I would run out of my own abilities. I had loved
being the center of the lives of the people around me, but in doing
this I'd been unconsciously trying to *be* God in their lives. And
only when I'd failed to control their feelings and destinies and my
own, was I ready to do business with a God who loves people as
they are, fulfills them and heals their brokenness. I remembered
that Doris had used the expression, "God heals all our brokenness
if we'll let Him." Already I was beginning to find this true.

One day I was talking to a friend who had come to visit me. She
was from a very prominent family and had everything. But when I
whispered to her what had happened to me, she wept, opened her
life and shared with me all its hurt and misery. As she got up to
leave, she said "I wish I had what you have, Hedy."

When she left, I laughed quietly to myself. What I had was
nothing but a helpless, broken body, a lost career, no hope as an
artist, no money, no man to love me as I'd always dreamed of, not
even the love of my own father. And yet as I lay there quietly, at
peace with the world I'd been so frantic to win, I felt somehow
that I did have everything. As a matter of fact, at that moment I
was actually grateful for all the things that had happened to me,
grateful to be in Wesley Memorial Hospital, grateful for all the
tragedy in my life.

I almost felt guilty when people said they felt sorry for me. Because I knew that I had found that thing I'd always been looking for. Tears of thankfulness came to my eyes as I realized that if I never got up or took a step or painted, life would be worthwhile. I had found its meaning. It *was* like a second birth.

But it wasn't only my soul which was changing. The doctors thought I was a little crazy when I told them that whatever state I was in, I was thanking God for it. They had to admit that my new faith made me a lot easier and more pleasant to work with. But what really caught their attention were the changes which began to take place in my body.

I had decided that if God could perform the miracle of healing my shriveled and despairing inner life, He could heal my body too. And I began to pray that He would do it quickly.

I had perked up so much that the doctors sent the physical therapist by. She worked on my fingers, one finger at a time, very gently. But inside I was almost amused at this. I had much bigger ideas. I wanted to move my arms and legs, to jump up and down and go tell people about this God I had found and help them find Him too. I had something to say and I was going to live to say it. The doctors were disturbed by my "impossible" hopes and plans, remembering the awful depression I experienced in December. They did not see me as being out of the woods even with regard to *survival*. And here I was planning to evangelize the world.

But I kept telling them they didn't know this Jesus Christ I'd met. Within a very few days I had advanced to the place where I was squeezing a small rubber ball in my left hand, even though each time this exhausted me in a few minutes. But I wanted to get well. So I squeezed the ball until my fingers couldn't move, and in a few minutes would begin again.

A couple of times back in December they had tried to lift me with sheets in order to put me in a wheelchair. It had taken four attendants, was painful and gave me very uncertain and helpless feelings. I hadn't wanted to get up that way. After that I had only asked them to get me up about four times. I'd spent most of my days and nights in bed. But now I *begged* to be put in the wheelchair every day. I had heard there was a physical therapy department downstairs. And I figured my recovery would be speeded up if I could get down there. The doctors had said I couldn't go, I didn't have the strength. But I begged to go, having no idea how weak I was. It didn't matter, I was going to get strong—whatever the cost.

"Please doctor," I said in my bullfrog voice one day, "what can it hurt for me to *see* the physical therapy department and talk to the therapist? It might calm me down and make me a much more manageable patient."

He shook his head and nodded it at the same time. "O.K., I give up," he said, and went out still shaking his head. They sent the body specialist from the physical therapy department. Her name was Jenny. Of all things, she turned out to be a Christian too. Jenny was very excited about what was happening to me and believed with me that in spite of all the odds against it, God could heal me.

People kidded me and made fun of my voice because it was so low and hoarse coming from such a tiny body. I laughed with them. But always having been very proud about my performance, I was sensitive about talking to strangers in my bullfrog voice. I could talk to Jenny easily, though. And we even prayed together in a secret conspiracy with God. She agreed, against her better judgment as a technician, to give me all the therapy I could take so we could speed up my trip toward freedom.

My right side was still virtually useless when I began. I did every exercise to my exhaustion point. At night I would lie awake and pray, thanking God and telling Him again and again, "I love you Father! I love you! I love you! Thank you for loving me and sending this strange new life into my life! Oh, I love you so much." And I'd fall asleep, exhausted, but more contented and at peace than I'd ever been.

The day soon came when Jenny took me downstairs to the therapy room. By this time my leg casts were off, but the heavy body cast looked like a white suit of armor. The attendants put me on a table and tried lifting my legs and arms with weights. I was filled with excitement and was hoping I could lift them myself when I learned how it felt for them to be raised. But the pain was so excruciating that I involuntarily cried out—something I'd promised myself I wouldn't do. My arms and legs were just limp rubber—there was no movement at all by my own efforts. But when they started to unhitch the weights I begged through my tears for more. I knew God was going to let me get well, and I was determined to experience any pain and effort to break through the barrier of my paralysis.

Later I discovered that no one had any hope of my walking. But as one of them said, "Hedy, we simply couldn't resist your hope." So they humored me by letting Jenny work with me while they were hunting for a permanent custodial type place where I could receive enough therapy to keep my muscles from atrophying and my joints from contracting. They saw this therapy only as a defensive, delaying action. But they couldn't find a place which would take a case as serious as mine.

I didn't know the impossibility of what I was trying to help God do. So I was quietly releasing enormous amounts of energy and hope into every small detail of every therapeutic exercise. Modeling had taught me the value and discipline of practicing every movement a thousand times.

And medical miracles began to happen, which the doctors never could explain. Within hours after the wreck a surgeon had inserted a plastic throat since mine had been crushed irreparably. In the midst of my new burst of life I was sent back to surgery for a surgical procedure involved with the opening in my trachea. The plastic throat was taken out and to everyone's amazement my own throat did not collapse as it had always done in previous surgeries. They waited. The throat still didn't collapse. And the doctors decided to experiment, keeping me under a careful watch, to see if my "new throat" might in fact be usable.

After several days of very careful watching, the chief surgeon said, "I don't believe it. Your throat's not very big, but you can use it. It's some kind of damned miracle. But for God's sake slow down, Hedy."

In a few days I was allowed my first bite of solid food—a spoonful of vanilla ice cream. It was a strange and exotic experience, the taste, the feel, the smooth texture—after I'd thought I'd never taste food again. All this time I'd been fed with a tube through my trachea. I was so grateful to God, and could imagine how food must have tasted to the first woman God made. It would be weeks before I could safely have any real solid food, but I didn't care— this was thrilling enough.

This miracle was simply more proof to me that God had amazing things in store for my life. I had a kind of confidence in the future which was very different for me. But this confidence and my exuberance almost cost me my life the following day.

An old friend Larry Sands, a country western singer and composer from California, was in Chicago at the time I got my new throat and he came to see me. Larry laughed at my bullfrog voice in a good-natured way. And I told him about what God was doing in my life. Larry was amazed. He'd become a Christian too and had been writing songs to glorify the Lord and celebrate his new hope. I asked him to sing for me. He got his guitar and played and sang for about an hour. His songs were so beautiful that the nurses turned on the intercom and the music went throughout our part of the hospital. I couldn't believe the warm conversation we had. It was as a sister and brother in God's family. Larry Sands a Christian! What a surprise! We had a wonderful visit.

When visiting hours were over, I called him close to the bed and whispered in my frog voice, "Larry, what I'd like more than anything is some pizza." I asked him if he'd sneak some in to me.

He laughed. "You're crazy, Hedy. But if you really want pizza, I'll get it for you." And he went out and sneaked some into the hospital, not realizing that I could easily choke to death on a piece of solid food.

The next morning the medical staff found out and couldn't believe I'd risked my life to have some pizza. The doctors took a lot of kidding around the hospital those days about their crazy Christian patient who was going to get well in spite of them. And having found the love of a Father at last, I was almost irrepressible. My search for intimacy with a man was forgotten among the opening blossoms of hope and meaning.

29. I Want to Go Home!

As I BEGAN to improve more, I was allowed more visitors. People I had known before came. Only now I discovered that many of them were Christians. And at first I wondered why they hadn't let me know before the wreck. But then I remembered how I had carefully avoided anyone who talked about being a Christian. I'd thought they were pious and that they felt superior to me because I wasn't "a believer."

But something mysterious had happened. I saw them with new eyes. I could feel their warmth and love now. I guess I was able to receive it for the first time, since I *felt* lovable because God loved me.

I wondered why all these people were coming. To my utter amazement, I learned that the entire congregation of a large church, the North Shore Church—one I had never even visited—had been praying for me to get well for months. One of the ministers had called on me regularly through my depression. He was a wonderful man and I looked forward to his coming every day. I was amazed that he came so faithfully when I wasn't even a member of his church. Several small prayer groups had prayed especially for me since I'd been in the hospital. And during my darkest days that church had had a special prayer service for my recovery.

As these Christians came to visit, they told me that people in different places all over the country had been praying for me!

I felt the love of God coming through these people and knew a sense of being a part of a loving family. It was like the carnival, only these people had hope and purpose in their lives. I had never known a church like this, but as I thought about their response to me, I realized that maybe the church was supposed to be a family. Certainly, knowing that God loved each of us should make us love each other.

Maybe it was no accident that I hadn't died all those times I should have, and even wanted to. Maybe the prayers and love of these people, who were also discovering the meaning of life, had sustained me in a way I couldn't even begin to grasp.

I was overwhelmed at the goodness and love which began to flood into my experience from all sides. The Deer Path Art League dedicated a cookbook to me. And the proceeds went toward the payment of my huge stack of medical bills. Sunday school classes in the North Shore Church, which had "adopted me," made things for a bazaar and gave the $2,500 proceeds to help pay bills.

For a litle girl who always felt that no one loved her, the church was an overwhelming demonstration that God could provide not only the love of a Father but another kind of love—the love of His family in one particular congregation. And I figured He picked a church I'd never been inside so I'd *know* I hadn't *done* anything to earn their love.

During this time, my physical condition improved continuously. I had several successful operations and was getting more and more able to move certain parts of my body. Way too soon I begged the doctors to let me try walking. Finally they agreed to let me try crutches, though they were sure I would never be able to walk. And sure enough, I failed—and failed. I didn't have the strength to hold and move the crutches and myself too.

After four days of trying and falling every time I could get someone to get me up on the crutches, my arms were so sore under the shoulders that I told God in tears that I didn't think I could ever walk on crutches. And it was as if He said to me, "Hedy, who said anything about crutches?"

I quit trying to use the crutches and told Jenny, my physical therapist friend, that I wanted to walk without them. I'll never forget the sad hurting expression in her eyes as she shook her head. "Hedy, *please* slow down. God's given you so much. Please don't throw away the crutches. It's only been *four days!*"

I looked at her, my dear Christian friend and said, "Jenny, don't you *believe* God can let me walk if I have enough faith and guts?" What could she say?

So she wheeled me down to the physical therapy department when no one was there. She stood me up between two parallel bars and put one hand on each bar. I still had my body cast on but my arms and legs were free. There was a mirror on the wall at the end of the bars. I looked at myself in the mirror and said to God, "I'm going to watch you and me walk. I'll meet you at the mirror." Even if the pain and effort killed me that hour, I was going to walk the length of those hand rails.

Jenny was silent as I began. I lurched, but said "no" when she started to stop me. Inch by inch, with precarious balancing and continuous near falls, I very painfully flopped one leg an inch or two, then the other, ignoring the pain, the time, the exhaustion, keeping my eyes on the mirror. I walked the length of the bars—and collapsed into Jenny's arms.

"Oh, dear Lord, I don't believe it!" she breathed as she put me in the wheelchair. I sat there trying to get my breath as she ran and got the orthopedic surgeon from down the hall.

When he and his staff saw me repeat my performance the next day, he said, "Hedy, I don't believe it. You walk like a drunk. But you walk!" He was almost as excited as I was—but not quite.

The next few weeks I remembered and put into practice some of the secrets I'd discovered so laboriously as a model years before. I had learned then how to walk with the appearance of being in total control. For instance, by keeping one's knees slightly bent, with seat tucked in, a person can maintain more total balance. Now, at a much more primitive level, I learned to memorize and control each motion which worked.

But the handicaps seemed enormous. My right side was almost totally numb. I could hit it and not feel a thing except the tingling one feels when an arm or leg is deeply asleep. After weeks of practice I could make some motions, even with my numb leg with as much poise as if I could actually control the leg directly. But if I forgot for an instant to control my motion by the way I would shift my body, then my right leg would flop aimlessly in front of the other.

Almost every day I'd get so discouraged that I'd cry and want to quit. I'd rasp, "God, why are you putting me through this? You know I'll never walk right." But it was as if God kept saying to me, "Hedy, do you *want* to be healed?" And I'd quit crying. Then I'd get back up and call together all the concentration, born of pride and fear, which had made me a good model at such an early age.

When I was at last ready to begin to eat regular food, I couldn't feed myself. My right arm was almost useless. So I practiced until I could use my left with an appearance of casualness.

Now I was spending most of my days in a wheelchair, but I refused to learn how to operate it properly since I had made up my mind I wasn't going to spend much time in it anyway. This caused great concern among the people around me, who thought I'd be spending much of the rest of my life in a wheelchair. But I kept reasoning, and believing with all my heart, that if God could save my life and give me a message of hope for the hopeless people in the world, then He could certainly put me on my feet and out of a wheelchair.

I was continually being surprised that the Christians around me *said* they believed God heals people. But at the same time they almost discouraged me from having that faith. With my lifelong naïveté I had just assumed that all Christians felt as I did. And I believed completely that God could and would heal me.

As I look back, I am amazed at the clarity and direct strength which came to me with my faith. But since then I have realized the thin line between a presumptuous testing of God and a simple trusting of Him.

I was learning more about God and the Christian faith every day through reading the New Testament and from Christians who came to see me. I especially enjoyed talking to the visitation minister from the North Shore church who had brought me the Bible.

This minister knew and loved God. We prayed, and I asked endless questions about Jesus, about the Bible, about the church and living as a Christian. I felt as if the world was beginning to make sense. Nature, beauty, art, love, food, hope, play, relationships—they were all a part of God's design. And here was a way to enjoy life with others instead of competing with them or trying to manipulate them.

My children's visits changed, too. I was beginning to teach them about God. We prayed together and all tried to give Him our lives. I didn't dream that before long they would be teaching me about Him.

One day I was sitting in my wheelchair waiting for Jenny to come take me to therapy. Looking out of the window I noticed the brown grass was turning green and the leaves were beginning to come back on the trees. The window was open a crack and the light breeze smelled of earth and of spring.

Suddenly I wanted to go home. The grey-green institutional walls of the hospital and the smell of old antiseptic and pine oil floor cleaner—all this seemed so sterile and impersonal. I realized that somehow I was becoming a person instead of a bag of tricks performed to win people's love. And I wanted to go *home,* the place for a "person." All I had was my apartment. But it had my furniture in it and it was a home to me. Then Jenny came in.

"Hi, Hedy! How's my olympic decathalon champion?" She smiled.

"Jenny," I said seriously, ignoring her greeting, "I'm ready to go home."

She looked up at the ceiling shaking her head. "Please, Hedy, *please* don't say that to the doctor! He already thinks you've gone nuts. Say that, and he'll know."

But I was serious. When I told the doctors they just laughed or avoided the subject or kept putting me off. But every day I asked, "When can I go home?"

Finally one of them said, "Hedy, we ought to let you go home so you'd see how impossible it'd be. You'd be back in two days." He was trying to be kind and patient, and I knew it.

When I asked why, he said,

"Well, in the first place you don't have any money and you'd have to have round the clock nursing since you still have to be in a wheelchair most of the time. You couldn't even get a pan out of the cupboard or take a bath by yourself. You'd have a hundred responsibilities you haven't even considered—like answering your telephone, people coming over, taking care of your kids, not to mention housework and grocery shopping. And besides, you'd need special medical equipment and would have to come back to the hospital for therapy every day. How's that for starters?" And he looked at me over his half glasses with a little shake of his head.

I knew he was right and wanted to cry and shake my fist at him at the same time—it didn't matter that it wasn't his fault. I felt that old despair creeping over me. But then I stopped, prayed and made a decision. It didn't matter what they thought. I was going to work out a way to go home.

When the doctor had gone I turned to the nurse. "Please tell them to bring my paints." They never had. But now I was going to paint again. I'd sell my paintings and make enough money to have the help I'd need at home. Surely I could learn to hold a paint brush with my left hand since I couldn't with my right. God could help me learn to paint again, left-handed. Unfortunately, I told everyone around me that this was going to happen.

At that time I could hardly negotiate a spoonful of food to my mouth. My first attempts at painting with my floppy left hand would have made a good slapstick comedy scene if it hadn't been so important to me to make it. Being barely able to hold the brush, I couldn't keep it steady even with my left hand. Claw-like, my hand and the brush shot out and hit the canvas, skidding across it, out of control.

I looked at what I'd done. "I can't do it," I heard myself whisper. "I'll *never* be able to." The brush was still in my hand. Everything in my universe stopped in those seconds. The future hung in mid-air. Then I looked up from the canvas and out the window. And it was as if God said to me, "Are you sure we can't, Hedy?" I looked back at the canvas. And then I began.

I wrapped the fingers of my left hand around my right wrist so

I could hold the brush more steady. But I couldn't seem to point it in the direction I wanted it to go. And finally when I got the brush going toward the canvas, it would swing away or skip across the canvas and off, getting paint on my cast, the bed, my hospital gown and anything else nearby.

I had told the nurse I *would* be able to paint and that I *could* take care of myself. And when she smiled at my mess, I was furious, I hated her—and I was embarrassed. But beneath the embarrassment was frustration, a realization that maybe the doctors were right and I wasn't going to be able to do it. My heart sank again.

In order to keep trying something that seemed so obviously doomed to failure, I developed a sense of humor and laughed at my funny mistakes and messes. For instance, with lipstick. When I first tried to put some on, I was red from one ear to the other— even on my forehead. And we all laughed at that too. But beneath the laughter, I was testing ways to hold things—especially the paint brush. Finally, by holding my left hand at the wrist with my numb right hand to steady the brush and trying again and again, I managed to get raw colors on the canvas. I was going to finish that painting.

I wished I had spent more time on the individual finger exercises in therapy. But now I went through my daily checkups and therapy routines as fast as possible so that when everyone left I could get back to painting.

They had brought acrylic paints. So when the paints would dry, I'd start again on the same canvas, day after day, a blob of color, a flower, some green—like a field. Each day I was more determined as I found a little evidence of control, definition, and saw the composition beginning to form on the canvas. But concentrating even for a few minutes was exhausting, since holding the brush steady was a matter of total mental and physical effort. I'd get discouraged, cry, and feel like a stupid fool for trying something I could never do.

About ten days later I woke up one morning and saw my canvas leaning against the wall at the end of my bed. I lay there waking up slowly, and suddenly it dawned on me, *"That's going to be a painting!"* The sense of relief was wonderful. My belief seemed to be confirmed. With a lot of hard work and dedication, a lot of agony, I could make a living and keep my children with me. Now, I can't imagine my not realizing just how much work, how many hundreds of hours it would actually take to get from these few jerky primitive splashes on the canvas to a painting of the quality I'd need to sell for enough to make a living. I almost gave up a hundred times as it was. But I think God must have protected me from knowing how hard it would be, or I don't think I could have kept trying. Besides, I wanted to keep Susan and Janie, and painting was my only hope. So I did keep trying.

And I kept asking questions and attempting to figure out how to get permission to go home. Somehow, I felt that God would not only take care of me but that there was something He had for me to do that I couldn't do in the hospital. I was learning more *about* God every day. But more important, I was learning to *know Him* and to trust Him. If I were willing to do what I thought He wanted me to do and to trust Him with the outcome of my efforts, I could somehow make it. Maybe I'd be wrong about what His will was. I knew that of course. But by trying to do what I *thought* it was, I'd learn about life. And since I could now be forgiven by a loving Father, I could afford to risk making mistakes—even about what His will might be. After a lifetime of being afraid of making *any* mistakes, this freedom was like being let out of a cramped cage.

As I thought about home, I felt more and more that going home was that act of faith which would force me not to settle for being the invalid everyone thought I'd be. I tried to be realistic about what I was facing. No. I guess that's not true. I tried to suppress and minimize the problems I'd face. But some of them seeped through into my consciousness.

I wanted more than anything to have a life with my children. Would I be able to care for them? They were so quick and their lives moved so fast. And everything I did was painfully slow. I kept forgetting that it was actually less than a year since the wreck.

None of the clothes in my closet would fit me, I'd lost so much weight and still had the body cast on. My car had to be sold to pay bills. Most of the money I'd gotten in the divorce settlement had gone to pay nurses. And the hospital had filed a lien on everything I owned. Although I didn't know it at the time, Findley had spent a lot of his own money getting things I needed, buying presents for the nurses and helping in a dozen other ways. If I went home, Findley would pay some child support. But there would have to be money for food, clothing, medicine, and a thousand other things I couldn't even think about.

One day the doctors, when they saw all that I'd done toward recovery through faith and working at it, decided to let me give living at home a try. When they told me, I was as scared as I was excited. I was to be on welfare at $80.00 a month. The doctor's report said I couldn't possibly work at anything for two years. But my nursing care, which had to be paid daily, was $90.00 a day. I was the only one who believed that in the hours I'd have alone I would paint and sell my paintings. I couldn't have dreamed in my wildest imaginings what help and opportunities lay just around the corner when I got home—or what discouragements and terrors.

The day I was to leave, the chief surgeon came to see me. "Hedy," he said, "we don't really know how you've come as far as you have. It's a miracle of some sort—really a whole series of miracles. But if this turns out to be more than you can handle, let us know and we'll bring you back here."

The staff had arranged for a machine which would help with my breathing and the cleaning of my trachea, for a wheelchair, rails, bars and special bedding equipment which the county was going to put in my apartment. And I realized how far out of their way these wonderful doctors had gone.

He smiled at me like a daughter, and I thought tears were going to come to his eyes. Then he cleared his throat and went on.

"Oh yes, Hedy. The Lake Forest police chief called and said that Danny's parents have gotten him out on bail. And if you ever hear from him you're to call the chief and he'll send someone right to your place."

He leaned over and kissed me on the forehead. "Goodbye, Hedy. I hope things go well for you always. And . . . this God of yours . . . he's one hell of a good doctor."

As they wheeled me down the hall with my bag, I couldn't wait to see what life was going to have in store. I had nothing, but I had the key to everything important, because I wasn't going home alone. God was going with me.

30. Ugly, Crippled, Scared, Mute and Broke — But Home

THE DOCTOR'S WARNINGS had seemed exaggerated in the glow of my new faith. But when I got home the problems were plenty real.

Now I can see that there is a strange "blindness" which is part of a conversion experience. It's like a honeymoon period in a marriage that seems to blot out a lot of the built-in difficulties of living while the honeymooners are getting adjusted to loving each other. My first days with God were a lot like that. In some ways I had almost seen God as a great magician who would do my will in solving all my problems.

But whenever I meet people in the honeymoon period, I try never to discourage them. Because the hope and motivation born in these first few days as a Christian were real for me and allowed me to make it through those otherwise impossible days and nights. I had hope, and I had meaning. There was the presence of a loving, encouraging Father urging me to come ahead with Him, and He picked me up and carried me in His arms in sleep when I felt exhausted.

Findley had agreed to let the children come back and stay with me. In fact he stayed at night for a while to help us get settled. He treated me like a child and did everything the nurses would have done when they weren't there. The girls were eight and eleven. I had dreamed of the day I could be their mother again and make up for the time I felt I'd neglected them. In my fantasy I had seen myself a hundred times cooking their breakfast and seeing them off to school, pretty and happy.

But one morning when Findley was gone, the nurse was late. I was too weak to get up and had to wait for my little Janie, who was already awake, to come in and help me from the bed to the wheelchair so I could go into the bathroom. There, it took both the girls to lift me from the wheelchair onto the toilet. Then they held me next to the sink while I brushed my teeth, put me in the wheelchair and rolled me back into the bedroom.

They went to the kitchen to make some coffee for me before they went to school. This wasn't what I'd planned at all. And for someone as independent as I, this having my babies taking care of me was almost worse than the physical pain and frustration.

I called in my whisper for one of them, to tell her I wanted more coffee. And I'll never forget the look of fear and concern on her face as she ran in my door. They almost apologized for having to go to school and wanted to know, "Is there *anything* we can do before we leave? Anything you need?"

As I saw their faces, I couldn't have asked for a thing, no matter what I'd needed.

The first week after Findley left I had nurses around the clock. But I knew I was sinking into debt so fast that I let the night nurse go—even though it meant that the children had to take care of me at night. Everybody fought me about this, but I knew that it had to be. The nurse taught the children how to clean my tracheotomy and prepared them to handle things that might come up in caring for me. I'll never forget their serious, intent faces as they nodded their heads when they understood each procedure. And they will never know how proud I was of them. They bought me a silver whistle with a chain to go around my neck, so I could call to them when they were out of the house or in another room.

After their first night of nursing me, when they had done the dishes and tumbled into bed, I lay awake, looking out of my window at the cool spring night.

"What was I thinking about, God?" I thought. "There is no way I can take care of these children."

I'd always been so strong physically that I had forgotten the extent of a mother's duties and responsibilities: getting them to school when it's raining or too cold to walk, helping them with their homework, taking them to Bluebirds, dance class, picnics, birthday parties, their own doctor and dental appointments—not to mention cooking and seeing about their clothes—and a hundred other things. Now I had to depend on other people for help. Some of the neighbors were very thoughtful. The Sutherlands next door often drove them to school in bad weather.

And I had to get some money. There seemed to be no way to stem the rising tide of bills. "God, what can I do?"

As I said that, I remembered a statement Jesus had made, "Sell all you have and come, follow me."

The next day I called several friends who were interested in my paintings and told them that everything I had was for sale, if someone would come and make an offer. These friends began to bring people by in a way that didn't disturb me at all. The nurse would let them in, and the friends would go through all my paintings and sketches. I managed each week to sell enough for another day or another week.

On an impulse I called Lucy and told her that if she or Daddy wanted to buy anything I had—furniture, knick-knacks or anything—to come and make an offer. To my surprise, two days later she came—with my father. I hadn't counted on his coming and was a little flustered. They bought some lamps and vases and we visited a little over coffee. After they were gone I realized I didn't *have* to have my father's approval to be whole now—but I told God it sure would be nice to have a sign of it someday.

Because of the word we'd received that Danny had been released from jail, the nurses were very careful who they let in the door. The same nurse, Henrietta, who had seen Danny try to kill me before, had become a dear friend and was with me most of the time. But I was much too busy to worry about Danny. And the energy I used up to do things was enormous. Each day I was de-

termined that "today I'll get through all my therapy, duties, maintenance tasks and *paint!*"

But the days were exhausting. The doctors had been right of
course. To do what I had set out to do was humanly impossible. I
hadn't been counting, though, on merely human power. And in
looking back I realize that there *is* a kind of physical energy and
drive released through faith which must have a great deal to do
with unlocking the physical forces of healing and growth—a
physical drive and energy medical science depends on constantly
but can evidently neither cause nor maintain. But looking back, my
daily schedule was an impossible combination of effort, pain,
frustration and despair, mingled with moments of the joy of new
achievements and the hope that I might get better.

Every morning the nurse would bathe me in the bathtub. Each
time I would insist on trying to raise myself without help. But
every day, after several tries, I would topple over. She would have
to catch me with her strong arms and get me covered and in my
wheelchair before the ambulance arrived to take me back to the
hospital. Because I had an hour of physical therapy every day, plus
an appointment with at least one of my many doctors for x-rays,
examinations, change of bandages where they had taken out my
plastic throat, or questions concerning the use of various parts of
my body.

Being an outpatient in the public department of a hospital takes
a great deal of time. Each time I went I'd have an appointment for
a particular problem and would go to the appropriate floor: orthopedic, neurosurgery, eye, ear, nose and throat. When I was wheeled
off the elevator, I'd be in a big open room which appeared to me as
big as a football field. There were rows and rows of folding metal
chairs like those in an old junior high school auditorium. The
chairs were filled with the poor, the miserable, the dispossessed of
all ages, races and nationalities. And the smells: body odor, bad
breath, unclean wounds, antiseptic, and the vague smell of poor
people's clothes permeated it all.

The waiting period for a doctor could be anywhere up to four
hours after the appointment time. I often looked at the blank green

walls and then at the people: hacking coughs, sad eyes, stooped shoulders, hopeless looks and silent tears; some of them clutching another person's arm for some kind of security.

I soon realized that many poor patients couldn't work. This waiting was their life, day after day, as it was mine. One day as I sat there, I thought of my friends at the carnival, and remembered that same look of hopelessness. Except now I knew a secret. I knew that there *was* hope and Someone who cared. And I wanted to tell these people, to shout it to them, to reach out and touch them with the love I felt. I wanted to tell the people at the carnival—the whole world. Where were the Christians who were supposed to visit the sick and announce the good news?

As I sat in the midst of the groaning herd of miserable human wreckage, a real part of it, I knew the time had come for me to get well and tell the world about Jesus Christ—at least the part of the world I could reach with my whisper. As a first step I would somehow *force* time into my day for painting, though I didn't see how. I wanted more than anything for my life to have, to *be* some kind of message to people who have no hope.

Pepper came from Milwaukee for a visit, bringing eight sacks of groceries. She hunted up all my paintbrushes which were "glued" together in twisted curls of solid lacquer. She painstakingly cleaned them all and brought them in to me, seeing that everything was set up to paint. Then she just stood and looked at me. I knew she loved me. She had written every day since the wreck.

I shook my head, knowing she expected me to begin to paint.

As I looked back at her, a wave of warm feelings of love and gratitude flooded over me. She really believed I could do it.

I picked up a brush and looked at it. A fear swept through me. What if I couldn't paint now. I hadn't had a paintbrush in my hand since I'd come home. Pepper just stood there saying nothing —damn her. I turned to the canvas. She had loved me into it. And life was beginning again.

Over the next days, which stretched into weeks and then months, I felt solid strength beginning to seep back into my body, and my emotions.

I began to paint, blocking out everything else for an hour, then two, sometimes all night, or only a few minutes. But I turned my intensity up to a white hot pitch to concentrate. At first the paintings came slowly. It was so discouraging I couldn't imagine why I was continuing. Just mixing the colors for the first painting took hours to get them right. I was three months finishing the first good painting. And I was thrilled and so grateful that I wept when I sold it for $450. I took a giant step toward wholeness and independence that day.

Through the curtains I watched the woman who had bought the painting put it in the back seat of her car. And I said a prayer of thanks to God. I realized again that all of my past experiences had been necessary elements in training me for this time of getting well. I was especially grateful for the almost unbelievable motivation and discipline I'd been given which allowed me to learn to control my body. I would recall each motion, reconstructing in my mind the way I moved my hands, arms, legs, whether in painting, working, or walking. Then I'd memorize each motion and the sequence of motions. So that long before I should have been able to, I was getting around and appearing to be doing things effortlessly—which in fact were like delicate balancing acts. No one knew when they saw me walk gracefully across a room that they could have literally knocked me off my feet by an unexpected nudge with one finger. And yet I found that the concentration and effort to make it appear easy and natural actually speeded up the process of healing. This was because I was "grooving" correct movements in my muscles' "memories." I don't know if this is the right way medically, but this is the way it happened.

Within a few weeks after I left the hospital I was spending almost half the time during the day out of the wheelchair and on my feet. Some weeks later they cut off my body cast. I can't describe the relief that brought. Not being able to scratch an itch or feel anything close to my body but warmth inside the plaster had been a discomfort I hadn't been totally aware of until it was gone. But I knew I was going to have to try even harder before I could become strong enough to help other people find the life I wanted to share so much. Now my paintings were coming faster. I sent one of the first to Wesley Memorial for the blank green wall in the public patients' waiting room.

One afternoon I was putting the finishing touches on a painting. The nurse was off duty because Pepper had been visiting from Milwaukee. After Pepper left, I completed the painting and began to think about what it was that I had to share with people out of my life. Mostly failure, it seemed, in spite of all the outward marks of success I'd chalked up. I had gone from one person, one situation to another, demanding total commitment, total success, trying to achieve enough to win my daddy's love.

And not realizing the impossibility of my demands on other people or myself, I had thought I was simply not achieving enough to win the love I demanded—and so had been on a crash course with failure. Then came the impact of the wreck and my paralysis. It was as if the shock cracked the protective shell I had built so carefully to hide my fear and inadequacy from the world.

In the hell of total separation, in my tomb of paralysis, I had gotten a good look at my life and seen that it was a dry, dead wasteland. Finally, when I had nothing left to try, I was ready to give it all to God. And now, slowly, almost imperceptibly at first, out of the black stubble of the past there were tiny beautiful shoots of green, of new life and hope. And with them the look of the living in the land of the dead. So this was the good news I had to tell a world of people whose lives had also become a wasteland of discouragement.

But with health there also came bubbling to the surface of my consciousness some feelings I'd repressed since the accident. I had been looking for another kind of relationship besides that with my father. I thought of the children, of Buzzy, Findley, Pepper and Bill—everyone who had been close—especially Danny.

Yes, in all these relationships I wanted something else—sometimes even more than a father's approval. I'd wanted a kind of close sharing of souls with another human being, especially with a man, an experience of total intimacy. I'd longed for a relationship in which I could really let my hair down and be totally natural about

who I was, with all my secrets, my childish dreams and my paralyz-
ing fears and guilts about not being enough. But I'd only had brief
glimpses of this kind of closeness.

Because the only drive *more* consuming than this need to be
known and loved was my desperate *fear* of being known.

Now that God had in some deep way laid to rest the need for
an impossible love from my father, this other need—for closeness
with another person—came into sharp focus. But for now I reminded myself, I was very lucky just to be alive. I was happy and
feeling very secure with God. And I felt a peace about the future.
God would help me through it.

As I was thinking these thoughts, the telephone rang. Still in a
pleasant state of peacefulness, I answered it myself and whispered,
"Hello."

"Hello, Hedy, this is Danny."

31. A Long Walk into the Night

SINCE DANNY HAD gotten out of jail, Henrietta had started bringing a revolver to work. She hid it under the pillow on the couch near the front door. Every time the doorbell rang, she'd tiptoe to the window so she could see out before opening the door—which we kept locked all the time.

But now Henrietta was off, and Pepper had just left for Milwaukee. It was six o'clock when the telephone rang, and I'd be alone with the children until seven the next morning. I realized all this as I heard Danny's voice.

I started to hang up. I'd known in the back of my mind that I would hear from him again, and I couldn't get those hate-filled, ice blue eyes out of my mind. But something in his voice made me keep listening. I could tell that he was or had been crying. He was almost incoherent and sounded so helpless. I knew I should hang that telephone up, but it's always been nearly impossible for me to break off a relationship.

"Hedy, baby, I'm sorry. I'm so sorry. I just can't live any more. I can't carry this responsibility."

Danny's tongue seemed thick, and he began to sob. In spite of everything, I wanted to comfort him. But when he continued, there was determination through the tears.

219

"I'm going to come over, Hedy. I don't want to live any more and you can't live that way. I won't make a mistake this time." He was crying again. "Hedy, I promise everything will be all right. I'll be right there. It will only take a little while."

While I tried desperately to keep him on the phone, Susan walked into the room. I asked Danny to wait a minute and sent Susan to the apartment downstairs to use the neighbor's telephone to get help. I didn't know if she'd think to call the police or friends. But I kept talking to Danny, asking questions about what had been happening to him. In just a minute Susan was back— the neighbor's teenaged daughter was on the phone! She'd be off in a little while, she said, and would come get us when the line was free! She was the only one at home.

I couldn't believe it. I put my hand over the phone and told Susan to run next door to get Dr. Sutherland to come over or tell me what I could do while I kept Danny on the phone. I didn't want to call the police if there was any other way—I knew he was out on bail. Strangely, I still felt love for him and couldn't bear to hurt him. I knew I was being irrational, but my mind was racing for some other solution. Susan ran next door, but just then Danny hung up.

In a few minutes, she came back, breathless.

"Mommie, the Sutherlands have gone out somewhere."

I picked up the telephone to call for help but was somehow paralyzed. Though I knew it was crazy, I couldn't bring myself to dial the police. The minutes seemed endless. Names were flashing through my mind in rapid succession, people who might possibly help. But I couldn't settle on one and kept discarding them for various reasons, trying to get a new name. Finally I called one of my doctors. He was definite:

"For god's sake, Hedy, call the police! That boy's crazy!"

But just as I hung up, the doorbell rang. And I turned to ice.

I told the children to go to their room and stay there, no matter what they heard.

I sat for a few seconds not knowing what to do. Then the door-bell rang again, this time more insistently. Now I heard something that sounded like the police reports that come through the radio of a police car on T.V. Cautiously I looked out the window. Even though it was dark, I could see that there were two patrol cars in front of the apartment building.

The children too had seen the police cars from their window, and they came running out. The three of us went to the door and little Janie yelled for me, "Who's there?"

"The police. May we talk to you?"

We opened the door, and two uniformed policemen from the Lake Forest Police Department came in, after showing their identification.

"Mrs. Robinson," the taller one said, "Do you know Daniel Baker?"

"Yes," I answered and began crying, "and thank you for coming! I'm so glad you're here. I didn't know what to do."

But before I could explain, the officer cut in, "Mrs. Robinson, Daniel Baker has been under house arrest. He was released to his parents with the stipulation that he was to be under the care of a psychiatrist.

"About thirty minutes ago his father called and said Daniel had started to leave the house. His father tried to stop him but Daniel knocked him down at the front door and left, running. He was evidently under the influence of narcotics."

Then Danny's mother had gone upstairs and found a note on his bed. The policeman came to the point. "In that note, Mrs. Robinson, he told his family goodbye, that he loved them very much but that he'd never see them again. He'd been talking about you the past few days. And they felt sure he was on the way to your house. We have no way of knowing if he's armed. But in any case we're going to stay until he gets here."

After moving their cars out of sight, the two patrolmen came back to my apartment, locked all the doors and arranged the lighting so that it looked like I was at home, but Danny wouldn't be able to see into the apartment when he arrived.

The officers were stationed so they could see out but not be seen. There were others hidden outside around the house and in the area. The police radio was sitting on the dining room table in the middle of the apartment. They could get reports of Danny's progress in the two miles he had to walk between our houses.

The tall policeman gave directions to the children to be quiet. "You can sit at the dining room table," he said. "But at the first sign of Mr. Baker you run into your room and lie down on the floor till we call you."

After a while I took the children back to their bedroom. They had decided that they should pray. I asked if I could stay. We all three held hands and I was moved to tears as I heard those little girls talking with God. Janie said, "Please help Danny, God. He's so mixed up and so unhappy. Please do something to help him."

This was the man they knew might be coming to try to kill their mother and maybe hurt them. They were so serious and wide-eyed and asked me if there was anything else they should pray for.

"No," I said, "I think you've done the most important thing." I kissed them goodnight and went back toward the dining room, bemused and amazed. It never occurred to the girls that God wouldn't take care of *us*. After all we had given Him our lives. Danny was the one who needed help—he didn't know God. And they were right.

While we waited, I told the policemen what had happened, starting with the wreck and how fortunate we felt to be together and have God in our life—that it was worth everything, even that night. The policemen had a very nervous reaction to my calmness. They smiled in a way I would see many people smile in the next two years, as if at a little child.

"Mrs. Robinson," the short one said, "What would you have done if we hadn't come? How would God have helped you? Would you have called us after Danny Baker killed you?"

He wasn't being sarcastic. He was serious.

I said I didn't know, but that they *had* come in fact. And I felt that it was all part of the way God helps people, although I was pretty new at the God business and there were a lot of things I didn't understand.

As the evening turned to night, the time seemed never-ending. Each minute was like an hour. I found myself serving endless cups of coffee. One of the policemen kept asking questions about how I'd gotten well and what it meant to me to be a Christian. Two more had come inside, and they took turns by twos at the windows overlooking the terrace. It must have been about two o'clock in the morning when I realized we hadn't received any calls from the police department in the last hour. What was going on out there in Danny's brain? All of us became more tense as the minutes ticked by loudly from the clock on the buffet.

By this time we were just sitting silently staring over another tired bitter cup of coffee—each with his own thoughts. I was trying to pray, but couldn't figure what to pray for that would solve things for all of us. So I finally just turned the outcome over to God and relaxed. I was very drowsy. In the background I could hear the hum of the children's voices still talking in their room.

Suddenly, with no warning at all, the doorbell's loud ringing shattered our thoughts. The two policemen at the table jumped straight up with their revolvers drawn. Now totally alert, I headed for the children's room as fast as I could walk and told them to lie down on the floor, as I shushed them with a finger to my lips.

The front door opened and I could hear the sound of masculine voices. I strained my ears expecting the noise of a scuffle, but there was no ruckus, just calm voices. I inched down the hall and looked through the door into the dining room from which I could almost see through the living room to the front door. All I could see were more uniforms, so I went on in.

Two more policemen had arrived and were reporting what had just happened.

"We saw him walking down Green Bay Road a few blocks from here. We pulled up beside him, and he took off running up a driveway between two houses. We challenged him to stop, but he just kept going, until he was about to disappear around the back of the house. Then he straightened up as if he'd been hit between the shoulders and crumpled up in a heap on the driveway. By the time we got to him he was dead."

As the reports would show, his heart stopped beating from an overdose of narcotics. In Danny's pockets, hand, and shoes were all the going forms of drugs.

When they said he was dead, an enormous sense of relief flowed through my whole body. I had repressed my fears so completely that I didn't feel them until that moment. And I sighed clear to my toes. It was somehow like the moment a few weeks earlier when they had unbolted the halo cast and cut the plaster prison off my body.

I thanked the police, and finally the last one left. Standing in the doorway, I looked up at the moon through the top of the big willow tree beside the porch. This was another of those turning points in my life. I remembered that night years before when I was fifteen and sat on my sister's front porch crying, feeling that my childhood had died, but I was not sure what womanhood would be like—or if there would ever be hope.

But now I knew. There *was* hope! Through God's acceptance of me, and now through Danny's death, God had unlocked me from the past. I stood in that doorway on the threshhold of a whole new exciting future. Leaning on that porch rail, I saw God in the moon and stars and felt His presence in the darkness around me. His breath moved the willow tree branches. The night was filled with His Spirit brooding over the whole world. And He'd loved me, Hedy Robinson, enough to save my life so I could tell people and show them how much He loves them. I looked up and said, "Thank you, God! Thank you! Thank you!" over and over through the tears of release and happiness.

Now I was free to be God's person. And I wouldn't be afraid of anything. I promised out loud in my whisper voice, "God, I'll do whatever you want me to do to help people—regardless of how frightening or hard it may be!"

32. Death of the Past — The Burial

THE NEXT DAY I asked a friend to take me to Danny's parents' house, where I tried to comfort them for several hours. Danny's younger brother, Billy, had come in from California. I told them I wished I could help them some way and to let me know if I could do anything.

The following day Danny's mother called. She was crying.

"Hedy, I've been to the funeral parlor and Danny doesn't look good after the autopsy. His lips are swollen and his hair isn't combed right. Would you please go to the funeral home with Billy and me? Maybe you could help make him look right."

I remembered my promise to God and my offer to her. I shuddered involuntarily as I pictured myself doing what she asked. But she was a good woman and had been through a lot with Danny too. So I said gently, "All right, Mrs. Baker, of course I will."

On the way to the funeral parlor, she handed me a gold ring and a gold neck piece that I had made for Danny.

"Hedy, do you want him to take these with him in the casket?"

"Yes."

"Then would you take them and put them on him?"

"Yes, Mrs. Baker, we'll do that," I said, taking the gold things she was holding out to me. Then Billy and I went into the room where Danny's body was.

When we got to him, I simply refused to acknowledge that that cold chalky form was Danny. And afterwards, when we walked out of the funeral parlor, I actually felt the death of the past.

As I rode home from the burial service, I realized again how Danny with his gentleness had somehow symbolized for me the hope of a spontaneous and real loving relationship. But something essential had been missing. What was it? We had mutual attraction, we had special shared time alone, we could give and receive love. Then I saw again how I had kidded myself rather than face the fact that some kind of sharing of secret hopes and fears *had* to be one of the main ingredients of intimacy. Except for our first night together, Danny had hidden most of the inner details of his life from me. And I had withheld much of my life from him, as I now realized I had from myself. So we had blocked the open interflow of shared history and feelings through which our love and intimacy could have breathed and survived. We had briefly known and loved each other emotionally, but we hadn't been open together.

"But," and I smiled to myself as I thought, "the question of intimacy with a man is certainly a remote one now." I weighed about eighty pounds. My hair had been shaved off a few weeks before when they had removed the bolts. I hardly looked like a woman, more like an odd little girl.

In fact, a few weeks before when I was in my wheelchair in the hospital elevator, a man had patted my arm and said awkwardly, "That's all right, sonny, everything will be all right!" *Sonny!* At that word I had felt a shock of disbelief and then awareness that I was light years away from any glamour I had projected as a woman.

But at least now because of my physical handicaps, I had, for the first time in my adult life, a vacation from having to deal with men as men and my search for intimacy with one.

When I got home from the funeral, I began to think about my new life and what I might do. My apparent ease of movement was far ahead of my actual strength and ability. But with great effort

I could get around by myself for several hours. I was painting almost as well with my left hand as I had been able to do with my right, and there was a new serious quality in some of my work which God must be bringing into my painting from the pain I'd been through.

I had a feeling of expectancy as if the decks were being cleared in my life. What the future held I wasn't sure. But it was as if God were telling me that my time was coming, and then I'd understand. But for right now I had work to do.

I knew I had to have an art show.

PART SIX

PLEASE LOVE ME

33. Walking on Water — At Sister Bay

BESIDES THE PAIN, God was showing me a loving, unselfish side of life through the people in the church—a kind of loving care for strangers which I'd never even known existed before. How was I going to capture this in an art show?

I had come out of the hospital at the end of March with nothing except an enormous backlog of unpaid bills. I was having a lot of trouble living on my meager income. At times during those first months, my gas was turned off, we had no hot water, and we went several days without electricity. But in the midst of this the Christians came, and food mysteriously appeared on the doorstep from out of nowhere. Some offered to take the children places they needed to go. Some just came to offer good wishes and pray. Others asked if I had any paintings or sketches left—they had a friend who was interested in buying one.

All this was even more amazing to me, since I felt I had absolutely nothing to give them. I felt so unattractive, and I couldn't entertain them or earn their love and attention in any way. Since I'd always felt that if I didn't perform, others wouldn't like me, I couldn't get over their thoughtfulness. These Christians really seemed to care for me.

It was as if God were saying to me again that "the love of your heavenly Father, which you've always longed for, does not depend on your being a movie star or a big civic worker. As a matter of fact, it doesn't depend on any performance at all." It was such good news I simply couldn't believe it.

The embarrassment at being poor which had plagued me as a child was gone. At a time when I should have been mortified by being helped so much and by not having any money, I found myself joining the children in praising God, thanking Him and feeling in a real sense richer than we'd ever been.

About a week after the funeral I'd been allowed to try driving a car a few times. I still walked erratically and couldn't control the swing of my legs too gracefully, but I found I could hold down a gas pedal and put on the brakes with my left foot. That same week the material practicalities of life suddenly became acute. It was late in the summer.

Financially I *had* to do something. My oil paintings and sketches were gone. Just at that time two representatives from the Deer Path Art League came and said,

"Hedy, if you'll do a show, we'll sponsor you. We'll do the invitations and make all the arrangements."

At last, a chance! Now that I had something tangible to motivate me, I could begin working my way back to being a whole person, standing on my own feet financially. But people kept coming to my door to talk, to visit, and to help. And I loved them. How could I escape my loving Christian brothers and sisters long enough to paint a whole show? When the committee representatives left that night, I prayed for a way to find time to paint, and began on the first picture.

Two days later Pepper called from Milwaukee. Pepper paints and sculpts, and for years she and I had rented and shared a cottage in Door County on the beach of Lake Michigan outside Sister Bay. We'd taken our children and watched them play as we worked together. Pepper was very athletic and years before had taught me how to swim and to build up certain parts of my body by doing exercises in the water.

Anyway, she called very excited and said, "Hedy, we got the

cottage for you. And if you can't make it up those steps"—the cottage was built on piers—"I'll stay and carry you up and down. But the water will build up your legs. And you can paint totally undisturbed. Maybe you can get some rest and get strong again. And—this is our get-well gift to you."

"How wonderful of you, God," I thought, "and how dear of Pepper and Bill."

When I called Findley to ask if he'd keep the children, and how he thought I could get up there, he almost had heart failure. "Hedy, you're *crazy!* Living on an empty beach in the off season, alone—where you couldn't go for help—or even scream for it. You've lost your mind!"

But I was determined. I called another friend to see if she could take me. But she was going to be on a trip. I was stumped. Then I thought about renting a car and driving myself. I could do it—it was only a hundred-mile drive.

The next day at the hospital Jenny also thought I'd lost my mind for even thinking about such a trip. The two doctors I had appointments with that week confirmed her opinion. Everyone was in complete agreement: "It's impossible."

This didn't discourage me at all, since those people had said the same things about my walking, painting and going home. And I felt that I was *supposed* to go and that God would help me again— since I was convinced that he had arranged the whole thing.

I know how naïve this will sound, but anyone who has not been where I'd been and seen God bring me back from death and worse simply cannot understand the nature and strength of my faith during those days. I had that same indestructible feeling children have. God had a plan for my life and I felt I'd be protected until it was finished.

Findley never agreed to my going, but he did finally say he'd keep the children. After all, we weren't married and he couldn't really stop me.

The hardest thing for me to put in my suitcase was the swimming suit. It took sheer guts to put that suit in, a little bikini to go over a body that was nothing but bones, loose flesh, and muscles that seemed to be made of gelatin. My bony knees were covered with skin which was mostly scar tissue from bones that had been sticking through. My forehead had holes where the halo had been screwed on, my throat was scarred from ear to ear. At the base of my neck where the tracheotomy had been, there was a huge scarred dent. And on down I was still asking myself where my breasts had gone. When the cast had come off, my chin was on my chest and I saw that I looked like a newborn child—just ribs. A far cry from the sixteen-year-old beauty queen. Miraculously my face was almost unchanged from before the wreck. But I knew I had to start from where I was if I were going to build my body back. Pepper had said to bring my suit. And God had already done so much.

So off I drove in a rented Gremlin, never having felt a clearer sense of myself and of the meaning and purpose of life—to glorify God and enjoy Him and His world forever. I was simply "Hedy" now. And whatever I looked like to the world, I was a perfect child of God because He loved me. If I was good enough for God—I was good enough for anyone.

One of the strange things to me was the way people treated me since I'd gotten out of the hospital. As word of my conversion and unusual healing got around, people accorded me a kind of awe, as if I had been touched directly by God. And although it was strange, it seemed natural to me, since I felt that I *had* been touched by God in an unusual way. But people, even doctors, apparently felt that I was being somehow guided, and they hesitated to stop me when I felt I was supposed to do something. I don't know if I repressed all bad thoughts during that time, but my mind was filled with faith and with good, beautiful feelings about life and people.

I'd made the drive to the beach every year for seven years. But now it almost felt like the first time for me. The September countryside was beautiful and familiar. The closer I got the more excited I became, but also the more exhausted. When I finally reached the city limits of Sturgeon Bay and turned down the old familiar road, I knew it was only a few miles further, and I wanted to cry.

I was so tired I had to stop and rest. I could smell the marsh water, hear the gulls and could almost taste the whitefish. I'd never thought I'd see that beach again.

After an hour I started down the road. And finally, there was the old red and yellow cottage. As I drove up on the sand behind the house, I wondered if I'd get stuck again. But I really didn't care, because I never wanted to leave. It was like heaven to me.

The house was more than ten miles from a grocery store. There was no telephone, and the water came within fifty feet of the door. Across the front was a porch where I remembered staying up all one night with Pepper because the moonlight and stars above the water had been so beautiful we couldn't go to sleep. I especially remembered our talk that night because it was probably the only long, honest one I had had in my whole life. Pepper was a real friend. As I sat in the car remembering, I wondered if anyone else had a real friend.

Pepper was there waiting and helped me get settled. I was completely drained when we finally got everything out of the car that night and I stumbled up the front stairs into the cottage. I fell into a bed and slept like a baby for twelve hours.

I started each day walking out on the porch, standing at the gray wooden rail looking at the sun rising over the water. The first morning the sun came up through a fairyland castle of towering clouds, turning them pink and orange and white. It was like the city of God rising out of the sea. I had chill bumps all over me and knew that God had met me in this strange desert appointment at the edge of the sea.

After breakfast those first few days, I would put on my jeans and a sweatshirt, or sometimes a pea-coat, and hang my whistle around my neck. I always wore it to remind me of the children's love. Then I would take my little tape recorder and Pepper and I started walking. When I first arrived at the beach, I visualized myself walking in water up to my knees so that my legs would become strong again. I thought, "When I get home no one will know me." But somehow I'd forgotten how cold the water was now that summer was over.

I wanted to tell Pepper all I'd learned about God, about my tendency to hide my feelings, and my fear of rejection, but we didn't get around to it—probably because it was still too scary for me. That disturbed me after she left. She stayed two weeks. After that I was mostly alone.

At first when I'd tried to walk in the sand with Pepper hovering over me, I could hardly move my feet and felt as if I had a ball and chain on both legs. Every few yards I'd have to stop and sit down to get my breath. But then I'd start out again. Day by day, pawing, staggering, tripping, losing my balance and often my determination, I walked an hour every morning and an hour every afternoon in the soft sand dunes at the upper edge of the beach. At the end of the walk I would sit down on a log and try to get my breath. That was when I'd practice speaking into a microphone with my tape recorder.

By this time I'd developed a pretty good whisper, but it was often foggy, gurgly and indistinct. My younger daughter had said the week before, "Mommie, you sound just like a bullfrog."

Then looking at my face, she quickly added, "But that's all right, Mommie, I love bullfrogs!"

I'd taken Janie's serious face in both hands and looked into her eyes, which were so like mine. I kissed her on the forehead and we both laughed and hugged each other. I felt filled with warm gratitude for those loving children. This made me even more determined to get completely well.

And I wanted to speak clearly enough so that people could understand exactly what I was saying. There was so much I wanted to say. I'd found the thread that held together the fabric of all meaning, God. There really was a loving Father, and He loves all of us as we look for life and its meaning. I wanted to introduce everyone to Him, everywhere I went. I'd already had the experience of wanting to go up and hug anyone who looked unhappy and tell them how much God loved them. I wanted to tell them that I loved them too, and that no matter what or who they were, they had a chance at life and peace and purpose.

But often when I'd tried to talk to people they simply could not understand my garbled whispering. They'd become embarrassed and couldn't hear the good news I was trying so passionately to tell them.

So on the dunes I started talking into the tape recorder about God and the love I felt for Him and for life. After Pepper left and I was alone, I would listen to the tape as I got ready for bed at night, hearing the seagulls in the background. And in my mind's eye I could still see the sandpipers running into the lace edge of the water as the wind blew it up on the shore.

God's Spirit seemed to permeate the sights and sounds and even what I was saying.

I was having a love affair with God and His world, and I began to write poetry. I wrote with freedom because I knew my love would be received and returned. As I was writing a poem one day, I wondered if maybe the experience of closeness with God might be as rare as intimacy between men and women seemed to be—and for similar reasons: we are afraid to trust. I saw that my trusting played a large part in my relationship with God—I trusted God's love and therefore trusted that my love and offerings of myself would be received by Him. Then I realized that I had never trusted a man that much. Maybe that had a lot to do with my frustration in the search for intimacy. But I had come closest to being open with Pepper, and she was a *woman*. That thought stopped me. Maybe intimacy wasn't tied to sexual attraction as I'd always thought. Maybe it was something bigger, like the closeness with God.

As the weeks went by, I could feel strength flowing back into my body. My voice improved enormously. I started reading my love poems to God into my tape recorder, as I sat on a big piece of driftwood on the dunes. I spoke and played them over and over, trying to improve the way I talked to God.

In the afternoons I painted. Almost from the first, I could sense that if God's Spirit were in everything in my life, He must be in my paintings too. Strangely, God had left me absolutely no vocational choice except to paint. With no voice, any work having to do with the telephone was out. I couldn't work on my feet. I couldn't type, since my fingertips were all numb. I had to paint. This must be what God was telling me.

I began painting canvases for the poems I had written to Him, about Him, for Him. It only made sense that if He was the Creator and Sustainer, then His "tint" would be in every basic color. And all of life would someday, somehow, fit together. I was overflowing onto these canvases—my love, my tears, my happiness.

Now I found myself painting almost as rapidly *every* day as I had on *any* day before—even though I was working with my left hand, held and guided by my right. A lot of the work was with a palette knife. Within three weeks my left hand was working by itself. And the paintings had changed without my even knowing how. They seemed stronger somehow, even though the colors were softer. The canvases almost spoke. I couldn't believe the work was mine. Then I laughed as I remembered that my Resident Teacher was known for His "creative bent."

By the time I was ready to pack and return to Chicago, I found that I'd been more prolific than ever before. And I saw that I would have more paintings for this show than I'd had for my first. That one had taken a year and a half to paint! And these paintings were much better.

When the car was packed, I stood on the porch with the breeze blowing the tears back down my jaw. "Dear Lord," I said to the empty beach, to the waves and to the sky, "No wonder no one can believe you. We have been looking among the puddles and streams of life and you are the very ocean itself. I do love you so! Take my life now and do what you want to with me, whatever the cost. I am ready to live for you now."

34. A New Stage

As I WENT to pick up the children at their father's, I was still happy and expectant. I knew I had the core of an acceptable art show. There were thirteen paintings and the beginnings of five more. But more than that, I was coming back with a future. I now had a way to make a good living and begin to pay off my medical debts.

Physically, I was almost transformed from what I'd been a month before. The wind and sun had put color in my cheeks. I had gained weight, good firm weight. My legs had almost doubled in size, and were stronger than I'd ever hoped they would be. I'd begun to fill out all over. My hair was at least an inch longer, and looked as if it had been very stylishly cut especially for me. Most important of all, I was no longer ashamed of my voice. People could understand almost everything I whispered.

It seemed to me that my life was a basketful of miracles. And they'd come as I'd simply tried to do what I thought was God's will for me. Where was He taking me? I didn't care. I had already decided that the journeying with Him was the important thing anyway.

Two days after I got home from the lake, before I'd even gotten resettled, there was a knock at my door. When I opened it, there stood a kind-looking middle-aged man who introduced himself.

"My name is Herman Bandy. I'm a minister at North Shore Church. I've heard so much about you from our visitation minister I just wanted to come by and meet you."

I just stood there dumbfound. Herman Bandy—a minister from the church where all the people had prayed for me coming to see me!

Finally I came to enough to invite him in. We sat a moment and looked at each other. Then I realized I didn't know what to offer a minister to drink, especially a conservative minister. I finally asked him if he wouldn't have a cup of coffee.

Mr. Bandy's official call was a real sign to me, happening when it did. God had accepted me. Now His people were officially reaching out to include me in His family. Mr. Bandy wanted to know how I was feeling, and it was obvious that he was curious about what had happened to me. I looked at him a few seconds, then shared from beginning to end all the good news I'd had since that night I had become a Christian.

When I finished, he smiled and nodded his head approvingly. "That's what I wanted to hear, Hedy. Your whole story sounds like Romans 8:28 to me."

"Oh really?" I asked, "what's that?"

Mr. Bandy quoted "We know that all things work together for good to those who love God."

"Yes," I answered excitedly, "they really *do,* don't they!"

Mr. Bandy got to the main point of his visit.

"Hedy, next week the North Shore Church is having its annual revival." As he paused to let that sink in, I realized I had no idea what actually went on at a revival. The word had always had a kind of carnival sound to me. I'd always pictured tents and off-key piano music with hell-and-brimstone-angry-preachers—ranting and pointing their fingers across the sawdust and metal-chaired crowd. So I couldn't even imagine a revival in the huge building which had been pointed out to me as the staid-looking church where so many socially prominent people attended.

"Hedy," Mr. Bandy continued, "we want you to speak at our revival, to witness for Christ."

I just looked at him, trying to imagine myself in a noisy carnival-like setting. All I could think of to say was, "You don't want me to talk there, Mr. Bandy. How could they possibly hear me?"

"Has it occurred to you, Hedy, that if you whispered into a microphone, people might listen to you more carefully than to almost anyone else?" He smiled again, happy to see me beginning to grasp what he was saying. "They'll probably *hear* you better than they would me."

My first thought was, "Oh, no." And then I remembered the hours on the beach talking into the little microphone, whispering about God's love, and then turning up the volume that night and hearing myself perfectly.

"You really did plan this carefully, didn't you, God?" I thought. This was not at all what I'd imagined—being a public speaker. And yet I remembered the years of dramatic speech training when I was a teenager trying to get ready for the movies and television. I realized that *nothing* in the past is wasted when someone gives God permission to use her life. I laughed out loud. And when Mr. Bandy looked puzzled, I said, "I can see the headlines in the church paper, 'Bullfrog speaks for God!' "

"Then you'll do it?" Mr. Bandy asked.

"Wait a minute, Mr. Bandy, there's something wrong about this whole thing that I don't understand. Why on earth would you need me to speak in a church where everyone's already committed to God? What could I tell those people that they don't already know?"

Mr. Bandy looked at me to make sure I was serious. Then he smiled a kind smile and looked up at the ceiling, not quite knowing how to tell me. Then he raised his eyebrows and looked directly at me. "Hedy, people go to our church for a lot of reasons, many of them having very little to do with knowing God personally. Business reasons, to please their families, or because it's expected of them, or because they're lonely. But most people in our church don't know that miracles can really happen. And they need to know."

As I thought about what he was saying, I realized that before the car wreck, if I had ever considered miracles, I would have thought that they were only for people in the Bible, not for today. And I saw that I certainly wouldn't have known that miracles of healing can take place if I hadn't been through the experience of the past year.

"Oh yes, I'll tell them, Mr. Bandy. And thank you. Thank you for this opportunity. Maybe I've been getting ready for this for months and just didn't know it."

At the door Mr. Bandy stopped, something still on his mind. "Hedy, I think your testimony would have a lot more impact and would reach people better if you joined our church before you spoke."

I was puzzled. "What difference would that make?"

"Well, if they could identify with you as an ordinary person like themselves, someone who is a member of their church, your message would have a lot more meaning to them."

"Oh," I said, still not really understanding. But I wanted to serve God and this was a man of God. And I was thrilled that he wanted me to join the church.

Suddenly I couldn't wait for the opportunity to tell my story to other people. But when I told the children that I was going to speak publicly, they looked at me as if I'd gone crazy. That next week, I discovered that all my friends felt the same way. They could all remember the hours, the weeks of saying to me, *"Slow down, Hedy. Say it again. I can't understand."* But they didn't know what had happened at the beach.

My faith was so real that I was convinced God could do anything with me. But if I'd been the slightest bit cynical, I'm not sure my healing or my recovery would have happened. I've learned, however, that a life of faith, the kind that accompanies miracles, is like walking a razor's edge between the greatest power available to people and a naïve delusion. But at that time all I knew was that God had crashed into my life and performed in a way neither I nor anyone else I knew could have believed. I wanted to tell everyone they could have hope and be made whole in God because a strong and gentle Father loved them.

I was as excited as a child and told everyone I saw to come hear my story the next Wednesday night. I wanted all the people I knew to enter the strange, secret world-within-the-world which could be found when you gave up on your old self-defeating life and accepted the love and guidance of God.

My children and I spent the rest of the week talking about what going to the North Shore Church would be like. We were even wondering how the people in the church looked on Sundays. How did they act? What did they wear?

Never having heard a public testimony for Christ, I didn't know what or how much to say. Nervously, I called on Mr. Bandy at his office and asked if we could go over what would be appropriate.

He couldn't have been nicer or more helpful. He knew I was frightened and was very patient and encouraging.

Before I left he said, "Hedy, I have an idea. Since you are naturally going to attend the revival this week, there may be something very creative you can do that may never have been done before."

"Attend the revival!" I was planning to attend the revival *Wednesday night*. I realized that I knew nothing about the rest of the program for the week. And I certainly didn't have time to go to meetings every day.

"How many meetings are there?" I asked hesitantly.

Mr. Bandy explained that the revival would last for seven days. After the beginning meeting on Sunday night, each day started with a breakfast at 7:00, followed by a morning meeting. There were other sessions throughout the day culminating in a large meeting each night. He was very excited as he told me about his idea. "Maybe you could use your talents, Hedy, in a very special way."

Of course I wanted to use my talents—I'd prayed that God would let me.

"How do you mean, Mr. Bandy?"

"Well, maybe you could take a canvas and each day you could paint a portion of the canvas to represent visually what the revival has meant to you so far—as you experience it." His eyes were alive now as he could imagine his idea being carried out.

"This way in the morning meeting each day we could start with your displaying this painting so the whole congregation can see how the revival is developing through your eyes." He finished, his eyes bright with excitement, and looked at me for my response.

That dear, kind man didn't realize that what he was asking would take most of every night as well as parts of the day for any artist. Thrilled to be asked, I said "yes."

I was so glad to be considered of value and a part of things. Here I was being treated like a real member of the family and I hadn't even joined the church yet. But it was going to be an impossible week, and I'd have to put off my own work for seven more days. I had to make a living plus get ready for my new show. Suddenly, though I was happy, I was confused and very tired. How had I gotten the idea that God's work was just living for Him and loving people? Now it seemed that "God's work" had a lot to do with religious programs. But I realized I was very new, and I was thrilled to be wanted and to be included in such an important way.

Right at that time we were at the depth of our poverty. As a matter of fact, that week our gas had been cut off again, and we heated the water to bathe for church on top of our electric stove.

My children wore their fanciest dresses. But I had nothing that fit except blue jeans, T-shirts and a ragged bikini bathing suit. So I used my mother's credit and bought a very lovely and expensive dress in which to speak for God for the first time. I was sure I could pay her back after my art show.

On Sunday morning at the end of the service, my first in that congregation of several thousand people, I walked slowly down the aisle and joined the church.

35. The People of God

THE REVIVAL OPENED with a supper at six o'clock Sunday evening. As I came into the church with my two children, I was very proud to be a part of these beautiful people. We were early and were told to go downstairs and join Mr. and Mrs. Bandy at their table. We walked into an enormous room with several buffet-cafeteria lines, dozens of tables, and people, people, people. I had never seen so many people in a church.

I looked around with that strange feeling in my stomach—"I will not see anyone I know"—a shyness which I've always felt on entering a room filled with strangers. I was looking for someone I might have met and was very relieved to see Mr. Bandy motioning for us to come over to his table. The children and I sat beside him as he tried to make me feel at ease. But the thought of speaking to that same group three nights later gave me butterflies.

On Wednesday night, it must have been obvious that I was anxious, although I was thrilled to be there. But I would certainly be glad when this was over. My stomach seemed to have live partridges in it and I could hardly eat anything at the supper. In a little while the Wednesday night crowd was thinning and people were moving out of the cafeteria toward the "Sanctuary."

Mr. Bandy pressed my hand reassuringly. "This is our biggest attendance yet, Hedy," he smiled. "Come with me. Mrs. Bandy will take the girls with her."

Through some hallways and up a flight of stairs was a small room right behind the pulpit, where the ministers evidently waited before going out on the platform. While we stood there I asked him if he would pray with me before we went into the sanctuary. He did.

The shock of walking out into that auditorium made my legs almost give way. I felt myself swaying slightly by the time I reached the high-backed chair assigned to me, and I very carefully avoided looking beyond the platform. My overall feeling, though, was gratitude for the privilege of being there after I'd prayed for a chance to tell someone what had happened to me. My heart swelled with thanksgiving when the introductions began and the music started. All those men, women and children singing about their Lord overwhelmed me.

As I turned and looked out at the people for the first time, my heart was suddenly in my throat again.

All I could see were faces, faces, faces, from the floor to the ceiling above the balcony. I had never imagined this. There couldn't possibly be this many people coming to any church service. A sea of faces from front to back of a room which seemed to me to be crammed full. People standing against the walls, behind them a balcony full of children, parents and grandparents. I sat down feeling a little dizzy. I had no consciousness of who else might be on that platform or what their parts in the program were.

I heard, as from a great distance, some announcements. I was praying frantically, realizing there was no way out. Suddenly all those faces rose. And when they began singing again, there seemed to be twice as many of them, all focusing on me. I tried to look back at them but there were so many. I felt like I was swimming in a sea of eyes. When the singing was over my ears were at total attention waiting to hear my name called.

As I waited, pictures flashed by in my mind: doctors shaking their heads, nurses and friends all looking sad. I knew that it would seem incredible to any of them if they could see me tonight. I'd been told that ten months before there wasn't a doctor in the world who would have believed I would ever make a sound or get out of bed again. And I was about to walk forward and tell all these people in my own voice about a God who had some very unusual abilities concerning healing and medicine. Suddenly, I felt a surge of faith sweep through my whole body, and I couldn't wait to tell them.

When my name was called, I felt myself rising slowly and walking very carefully so I wouldn't look awkward. I'm sure no one could have guessed how fragile my easy gracefulness really was. I had goose bumps all over as I realized again what God had done for me. This was, I knew, one of the great moments in my life.

At the pulpit a complete peace came over me from head to toe. I looked into those hundreds of eyes below and up in the balcony. And I smiled at God's people. They were my people. This church was my new "home."

In my hoarse whisper I told publicly for the first time my story of becoming a Christian and being healed. When I finished, I stood there a few seconds—feeling the total silence in that vast sanctuary.

After the service that night it took me an hour and a half to get out of church. People crowded around from everywhere—many of them crying. I was amazed at their response to what I'd said, and to me. They hugged me and touched me. They loved me, and I loved them. At last I had found not only the loving Father, but I had been accepted into His family. For someone who had been searching all her life for acceptance, this response was almost more than I could bear.

By the time I got home I could hardly move. My limited energy was gone. All I wanted to do was sleep for twelve hours, then get back to my easel to make some money before all my creditors closed in.

When I got the children to bed, I wanted a drink in the worst way. But I wasn't sure it was all right to take a drink, now that I'd witnessed for Christ. I had read about Jesus drinking wine and even making it for parties. Now I felt that maybe my new family might not approve, and their love was too much to risk losing. So I had a cup of coffee and collapsed on the couch. I certainly had a lot to learn about being one of God's people. But I was totally committed to doing everything I could to be one.

Pretty soon I sighed, got up and went in the bedroom where I painted. As I faced a three-by-three canvas, I wondered where I'd get the money to replace it. I'd worked until five o'clock Monday morning putting the background on the canvas and doing the first part of the painting. And I'd had to attend all the meetings, beginning with the 7:00 A.M. breakfast, to know what to paint.

Excitement and concentration on what was being said carried me through the first two days. But by the time I got home after speaking on Wednesday night, I was a basket case.

It evidently never occurred to anyone that I couldn't start painting until I got home in the evenings after the last meeting. So each night I painted all night, getting about an hour's sleep. And every day I started again by attending breakfast at the church and then in the morning session presented my painting.

At noon of the second day, I'd skipped lunch and bought two more dresses I couldn't afford—using my mother's credit again, since mine was no good. I knew it was dumb to spend money I didn't have for nice clothes. But everyone in the church seemed so well dressed. I didn't mind having only one dress that fit, but I had to appear before the whole congregation every day.

I was able to finish the painting by the time the revival was over, and I presented it at the last meeting. Though I was very happy about the people's response, I was totally exhausted from the effort. Yet I felt I'd done what God wanted me to, and that was a good feeling.

When I finally fell into bed after the last service, my head was whirling with a kind of manic dizziness. As soon as I closed my eyes, scenes from the past week kept flashing across the screen of my mind. I was awed by what was happening to me.

As I drifted off into a restless sleep, I remembered how the people had been dressed. Evidently everyone else at North Shore had money, and most of them had gone to work during the daytime. But painting was my work. I wondered how an ordinary person could *afford* to be on God's programs when she had no money. I hadn't told Mr. Bandy how acute my financial situation was, so he certainly couldn't be blamed. But I saw that Christianity could get to be a very expensive business.

I was so tired and was about to drift off to sleep when I remembered saying goodbye to Mr. Bandy after the revival. I had given him the painting I'd done during the week. And I was very grateful to him. He had opened a whole new world to me by asking me to speak when I was so new and had so much to learn about the church. But more than that, I was grateful to God for sending a minister to my house who loved Jesus Christ and was really committed to Him.

And I couldn't get over God's people. I was ecstatic about the church family. It was like coming home after having been exiled all my life. They were very warm toward me and the children. Janie and Susan loved the attention and excitement of our new life.

Before the week following the revival was over, it seemed that word had gotten around in the church scene about the miracle of my life.

Mr. Bandy came to my door the next Wednesday evening on his way to church. "Hedy, I have another great opportunity for you to witness for Christ! There is going to be a conference at Lake Geneva Conference Center in Wisconsin and they've asked if you will witness opening night—before thousands of young people from all over the Midwest." He said the representative of the conference would contact me.

When the call came, I decided to be very frank: "I appreciate the invitation, but I can't afford to accept it—financially." I had no money at all. The registration fee for the conference, it turned out, was $85.00. And I had no way to get to Lake Geneva nor any way to get money for my expenses. There was a pause on the other end of the line when I said, "I can't afford to."

"Hedy," the voice said seriously, "how can you afford *not* to!"

I was confused again. I knew he was saying that I should be grateful to God, and I was grateful. I also knew that people from God's church had raised money to help with my medical bills. But this man didn't understand that I actually had no money *at all*.

He said he'd see what he could do and call me back. Later that evening he called and said he had the money for my travel expenses and conference fees.

I went to the meeting out of gratitude to God. But I lost another five days of work plus the two days getting ready to go and coming home. And I couldn't afford those seven days. Yet I wanted so much to be God's person and felt guilty thinking about my own needs. I was genuinely grateful for the opportunity to speak for God. And the response at Lake Geneva was similar to that of the people at North Shore.

After that, the telephone began to ring off the hook. People wanted me to speak in all kinds of churches, at conferences, women's meetings and Sunday school classes. And I tried to go as often as I could. I'd prayed for this chance to tell people about God and I'd really meant it.

Suddenly I was known and apparently loved by hundreds of people I had never even seen before. Yet I found myself being so busy performing for God that I hardly had time to *relate* to Him personally. It was baffling. Was God as interested in successful programs as His people seemed to be? I could see the good that was happening. Many people had told me that they had accepted Christ as their Savior. That made it very wonderful and worthwhile. I wanted with all my heart to be used by God. But I was totally spent just when I needed every ounce of energy I could muster to do the job God *had already given* me to do at the beach— paint for a living.

I was getting almost despondent about my vocational and financial life. With a sort of desperate surge of energy I finished the preparation for my art show. If I'd had much more to do to get ready, I don't know how I would have made it.

Just as I was getting terribly discouraged, help arrived from a very unexpected source. A writer came from the *Chicago Tribune* wanting to do a blurb on my art show, which was to be sponsored by the Deer Path Art League. I told her my story—conversion, healing, and all. She asked some very perceptive questions and seemed to be deeply moved about what I was convinced God had done for me.

After a couple of hours, she decided her story wouldn't be just an announcement of an art show. "What's happened to you, Hedy," she said, "should go into a full-length Sunday story. People need to hear about this. But I've been so involved I didn't take any notes. Could I come back tonight?" I invited her for supper, and we spent the evening talking.

The article she wrote was very powerful—a full-page story with pictures of me and some of my paintings. It changed my life overnight, but in a way that was to lead me to the brink of despair again.

On Sunday two good friends were helping me get ready for the art show that night. The phone began to ring. Christians called, there were crank calls, perverted calls, congratulatory calls. People came, all kinds of people. Strangers knocked at my door, expecting to come in. Because the writer had captured the miracles which happened to me, people wanted to touch me, to talk to me, to cry out to God for help through me. There was something happening I could neither understand nor control. That night the city had to send policemen to the art show, and one stood by me the whole evening. There were parking attendants to help with the crowds of people, and one of the television stations did a live special on the show.

Someone told me that my eyes were shining with a strange light. This was due to exhaustion, but it evidently made me look like a holy mystic.

The art show was almost sold out in three hours. I was ecstatic. Only one painting was left at the end of the evening and there were more than twenty commissions for future work. Suddenly it seemed that I had come back to life in a way I couldn't have dreamed possible. I was very grateful to God that night and very, very tired. Yet I was confused by the intensity and the sudden floodtide of people pouring into the already crowded space of my life. What was God doing to me?

36. "Christian" Rush Parties —
With Answers for Everyone

IT WOULD BE impossible for me to describe the next few months of
my life. As I think back about that time, I see a shifting crowd
of smiling faces and hear people saying, "Hedy, you've given me
hope. Thank you!" or "If God can do what He's done for you,
then I can believe in Him." I didn't know how to answer them.
But I was happy to be getting out of myself and helping these men
and women I'd never met.

Some people phoned, wanting to know if my story were true or
wanting to contradict it. Or wanting all kinds of help or advice. "I
know you paint," one woman, a stranger, told me. "Can you help
my daughter? We can't afford art lessons, but we know you're a
Christian too and will help her." Someone else asked, "Can you
just see my son's paintings? Can he come by?" Others just wanted
to come sit and watch me paint. I tried to take each call seriously.

A steady stream of people began to come for spiritual counseling
and advice—old people, young people, women and men. Some
came ostensibly for counseling, but I found out they wanted to get
to know me for various other reasons, some healthy, others unhealthy.

But many were just plain lonely. Being superconscientious, I
tried to help each person with the same care God had used with me.

I listened by the hour to strangers in trouble or people who wanted to know about God and who poured their lives out before me. And I didn't resent their imposing on my time, since I felt I had nothing more important to do than to love them and tell them about Jesus Christ. "This is what God saved me for," I thought, "to love these people!"

It was one of the happiest times of my life. I was trying to help someone besides myself, and I felt an almost continual sense of God's presence.

One afternoon after lunch when I'd been planning all week to paint, an old white-haired woman knocked at the door. Her clothes were worn, wrinkled and dirty, her eyes clouded and bloodshot. As we talked over coffee, she complained bitterly about her life. When she cried, I held her like a child and she asked, "What hope is there for a broken old woman like me?"

I told her about what had happened to me in the hospital and since. We prayed and she tried to turn her life over to Christ. She sat silently for a few minutes. I could almost see her body relax as she took a deep breath, and sighed with relief. As so often happened in those days, I saw a great peace come into an almost impossible life. She was quietly radiant.

Suddenly she looked at her watch. "Oh my," she said apologizing, "I had no idea how late it was." It was 6:30. The children had come in from school through the back door without disturbing us. I had no idea how much time had passed either. I was only grateful that another "hopeless" woman had found a new beginning with God.

This same scene repeated itself many times during those days. And I wasn't worried that I wasn't succeeding at anything. Life was amazing and I'd never known this kind of leisure to love people who could not help me in some way.

Amazingly, though I was running out of energy, I noticed that I was gaining weight through all of this. My figure was slowly coming back to a subdued version of what it had been before the wreck, although I was still considered by many of the doctors to be a semi-invalid. Not being able to lift an iron, I couldn't even iron clothes. And I was just barely able to hold my paint brush, or a coffee cup steady.

I don't know what my children got from me during that time. I tried to give them what I could. As I look back, it must have been very little. But they were thrilled with our new life and with my witnessing. We were all happier than we'd ever been, and were very grateful to be together and thankful that I was getting well.

But I didn't have time to paint. Not only was I helping people who came to me, but I was still speaking three times a week at churches or public places. Sometimes I talked to three different kinds of meetings in a single day. Having heard me once, people would ask me to speak on some other subject at a later meeting. Through articles in the newspaper and by word of mouth, I was invited to be on several television programs. When it came out that I had taken in over a dozen foster children into my home, people assumed I was an expert on that.

And the subjects broadened. Because God had healed me physically, now I was supposed to be brilliant and knowledgeable about medicine and able to give advice on just about everything. And feeling I was *supposed* to know, I tried. I was asked to talk about subjects I had had no real contact with, and would spend an entire day preparing. But at the same time, every day, I was having to go through the involved process of merely surviving physically as well as trying to take care of Susan and Janie. Often, I'd speak at night after a very trying day, and the next day be so tired I couldn't get out of bed. And since we were out of money, the pressure to work was building higher and higher.

I certainly didn't understand the mixed feelings I began to have about being used as a speaker at all these meetings. People were nice and seemed to like what happened when I spoke. Often I'd be invited to speak once and find there were two or three groups to address. I began to feel some resentment and didn't know why. Finally, I realized that I felt people were not accepting or considering me as a *person* but more like some sort of exhibit "A" with my whispering voice and my miraculous physical healing. I was an "act" they could use. I wondered how many ministers felt that way—that they were public property. The people who invited me certainly weren't unkind—they were very gracious in fact. I guess I was just surprised that no one except Mr. Bandy seemed to consider *me*—my needs or even my health. I was ashamed of these thoughts and felt very selfish, but they were there. I loved the church and all her people and was thrilled to be a part of Christ's ministry. But I was confused and began to see that in the name of love we Christians are often very thoughtless of those who try to minister to us.

Mr. Bandy had found out about my financial situation and told me I should receive an honorarium for speaking and that my expenses should be paid to and from the out-of-town meetings. After that I sometimes did receive the agreed-upon honorarium, but often I received instead a flower or a note of thanks. This really shocked me—that churches would not pay their financial obligations. And I began to realize that sin does not stop at the inner side of the baptismal font. I decided maybe that was why we keep needing God and His forgiveness.

One night getting ready for bed after an especially full day, I tried to think about all that had happened. Here I was a committed Christian. I had been filled with God's Holy Spirit. But something was desperately wrong at a deep level. I was supposed to have been freed from guilt now, yet guilt was an almost constant part of my life. When I was painting, I felt guilty for not helping people for God or speaking for Him. And yet when I witnessed and counseled, I felt guilty because I wasn't painting to earn a living and fulfilling my responsibility to my children. The contradiction bewildered me.

During the next two years or so, the press of people got so bad that I had to go out of town to get any painting done. I had to rent a place and hide in order to make a living. But when I was doing that, I was away from my children, and someone else had to take care of them. And, besides, this way of living was more expensive, which I couldn't afford.

The only thing I could do was go on each day. But I didn't know if I'd have the strength much longer. My children were sort of compounding the problem without ever knowing it. I would say to people, "I'm sorry I can't speak. I've been away from my children so much." But the girls would say, "Mommie, we want you to do what God wants you to do. And we think speaking is what He wants you to do."

Yet I was losing touch *with* God and with my own inner self in all the things I was trying to do *for* Him. I was feeding people emotionally and spiritually, but I needed desperately for someone to feed me, someone with whom I could be totally honest about my own needs and questions. I was starving for God and for some human companionship.

Mr. Bandy tried to get me involved with the other single adults at church. But my reputation as a public witness separated me from many natural contacts with eligible men—although I had begun to date. I tried to read the Bible every day, but I had less and less time for that because of the pressure of people who called early and late. I tried to go to church on Sundays to get some help, but I was speaking outside my own church three Sundays out of four. The ministers said I was being "used greatly by God." I felt good about this. But I began to feel a deep restlessness and frustration in my stomach about what was happening to my life.

I also felt an undercurrent of something which disturbed me in some of the meetings. But I couldn't get my finger on it. One time in the middle of a huge revival service with beautiful music, I looked around me at the expensive equipment and elaborate, well-planned meeting. It all had a faintly familiar and unreal plastic quality. What was it? Good lord, *Hollywood!* There was something here that smelled more of Hollywood than of the earthy hospital where I'd found Jesus Christ. But there was a big difference. In Hollywood all the actors were paid. Here the professional evangelists, preachers and musicians were paid. But often I was none of these. Even as I thought about this I felt selfish and ungrateful. I knew it was right to pay them. And I loved the church so much I felt bad judging it. Besides I saw that my own sins of judgment were worse than the things I was condemning. But I knew there was a grain of truth in what I had seen.

Looking back now, I can see that I tend to be especially naïve and innocent in any new world I enter—and it takes me a while to wake up and face the unpleasant parts of the truth.

I had really enjoyed being in the spotlight. But everything in me had been crying out for intimacy and personalness—something the church had promised to give in its fellowship. The people had been warm and loving. But I didn't seem to be allowed any ordinary doubts and problems. Instead, people had made me into a plaster saint—or perhaps more correctly, I had *let* them make me into a plaster saint, out of my own guilt, and my lack of understanding and honesty about my own situation.

This period of my life came to a head one day when I was especially tired and had to finish a painting after attending to a thousand details, like catching up on correspondence. A woman called at eight in the morning. "Hedy, we'd like for you to speak at a women's club luncheon meeting today. I know it's late, but we felt sure you'd help us out."

I just couldn't believe it. "Today?" This woman was bright, wealthy, a shiny Christian socialite and a person I'd known. I told her I couldn't because I had letters to answer and telephone calls to return, along with some work I had to finish that afternoon in order to get a painting completed. She said she would change the meeting by having the luncheon first. That would make it an afternoon meeting and I could come later.

Very discouraged, I said "It isn't just the *hour* of the luncheon. I simply don't have *time* to do it because of these other things I have to get done."

"Hedy," she said, "I think I know what would solve your whole problem. What you need to do is hire a full-time secretary to take care of these things for you!"

A secretary! I couldn't even afford myself and my children. How could I afford a secretary?

As that statement with its total lack of awareness of my situation seeped into my consciousness, something snapped inside! "Good lord," I thought, "Christianity is not a *game,* a social pastime. It's a *life-and-death* matter! I am *alive* because of Christ and His healing power. Yet we're making being a Christian a new social entertainment. And these women—who are fine people—don't even know I'm having a problem just staying afloat financially— to them I'm simply exciting spiritual entertainment."

I'd always thought of myself as a lady, and I'd never been pro- fane, but the one word that popped into my mind with a terrifying, irrational insistence, demanding to be said to her, was "shit!" I wanted to say it to her and to people everywhere who have as- sumed that all the world is wealthy—to those who use other people in the name of Jesus Christ without considering their needs. I wanted to scream, *"You!* You have no idea of my problems, be- cause you've never even thought of them."

Of course I didn't *say* it, because they expected me to be an angel, and because I wouldn't. All of a sudden I could see that this was my *real* problem: I was trying to be something pious and unreal to avoid disappointing people and being rejected. But I really wasn't pious. I only longed to be real and natural. I'd been very honest and direct in my verbal witnessing. But in my personal relationships to Christians I'd become dishonest. Because of my pride and fear of being revealed as not a good enough Christian if I were simply being Hedy, I had hidden my problems, my financial condition and my resentments of pious Christians. And a pressure was building within me to risk being totally myself with someone.

37. The Victory?

I COULDN'T SLEEP. It was 3:00 A.M. I looked up at my ceiling in the dark.

"What is Christianity, God?" I cried out silently.

No answer.

I'd gotten the message that once someone made a "total commitment" to God, then life was relatively simple. All you have to do is "do God's will." The only trouble was that "God's will" meant to many people "doing church programs." But what happened to a Christian's family life if she were always at the church? I *knew* that for a family to be healthy there *had* to be time for the natural conversations and give-and-take of daily living. God just had to be as interested in the relationships between a mother and her children as He was in Christian luncheons and teas.

And there was another enormous dilemma in my mind. I'd gotten the impression that "truly committed Christians" have what is called "The Victory." They lead "the victorious life." So if I had personal problems, it might be an indication that my commitment was not perfect.

Further, as a committed Christian, I was supposed to *always* respond with loving concern and total giving of myself, my time and my talents. I was told that when you had the victory through commitment to Christ, you don't have to worry about anything else because God will take care of all your needs. I translated this to mean that putting the earning of money before "God's work," for instance, was selfish and sinful. And I felt trapped.

But one of my very practical "secular" friends said, "Listen Hedy, the ministers who tell you not to worry about getting your expenses, have *theirs* paid by the church. And whether they're given anything for speaking or not, they're paid salaries for doing the same things you are doing for nothing." My friend went on to point out that many people who were on the boards of these churches, and who felt that I should give them endless time, didn't themselves give endless time they couldn't afford.

Still, I found it almost impossible to let anyone know my problems. I hid the severe needs and pain I was going through and acted as though everything was fine. I'd fallen into a Christian version of my old fear of being discovered as inadequate. And as I'd done so often in the past, I was blaming the people around me. God seemed to be moving in my inner life in a very threatening way. Now that He had gotten me converted and had virtually healed me physically, He seemed to be hammering away at the idea that maybe I had never really faced myself as a person and a woman. I was afraid to look inside and deal with what I might find. What if no one were down there beneath all my adequate and loving "behavior"?

How could I find out the truth about myself? I didn't know any Christians who talked about the need to look at ourselves and our possible self-deception *as Christians.* I knew that God wanted me to be free. Yet I was trapped and exhausted because of my old compulsive patterns and hiding of my imperfections. And these deceptions seemed to be encouraged by people who claimed "the victory."

Then a new—yet old—and very threatening problem began to reappear, totally unexpectedly, in a way that brought me to a complete crisis in my faith—and in my whole life. It began very naturally and innocently, as "a part of my ministry."

Once, when I was scheduled to speak at a church in downtown

Chicago, the minister offered to pick me up and take me to the
meeting. He was a fine-looking, sensitive man. We began to visit
as we moved onto Lake Shore drive. I was glad to be with him and
listened as I usually did with real interest. Thirty minutes later,
before we reached his church, this man had run through the usual
small talk and suddenly began to tell me about his personal struggles with being a minister. He confessed to me that he was having
problems with his wife and was almost at his wits' end.

My heart went out to him, and although I mostly just listened,
I really hurt for him. And I let him know I could certainly hear
what he was saying.

"Let's pray," I suggested as we pulled up at the church, "for
guidance for our own lives and ministries," and we did.

This scene began to repeat itself many times over the next few
months. I was nonthreatening since I was a woman and not or-
dained. And I tried to listen and help these men find hope and
meaning in the midst of their franticness and anxiety.

I was amazed at the loneliness and personal discouragement in
the lives of ministers, and was really grateful to be able to try to understand and to pray with them and help them go on. I had a lot
of deep compassion and sympathy for some of these men who were
forced to hide or deny their own problems and needs while pro-
fessing publicly that total honesty and integrity were the hall-
marks of the Christian faith.

Some of these pastors who lived in the Chicago area began to
call me and ask me to have lunch with them. "Hedy," they'd say,
"I really need to talk to you today, it's urgent." At some level I
began to realize that all was not "spiritual" in their interest, but I
couldn't—I wouldn't face that.

I also wouldn't face the fact God was making some great changes
in my physical appearance. I was aware of and was troubled by the
fact that my bullfrog voice had mellowed into a soft throaty whisper
which normally women use only in very intimate circumstances,
and I was often embarrassed at the responses to my voice. As one
friend put it, "Good lord, Hedy, you've got a pornographic voice!"
This no doubt contributed to something else which seemed ludi-

crous at the time, and which was a dubious blessing! I was selected as one of the fifteen sexiest women in Chicago by the *Chicago* magazine. I laughed about this—and was delighted, but didn't take it seriously.

But I repressed any "nonspiritual" aspects of my counseling with ministers. I seemed to be in a unique position to help. And I believed them when they said, "Hedy, God sent you to help me. Who else can I go to? Another minister might reveal my secret." Also, I enjoyed the personal contact very much. So I kept seeing several of these men.

Before long, though, I began to feel very uneasy about the overtones of man-woman intimacy which came into some of these relationships. Then one day I realized that I had begun to feel the real stirrings of physical intimacy in *my* life as I shared with these men, most of whom were married.

I tried to tell myself and God that it wasn't true. After all, how could I walk away from what was a genuinely helpful ministry to God's men who had no one else to go to? "Besides," I told God, "*I'm* certainly not doing anything to encourage their feelings."

But as I said those words, it was as if God shook me by the shoulders and said, "Wake up, Hedy! You've been through this before, again and again! Don't you remember Bert? Your own needs for intimacy with a man are so great that you're sending out unconscious signals—invitations to intimacy—to these men, then you're being surprised when they respond. Why don't you hear what I'm telling you and let me lead you to true intimacy, free of unconscious games?"

Over the shock and unbelief, I suddenly remembered the surprised look on the fat photographer's face and on Tom Heinman's and Bert's when I had pushed them away.

Had I really sent out unconscious signals? In little scene fragments from my past I saw myself as in a movie—turning my head and raising my eyebrows when laughing with Bert. I saw half glimpses of myself unconsciously moistening my lips during pauses in intensely personal conversations a hundred times back down the years. I'd never seen myself in this light before, as if I were unconsciously begging men to please love me, but consciously just being interested in them and keeping them at a proper distance. But these "woman" movements, I saw now, could have been interpreted as come-on signals, though I had not meant them to be suggestive—"at least consciously," a little voice within me added.

But what could I do? I desperately needed personalness. And I was coming alive again as a woman. The church had implied that along with its gift of a Father's love I could have my intimacy needs met through prayer and the fellowship of the church. But that was only a very partial truth.

The people at church *were* kind and loving in many of their attitudes, but they were not deeply *personal* in their sharing. One Sunday in a small class, a new Christian, a man who'd gotten converted in a revival, said, "Listen, I'd like to be more committed to Christ but I've got some serious problems that are about to drive me up the wall." Everyone was totally silent and he continued, "I'm afraid I may be a borderline alcoholic. Our marriage is in serious trouble, and I need some help. Are any of you going through stuff like this?"

No one said anything. Everyone was looking at the floor. Finally the teacher said in what I thought sounded like a pretty formal tone, "Maybe we ought to pray for George." Then the teacher led us in prayer, and the class broke up, leaving George totally stripped and feeling rejected. I could understand how threatening it would be to try that kind of openness, but I also understood why none of us said, "Yes, George, I've got a bunch of problems trying to be committed to Christ, too." *I* didn't because I was afraid of being misunderstood. So I talked to George privately and told him how hard it was for me.

After that I often was more lonely as a single person in church than almost anywhere. I felt we'd all be terrified to bring up our real inner frustrations, hopes, and dreams in the fellowship of the church. And I realized that there may be millions of us who are smiling and hiding our heartbreak and loneliness from each other in the church, while silently crying out for intimacy from each other. Why couldn't we love each other in our loneliness?

But if I couldn't be deeply personal with Christians at church, then why was I feeling deep stirrings of genuine intimacy with the ministers I was counseling, who couldn't be honest in their own congregations?

That was it! They *could* be *honest* with *me! Honesty* was the doorway to the kind of intimacy God made us for!! As I let that thought sink into my mind, I knew it was true. But I couldn't risk sharing *my* needs with them. It was also true in my personal relationships with all those people already closest to me—my children even. I had not shared my real frightened self with anyone but God. And thus I'd sealed out the possibility of genuine intimate love and understanding.

I wondered where I'd ever find somebody who would accept me as I was, or if I ever would allow myself to really let go and be open so I could find out. The problem was I couldn't seem to trust *anyone*. After all, Findley had rejected me physically, Danny had tried to kill me. And most people seemed to think of me as a religious symbol to be set apart.

The frustrating thing was that I also loved the image of being considered saintly. It was very flattering to me as a woman. But it meant that all kinds of people were always pressing against my life. I *always* had to have everything in perfect order, so I could never let anyone see the real me.

I'd been blaming other people for my isolated plight. But I had made any real relationships impossible by hiding my true self—"in the name of Jesus Christ."

38. A Coming-Out Party

I'D HAD IT WITH "religious" men. And I had been staying away from "secular" parties because I was simply too busy. Realizing that I had been isolating myself, I accepted my next invitation to a party. It felt good to be in a noninstitutional setting where no speech or performance was expected from me. The atmosphere was "Lake Forest social" instead of "evening Christian meeting." And it was a relief.

As the evening progressed an attractive man was introduced to me by the hostess. He was a very easy person to talk to and did not even seem to be interested in spiritual things. There was an immediate rapport between us, and it felt good to meet a man I could relate to easily without having to be "St. Hedy." We talked the whole evening. When the party was over he walked me to my car. The air was chilly, and he took off his jacket and put it around me. It was an easy gesture and spoke of thoughtfulness and chivalry. I felt very warm and happy as I drove home. Maybe I needed someone who wasn't all wrapped up in the church. The thought disturbed me, but I was certainly sick of a solid diet of religious talk.

I saw Harry almost every day after that. Because he was self-employed and materially successful, he had many free hours for long happy lunches during which we laughed and talked about what was going on in Chicago, his business, and fun places to travel.

Over the weeks we got to know each other better and better. Harry was bright, masculine, and seemed to like me as a woman, with feelings having nothing to do with my religious experience—although he seemed pleased about my reputation as a Christian woman.

Though Harry didn't know it, I was having to steal time from many other people and responsibilities to be with him. It was a great relief that our relationship was not dealing with intense problems. I felt Harry was a godsend in helping me recover my sense of the reality of normal living. I loved God very much. But I needed some distance from His demanding children. I had to get over my resentment and recover the sense of love and compassion for people I'd always had as a Christian—even for those who took advantage of my life and time. I put my discoveries about my own lack of honesty concerning my inner feelings on the back burner.

But as we got to know each other better, I felt uneasy that I couldn't share with Harry the most important thing in my life—God. This had never been a problem with Findley or Danny since I hadn't been a Christian. Now I was restless. What did I want anyway? Harry had everything a woman could ask for. And he seemed to be very fond of me. I put this question out of my mind and decided we could just enjoy dating. Being with him was a fresh breeze of normalcy, I told myself, in a world of smothering demands. And I loved the unfolding relationship, which was filling more and more of my time.

But my other contacts and responsibilities began to move in on me as I spent more time with Harry. Finally it seemed as if everyone were trying to ferret me out and pull on me from all directions. Many of my friends and counselees who depended on me for companionship and spiritual counsel were hurt that I was suddenly so unavailable. They called and wrote. Some even tried to stop by without notice.

As I began to feel that I was regaining my balance through my relationship with Harry, I started to reestablish contact with Christian friends.

But now it was Harry who didn't understand. He didn't have a life as filled with other people, and he couldn't imagine why I was suddenly not totally available to him for lunches and dates. As time had passed, even he had begun to treat me as if I were special because of my relationship with God, though he was not involved in the church as I was. But now his personality seemed to change before my eyes. He thought I was rejecting him and secretly dating other men.

In fact I wasn't at all. I was torn between my children's needs, household chores, the needs of my new Christian friends and counselees, doctor's appointments, and the continually pressing need to paint in order to pay my bills. Painting was the only talent I felt God had provided for me to use. I longed for the peace and solace that always came to me when I painted. But as I got back to answering the correspondence and telephone calls—often from strangers I felt I couldn't disappoint—I was again overwhelmed by the feeling I was letting everyone down, including God. I doubled my efforts to meet the needs of all the people in my life. At the same time I withdrew from the ministers I'd been counseling. But they kept calling, and with more urgency, and began coming to my apartment at all hours.

Even in my sleep I began to hear the voices of people I was pushing away, all wondering why I wasn't paying attention to them. Why couldn't they see what a strain I was under? I was still too proud to tell them that I was exhausted, and I was beginning to hate myself for that. But I also began to resent them for their insensitiveness and endless demands on my time. I resented even my closest friends—even Harry. Yet I felt guilty if I didn't try to meet all their needs.

I was sick of being lonely and on a pedestal because Christians —and now even Harry—had made me a "religious figure." I desperately needed a loving, understanding touch. I wanted someone to hold me, to say, "Slow down, Hedy. It's all right to be human." Not feeling understood, I isolated myself even more. But I kept going publicly.

Staying busy kept me from facing the truth about my life: that although I was supposed to have the victory, to have no problems and to be full of Jesus Christ, I had actually become lonely, miserable, cynical and bitter. Harry was caring, but he couldn't even understand the problem, since so much of it was involved with my ministry for Christ. I talked to people all the time about the freedom of God. Intellectually I still believed it. But something was really wrong, and it began to show.

Pepper spotted it first. She came down from Milwaukee and saw what was happening after being with me a day. "Hedy, you've got to get out of here and get away from all this. Something is tearing you to shreds inside. Please come up and stay with us for a while."

She looked at me a long minute, "Somehow, I don't know how, but you've left God behind. If you can get back in touch with God, get back to your painting, the things a *happy* you can do accidentally will be more help to people than all this frantic effort. I don't care how great they say it all is. Something about this kind of 'religion' just isn't Christian."

Pepper has a fantastic nose for unreality and is always very direct. "Those are fine people you're with," she went on, "but some of them seem like a bunch of prissy rich kids playing a game. And you're playing it with them, Hedy. You're getting phony. For God's sake and yours, can't you have your own faith? Do you have to have *all* these people around *all* the time?"

I looked at her and knew she was right.

She said, "I'm afraid of what's going to happen to you if you keep going this way and don't slow down. How are you going to look in ten years? And if you keep living this way, you're still going to be alone."

Again, I knew she was right. But I didn't get away. And the pressure built more and more intensely in my chest.

Several things started to change in the next few weeks. For one thing, I actually began to hide as I had never done before. And I was deliberately lying—something I thought I would never do. I told people I had engagements, or previous commitments, when I didn't. But with every lie, I got both more depressed and more frantic. Although I knew I was dramatic and had sometimes colored the truth, I had never imagined myself lying outright, one time after another. But now I was.

My actions contradicted everything I believed and had come to stand for. Was I running from something inside myself that was too frightening to face? Where was God? The God who was supposed to give me His support and certainty—the victory? And where were His people, who were supposed to love me, but who were instead only disappointed when I wasn't always available? And most of all, where was *my faith?*

While I was hiding out and lying to everyone, I began to find myself spiraling inside. The freshness left my face. I felt hard and cold inside. I began to doubt my faith. Yet I'd say to myself, "Look at all that God's done for you, Hedy! You ought to be ashamed!" And I was. But I also began not to care. I was just tired now, bone tired.

Through it all I still believed in the love of God as my Father. But it began to dawn on me that I *had* to find someone to open my life to, another *person* besides Christ, or my life would never be complete. Yet all the terror of rejection I'd hidden, all the shame about feeling unlovable and unworthy of love, all these screamed at me through another inner voice: "No, you *don't* have to ever reveal yourself, Hedy! That's dumb. And you'd never recover if you did reveal yourself and a man rejected you." *That* was true. But God seemed to be demanding that I face myself and trust Him by trusting other persons. That was the point. And that's what I couldn't do—trust God that much.

I was thirty-three years old, considered by many to be beautiful and bright. I had talent as a painter. And yet I was almost more alone than I could remember having been. I'd lost touch with living. And my eyes seemed clamped shut to hope about straightening out the strands of my life. Something had to change.

I decided to have another art show, I needed to come out somehow in a new way. I was sick of what Hedy Robinson had become

—a pious, victorious, plastic phony. I wanted to *live!* Jesus Christ was the one who had come to bring life, and I wanted to live again. All I'd become was a religious machine.

Once more I had run out of money. I walked around the house for a week, ignoring the telephone and saying, "God, I can't afford you. I can't afford you!" I shouted it as loud as I could whisper.

Finally, I rented a private studio without a telephone, and didn't tell anyone where I was. I painted day and night. During this time I would take the children to school each morning and go to work in the studio until school was out. Then I'd pick them up, make some sandwiches or a light supper, and we'd go back to the studio. I'd have them do their homework while I kept painting. During the next few weeks, we spent our days and nights living in a room that was about twelve by twelve, until I produced a show.

At my other shows I had worn lovely designer dresses. At this one I decided I was going to have a whole new image of myself—no longer the saintly religious figure. Something had happened at my art shows during the years as a Christian. Some of my Christian advisers had subtly suggested that "since you're a Christian, Hedy, it might be a good witness if you served fruit punch instead of alcoholic beverages at your shows."

Suddenly all this seemed incongruous when one thought about the earthy, wine-making carpenter of Nazareth. I felt that God wanted me to become myself somehow, the self he had made. But as someone had pointed out: "People do have their expectations about you, Hedy." And they did.

But now I wanted to make a break, to be free again. Whatever God was, I sensed at the deepest level in me that He wanted me to be alive, to be honest, to be a real and natural person, to be a woman, to be what I really was, instead of what any community expected me to be, including the church. I knew what I was thinking *sounded* like blasphemy. But it *felt* like it was from God. I wanted to laugh and not always be the serious saint who was smiling sweetly.

So I decided to have this show in my own home. With my new image in mind, I painted my dining room a Roman red with the help of several friends, and put fifty candles all over the apartment to produce a Bohemian atmosphere. I transcribed some French guitar music on reel-to-reel tape interspersed with John Denver and "Moody Blues." No one knew what song was coming next. A friend who was a guitarist and ballad singer came by and sang some folk songs at the opening.

The fact that the show was in my own apartment was very symbolic to me. It was called "The Birth of a Woman" and that of course was no accident either. I had painted every aspect of a woman's life in very personal terms. This was my coming out party, this was my own emerging. I was dressed in slacks in a very informal and relaxed way.

Only Pepper knew the background and the urgent necessity of the show. I was getting desperate to live as a person and didn't really know how. A kind of unhealthy religious death had settled over me. All the fresh authenticity and intimacy which God had lavished on me in the midst of my pain and despair in the hospital had been translated into a slick, Christian mannequin—who could lead people to Christ, but who didn't have time to love her own children, or exercise the gift of painting and creative imagination God had commanded her to use.

I used my own home as a gallery because I was sick of public buildings, impersonal crowds, and wanted some closeness with people. The invitations and announcements stated the beginning date of the opening, at which I served wine and cheese. And then I announced that the show would run for two weeks, and people could drop by any time. They came in ones and twos, simply to look at my work. I would visit with them, informally. And suddenly I was no longer a "program." I was inviting people to share my life and work. I was talking casually and having a glass of wine with those who came. It was a marvelous breeze stirring through the almost dead leaves rustling in my soul.

This way of "being" was worlds away from the breathless days and nights when I'd come flying in, "be the speaker" and then get shipped out again, exhausted. Now I was visiting quietly and personally with people. I felt love. And I wasn't defensive. Something like the sap of spring was seeping into my dry heart and limbs, and I felt God's presence stirring in my life again. I began to sense that living for God could be real and earthy, just when my life had begun to seem like it was filled with the glitter and tinsel of a roadshow carnival. Meeting after meeting when I had spoken, someone would rush up and say, "Oh, Hedy, I've heard of you. I *must* talk to you now!" But at my art show, people came to my door and said, "Hedy, how are you?"

It was an enormous relief to have someone walk into my life without making demands. People came to see what I was painting. And I got to show them something of the fresh, creative footprints of God in my life.

39. Two-Minute Warning

DURING THE NEXT few months I painted almost constantly. I shut out most of the religious meetings I'd been buried beneath before. That year I had seven shows, many in connection with Christian missionary conferences in several countries, where I would also witness. I was paying back debts and medical bills—over $50,000 worth, and there were always more. I was exhausted when I flew in from the last show.

When I got home, Harry called, and although I was very tired, I said I'd go out with him. Over dinner I told him about my trip and about an interesting older minister I'd met in Mexico. Harry's eyes narrowed.

"What did you *do* with him?" He asked.

"What do you mean: what did I *do* with him?" I said.

"Well, it sounds like you spent a *lot* of time alone with him, Hedy, and he's obviously in love with you."

I was furious. All I'd done was visit with an older minister who was in charge of the mission, and Harry was a mass of jealous accusations.

"Take me home, Harry." I was exhausted. I knew Harry's accusations were groundless. And yet I didn't have the energy or desire to defend myself. I just wanted to rest.

But why hadn't I been honest about being so tired? Why didn't I just tell people when I was exhausted? I always had to be Scrap Iron and hide my feelings. It was almost as if I thought at some level I wouldn't be acceptable as a Christian witness if I were *mortal*.

But I still kept seeing those who came or who pressed for counseling time. Not being honest about my own condition and needs began to fester in me like a boil. I still hated to give up my image of adequacy. And I kept on saying to people who asked—even when I was miserable and totally tired—"Oh, I'm just fine."

In spite of my burst of freedom in the art show, I still hadn't sat down and actually faced myself and this refusal to risk being discovered as inadequate. I still wanted to be the victorious saint. The knot of inner conflict tightened around my heart and made me strike out at the people around me.

My personal life began to be defensive in many ways now. I seemed to be *always* holding people off, pushing them away. But the situations only got worse. I agonized over the impasse—the more I honestly tried to say "no," the more a great cloud of misunderstanding came between me and others. I became afraid as I saw myself withdrawing from everyone. Evidently they heard a small "yes" beneath my "no," and kept calling me.

And with Harry I was scared too. I liked being with him very much. But I was becoming aware of the huge gap in the way we saw almost any situation because I was trying to commit my life to Christ. And his jealous accusations made even a personal friendship with anyone else seem dirty. So I pushed him away too.

I became almost sick with a feeling of dread when my telephone rang. Having had virtually total acceptance and approval since I'd been a Christian, I couldn't understand the hurt and anger expressed towards me when I said I couldn't see people I'd been counseling. I had repressed the fact that my appearance had improved, and besides, I couldn't see my own angry expression when I reacted to their requests—and that my anger was the outer mask of a nameless and growing inner fear.

One night I had a dream: hundreds of people were coming toward me all at once. There was anger in their eyes, flashing with hate and lust! I ran! But they were coming closer and closer, shouting obscenities and declarations of love and passion. Something told me that if I'd quit running, they'd quit chasing me. But I couldn't risk believing it. In my dream it was night, and there were horrible looking black storm clouds gathering around us. The people, particularly the men, seemed to be closing in on me with great leaping and shouting. They seemed like wild animals. A huge pin-striped cat was about to grab me. I tried to scream but no sound came out. Just as I was falling beneath them, I woke up, drenched with perspiration and trembling violently with fright.

As I was struggling with myself and trying to avoid admitting even to me that I was not being honest about my situation, some old feelings began bubbling to the surface of my consciousness—some feelings I'd repressed since the accident. I saw Danny in my imagination and instead of feeling sorry for him as I had at the time, I felt some real irritation! After all, he hadn't even offered to let his insurance company help me. The irritation kept unfolding until I was furious and bitter. I could feel the heat of my anger in my face and the skin of my upper arms.

Then I felt anger toward some of the ministers who had so selfishly devoured my time without considering my needs. Next I was furious with Harry for his insensitivity and accusations. I couldn't imagine the surge of feeling which came roaring up from the basement of my soul like a flood crashing through the doorway into my conscious mind! I was awed and consumed by the waves of my own rage!

When it was over, I realized that except for my anger with Buzzy and then with Bert I couldn't remember ever letting myself feel angry. I'd told myself I was too nice a person to be angry.

As a Christian, I was frustrated and confused by these enormous feelings of anger. Expressing them had felt like a scalding shower which left me aching, but clean somehow. Yet I couldn't believe that I was filled with that kind of anger. I really was getting in touch with some new feelings. But I was still in tight control of my life.

Why couldn't I give up, quit trying to play God, and relax? But I couldn't. There seemed to be no place I could run to hide from the demands of people. The quiet closeness I'd longed for all my life seemed nowhere in sight. Was there anyone, anywhere, I could relate to without having to be St. Hedy or Sigmund Freud? Was there a man who would understand without my having to explain myself, who could not be jealous and suspect me of being a devious fallen angel if I had a cup of coffee with a friend?

No one, it seemed, would let me be Hedy Robinson, woman, human being. And if I couldn't be Hedy, how could I find intimacy? How could I be God's person and bring closeness to others when I didn't have the courage to risk openness myself? Even though I had God as a Father, how could I ever find an emotional home with someone? There seemed to be no answer.

I felt myself slipping, sliding down the slippery bank of my desperation into despair.

The world closed in on me in a way I can't describe. I felt a hot heaviness like steaming wet blankets being laid over my whole body and face—smothering—heavier and heavier. In my depression there were times when I could hardly move. I buried the budding self-realization deeper and deeper in the swamp of my fears until all I wanted was to run away from the self I was afraid to see.

Then I began to take amphetamines to stay on my feet. After taking them for a week, I found that sometimes they didn't work. But I needed the pills in order to get up to give a Christian witness. I realize this will be difficult for some Christians to understand who have never been that desperate, that down, and that exhausted. It seemed incredible. Still no one knew what was going on inside me.

Finally I couldn't hide my inner chaos any longer, or the fact that I was falling apart. Several things began to happen to me physically. I'd started smoking incessantly and was beginning to have trouble breathing. I had repressed the fact that after all the operations, my throat was so small I only got about 20 percent of the air other people get when they breathe. All I knew was that if the scar tissue formed in the wrong way there was some danger of my throat closing again.

Also, I didn't know about the effect of amphetamines. Although they get people "up" for a while, in the long run they can lead to the most desperate kind of emotional depression—which I was discovering very quickly. With the depression came a whole catalog of physical symptoms. I began feeling weaker and weaker. Often after sitting down, I could hardly get back up. I was dizzy most of the time and stayed alone as much as I could to avoid anyone's finding out. An almost physical blackness came and went. Terror would blanket my mind, making me tremble or freeze with cold for hours or days. Then it would go as quickly as it had come, freeing me.

Sometimes I was so afraid I would stumble into my bedroom in order to hide. But I'd be so dizzy I could barely make it. If I'd throw myself across the bed, my throat seemed to collapse, increasing the terror, which in turn made sleeping almost impossible.

I didn't know if all this was happening because I'd left God, or what, but that thought added to my terror. And the effect of the amphetamines was to make me more hyper and push sleep even further out of reach. The vicious circle forced me into the deepest depression of horror and hopelessness about life I had known.

As totally spent as I was, I began to fear going to sleep. I was afraid I wouldn't wake up. If I dropped off, I'd often wake with a jolt to find the children standing by my bed in the middle of the night, their eyes as big as saucers. It seemed that when I did fall asleep, my throat would collapse to the extent that I made gasping, desperate noises, trying to get enough air. The look in their eyes confirmed my own fears that my throat was closing.

My coloring changed to a chalky white. My hands began to tremble and turn cold. My feet became icy, even in bed, and I knew that my circulation must be failing. One night when I couldn't sleep, I looked at myself in the bathroom mirror and couldn't believe what I saw. Sunken, hollow eyes—deeply lined forehead—age lines around my mouth. Surely, I must be about to die—the expression on my face seemed like a death mask. I shivered, and saw myself bent, slumped, old.

And something was radically wrong with my eyes. Maybe I was

going blind. It was almost impossible to work. After only a few minutes of painting, my eyes ached and I could hardly see anything. I'd have to stop painting, and then I'd cry and cry. But, when I tried to get up and paint again, my eyes would get swollen and start to burn. And everything was blurred.

By now I had withdrawn from everyone. I had a locked iron gate on the stairway leading up to my apartment. When I refused to answer my phone, people began to call on Susan's phone. But she quit answering too, since she didn't want to lie, and I'd told her to say I wasn't at home.

The weaker I got the more I didn't care about looking good or taking care of myself physically—which I'd always done before. Finally I caught pneumonia and was taken to the hospital. In my condition, the prognosis was not good. And for several weeks I was in an oxygen tent. During this time the doctors discovered that my breathing trouble and my numbness were largely due to the scar tissue in my throat. The tissue had thickened, and the opening through which I breathed was closing, although it was not yet really critical. They didn't want to operate because of my weakened condition. And they didn't want to cause additional scar tissue unless it was absolutely necessary. But they told me it was imperative that I quit smoking.

When I was finally released from the hospital, very weak and tired, I'd lost all sense of hope. I looked around the house and it seemed strange. I felt like I could never be at home there again. Without sitting down I called Findley.

Findley and I had remained good friends over the years, and I felt he still cared about me. When he came, I asked him if he'd have his lawyer draw me a new will. "I can't take any more, Findley," I told him. "I don't want to live." He just looked at me.

"I want to die a normal death. No one expects me to live anyway, and no one will be suspicious. I can't paint anymore. And since that's all I can do to make a living, the children will be a lot better off if I'm gone." He still didn't say anything. "I can hardly see, and by the time they come home from school, I'm so worn out from trying to paint that I can't be a mother. They need and deserve somebody to take care of them and help them with their homework. I can't do any of these things. Findley, I've had it."

I had heard that there were lethal drugs one could take which led to what appeared to be a natural death—they were untraceable in the body. I knew Findley had several close friends who were doctors, and I asked if he would arrange to get some of these drugs for me. He shook his head, "Hedy, you don't want to do that." But when he saw that I'd made up my mind, he finally agreed to try. He knew that I was serious and would do something anyway. But he told me it wouldn't be easy.

During the next few weeks, while I was waiting for Findley to get the drugs, I got my affairs in order. I made a will, checked on my insurance and made notes telling the children which personal things went to each. I tried to think of all the people who had helped me along the way, loaned me money or given me some special gift or encouragement. I made codicils to my will or wrote thank you notes to pay off debts and express my gratitude. At the end of two weeks, I had a neat stack of papers which would, I felt, settle all my affairs and relationships.

The night I tied a string around the will and these papers I had the peaceful feeling of having squared my accounts with the world. I walked out on the balcony and looked up through the branches of the big willow tree at the moon, wondering about life after death. Perhaps death might bring the intimacy I'd always sought. I didn't know and was really too tired to care at that moment. I went back inside, fell in bed and got the first decent night's sleep I'd had in weeks.

I'd been calling Findley all this time to find out why he hadn't gotten the medicine. First he said that he'd called his friend, but the doctor hadn't returned the call. Then, he said that when he did get hold of him, the doctor didn't want to talk about the drug on the telephone. They'd have to have lunch. But unfortunately, the doctor and his family were going on vacation. All in all, Findley put me off for about three weeks.

But the morning after I'd finally gotten my personal papers in order, I wouldn't be put off any longer. When Findley told me that his friend said he definitely would not help, I realized that he had been stalling.

"And *I* won't get it for you either," Findley told me just as I was going to ask him, "and I don't think anyone else will."

I looked at his eyes and knew he meant what he was saying. My heart sank as I realized my clear way out had crumbled. And I couldn't commit suicide openly. To make my children live the shame of that, on top of the other things I'd done to them, was unbearable to me. What could I do?

The despondent feelings which came over me then are difficult even to imagine now. By this time there was almost no let-up to the enveloping blackness. I was numb and just stared at the wall a lot. It was as if I were watching myself stare, feeling the numbness of my slack face. I'd have to do something sooner or later, but for the time being I just was not able to act.

One day I happened to answer the phone for two calls which opened a new door and seemed to wake me out of my suicidal nightmare.

My minister called and said I could use a friend's beach house on Sister Bay in Door County to paint in for as long as I wanted, in exchange for a painting they'd always wanted me to do of that beach with their two children on it. I couldn't think very well while we were on the phone, but told him I'd call back in a couple of days. The other phone call was from the manager of the most popular radio station in Chicago. "Hedy, we're going to have a contest called 'Ten Treasures of Man.' People have to guess the secret prizes, and one of them is going to be a painting by Hedy Robinson, if you'll sell us the painting!" He was very excited about this project.

These two calls opened the doorway to life for me, just a crack. Two people wanted me to do something creative and felt it would be worthwhile. I'd given up, tired of even trying. But their enthusiasm seemed to light a tiny spark of hope which began to glow in the darkness inside me. It was one of those fragile, delicate moments on which a whole universe hangs. From somewhere came my answers: "Yes, I'll go to Sister Bay." "Yes, I will do the painting." I called my minister back and accepted the use of the beach cottage. And the next day I took off.

As I drove up the familiar highway I knew in my bones that this was my last chance. I was going to try for life one more time, if I could find out how. But this last brush with death had made a change in my attitude. Before, when I'd gone to the beach, I'd always told people I was "going off to *paint*"—even if the real reason was that I was going to keep from having a breakdown. This time I told them frankly I was going off to rest. As strange as it seems, this was, for me, a new kind of honesty, and it felt good, since I'd never before been able to even admit that I was just plain tired.

I knew I was mixed up about life somehow and was afraid I'd lost forever the simple clearness I'd found by trying to commit my whole life to God. Somehow I longed, almost ached, to find out what really was the truth about myself—and to be that. My desire to be God's woman and my recent behavior didn't match. Getting ready for the trip, I'd begun to allow myself—force myself—to face how, in my need for acceptance and perfection, I'd been unconsciously playing all kinds of psychological games with people. Now I was tired of any kind of devious dodges—my own, or anyone else's. I wanted to see what my unconscious games were and quit playing them! I was going to find myself!

On this trip I decided I would paint if it came naturally, and if it didn't, I wouldn't. The last few months I hadn't been happy with my work, and this was very painful since art had always been a "place" where I could go and get refreshed. Always before when I had begun a painting which seemed to me to be creative, I noticed I would begin to breathe more naturally. A feeling of relaxation would begin to flow through my veins like a warm oil soothing my whole body. I'd have the feeling of being in a nest, a place just for me, in the midst of my paints and easels. And my sense of identity would come back, even in the face of terrible rejections and disappointments.

But the last year or so, an "automatic" quality had entered my living, which was reflected in my witnessing and finally in my painting. Rushing frantically to get paintings ready for too many shows had brought a slick commercial feel to my work—which I didn't like at all. But I knew what would sell—and I had to sell. The problem wasn't that the work was bad. But in trying to meet other people's demands, I was suppressing my own inner pictures and dreams that I had longed to splash onto my canvases and into people's hearts. During the past few months I'd felt inspiration slipping away as I'd rebelled from God's people. I also was dimly aware that I was rebelling from something He seemed to be trying to say to me. As the distance from God increased I couldn't recapture the creativity which had seemed so natural before. And when I couldn't be creative, I had begun to lose the desire to paint, or even to live.

As the miles slipped under the car, I saw that trying to paint only what other people wanted me to had stifled the flow of creative feelings in my studio. Even as a Christian I had been meeting the demands of people instead of the demands of God concerning His will for me.

As "un-Christian" as it sounded, it became clear to me that I could have been denying God by compulsively doing so many things for His people. I remembered Art Parker, the tall doctor at the hospital and how strange I'd thought it was when he'd said, "They have me so busy witnessing I don't have time to be a Christian." Now I could understand. I'd known since I'd met God in the hospital that I needed a regular intimate time with Him to keep the integrity of our personal relationship. And I knew that I had mislaid this integrity in the hurly-burly of Christian activities. Now I wanted nothing but reality. I'd settle for nothing less. I was going for broke! That meant getting back in touch with God and trying to find out what He'd have me do.

For the first time I didn't have to force myself to paint a show, since I could always end my life. Now I was free to live a little. And I felt a dawning sense of knowing or understanding about life. I smiled at the unexpected freedom the willingness to die brought. With that choice came a kind of leisure, a new set of eyes to see what was around me. The April sky was clear and light blue, the sun was bright and reflected a burning white light from the chrome around the windshield, as I drove through the bright spring day.

Before I'd left the hospital a doctor had told me the reason my eyes had hurt when I painted. When I concentrated, I didn't blink. I had been concentrating for long periods of time, trying frantically to work while I was depressed. My eyes had gotten so swollen and sore, I hadn't been able to see. Fear had compounded the problem. But when my breathing began to clear up, my eyes relaxed too. So I felt good when I arrived at the beach outside Sister Bay. I'd come for a retreat from the world. As it turned out, it was to be another first step into a new life. But this time was different somehow.

40. From Out of the Sea

THIS HOUSE, TOO, was right on the beach. The waves during a storm came almost up to the door. I loved Lake Michigan. When I was a child I had insisted on calling it "the sea." As the wind tore past my ears and the waves rolled up on the sand, they seemed to pound at the doorway of my heart, trying to get in, to pull me back to the center of life.

The frantic scenes and fears I'd lived with the past weeks began to settle out of my mind. And I heard in the waves and wind a steady rhythmic call: "Come back, and get in touch with Me, Hedy, with the essence of life. Don't be afraid. Let Me teach you who you really are."

Hesitantly, very slowly, I began to let life in along with smell of the sand and water.

Again it was off season and the beach was deserted and cold. But it was all mine. I felt exhilarated, as if I owned it all! Every morning I walked as the sun was coming up, sometimes squinting my eyes into the freezing wind or in the still bright morning sunshine. Often during the day I looked for driftwood. In the evenings I'd walk with our dog, Mandy, and watch in amazement as the sun disappeared in a cold orange furnace of color. I let the muscles of my soul stretch as I drank in the freshness and tasted the damp, cold

PLEASE LOVE ME

air. I cried as I stood looking at the sunset just because it was beautiful. And the hard clay of my heart was being made moist and pliable by the tears of relief and release.

The sunshine and wind blowing the spray on my face gradually softened and seasoned my skin, which had been like an empty pod. I was beginning to be filled once more with "greenness and health."

In those long walks on the beach, I started to face the contradictions in my life. It was somehow skewed. Why had I felt guilty when I was not "witnessing for Christ" or working at the church, and yet equally guilty when I wasn't painting?

One day, as I was walking, it came to me clearly that my gift and the need to support Susan and Janie constituted a Christian ministry which for Christ's sake was more important than being a "program for God." Why hadn't I seen it before? Painting *was* my ministry for Christ, my *primary Christian work!* Yet in my own need for acceptance I'd heard the implication that if I really loved Christ, I would always put the church's program first. So I had quit using the particular talent He had given me.

Wrestling with these apparent contradictions, I began to realize there was a sense in which I'd always considered my own legitimate needs as a human being to be selfish, therefore sinful. But if that were true, it would mean that God didn't love me or want me to be fulfilled in using what He'd given me. Maybe I had "denied myself" in the wrong sense. Though I'd been told from the pulpit that God loved me without any performance at all, I hadn't understood it in my heart until now. An artist picks up her truth from what's actually *going* on around her, not what is *said.* And what I had picked up in terms of behavior in Christian circles was that God's will involved religious activities rather than living in the intimate presence and communion with God's Spirit. But I saw that only if I lived in communion with God could I hope to relate in healthy ways to people.

I had not become a theologian as many people do when they start witnessing, though I'd tried to learn all I could about life and God from the Bible and from other Christians. But no one seemed willing to deal with these contradictions between what we said and what we did. And I'd gotten to be so unreal I didn't even know what I really thought or wanted out of life any more.

One noon I stood at the end of a rickety gray wooden pier, my face toward the sun, my eyes closed, but my heart open to God.

"What do *I* want, Lord?" I asked silently. "I've run after the approval of your people, and I'm sick and tired. What is *your will* for me—now?"

The answer seemed to come, "Hedy, just find out who you are and be that for Me."

In a few minutes I opened my eyes. I saw that I'd been afraid to tell God or anyone else my own true needs and desires, for fear they wouldn't be met. With a great sigh of relief I could almost hear God's voice saying, "Hedy, at last you're ready to be you. You're ready to quit ignoring what I made you to be, and to see the truth about your life." What a relief to admit to myself that I had some legitimate needs in my life and that they'd been placed there by God!

Every night, returning from my walk along the beach, I lit a fire in the fireplace and watched the flames for hours. It was as if the fire was communicating with the life and warmth I felt stirring in me—a subtle warmth I couldn't remember having known before. In those evenings I began to sense that something was starting to melt inside of me, like a prison door at the basement of my soul. And again I heard the call to open myself to another human being. That need which I had buried for so long beneath the efforts to win the love of a father and then the approval of people through my achievements.

But the intimacy I was beginning to sense now was different. It wasn't something I could manipulate. Rather it was more like the fire. It just had to flicker up as the flames did without my shaping it. Or like the sea, which moved into my life without my asking. It was a little scary to see that there was something about true intimacy which couldn't be controlled. But I found myself sensing a warmth and a closeness to God which was natural and into which I could simply relax. I realized I had almost never just relaxed,

even in my own presence. What if . . . what if I could relax
with a man?

A ripple of excitement ran across my skin. I hugged myself at
the awesome idea that I might relax and simply be with a man and
find with him this at-homeness and oneness with myself, with life
and with God. I was caught up in the awesomeness of the prospect. That really was what I had always wanted from people but
had been afraid to even imagine—because I'd realized instinctively
how vulnerable I would be in such a relationship. The idea of this
experience of relaxed safe closeness with another person was overwhelming—fantastic and fearful.

What was it? Presence and attitude, not performance. That
must be it. I had never really been "present" to people with my
real self. Instead I had tried to listen intently and to be interested
in them, to "perform" even by helping them—which wasn't bad,
but left me outside and alone. By playing the parts expected of
me, putting on a show of perfection, I had really missed out on
life, hadn't I?

A great sadness overwhelmed me because this natural intimacy
wasn't a part of my relationships—to be shared with people I
loved. How could I experience this wonder, this magic, which was
the password to open the locked inner doors of life? That was the
question that began to haunt my days and nights as I became ruddy
and stronger on the shore and by the fire. Out of these feelings and
this question came my first new painting.

Onto the canvas splashed the sea at dawn. There was nothing
else but the water sliding in and colors reflected from the sunrise.
Then, in the foreground, I placed two small shells, representing
the male and the female principles. All else was still. To this painting of a new and strangely intimate beginning I gave the name "In
the Beginning." In creating that painting, my heart and my whole
body confirmed the notion that the meaning of all of life might
stem from the kind of relationship I had only dreamed of—and it
somehow was brought about by God.

As I looked at the painting, I knew the experience was real. It
was the same sense of knowing I'd had in the hospital when I was

told I couldn't walk. Yet I had *known* in my life, in my bones, the possibility that I might before anyone else had even suspected it. Now it was beginning to dawn on me that there was an actual possibility of my lowering the lifelong inner barriers in my soul and touching another life and soul.

After this, the paintings came in a rush like hot popcorn opening. I saw each one first clearly in my mind. Their themes were the great archetypes of life, and I painted them with a naturalness and totalness I had not had before. My previously locked-in feelings were flowing onto the canvas. I did my first male nude—a breakthrough which expressed getting in touch with the total feelings of my life. The separate parts of all of living seemed to be coming together. Some hidden wall of fear was crumbling.

What was being born in me was not only life, but hope. And I saw that hope, rather than love, is probably the first medicine of God. For without hope, I hadn't even been able to receive love. I had let the religious trappings of the church hide me, encasing me in armor like a female knight. But this armor had kept me dry and untouchable in terms of my emotional, spiritual and even physical life. Now I was coming out! And although I hadn't experienced this intimacy in the world of relationships, I was experiencing it inside myself. So I knew it was real. Deep feelings were coming out of my unconscious onto the canvas. I hadn't had feelings like that in a long, long time . . . if ever.

Many of my previous pictures had been of people looking in or out of windows—often terribly lonely or seeming to be afraid of life—or of frightened little animals. I had painted them when my *outer life* was totally victorious and strong. But now that I felt weak and was not ashamed to admit it, my paintings had a very strong feel about them.

I tried to capture this paradox—of being strong through being vulnerable—by painting a very powerful lion totally at rest by the edge of a pool of water. I knew that no lion would probably lie that way with his back to the jungle behind him. Yet there was a great strength in this resting, vulnerable king of the jungle.

Another painting showed a deer who was afraid but was

somehow standing alone in an open clearing in the forest. The
effect on me was strong and vibrant. I began to sense that the
strange quest for intimacy in life had to do with this willingness
to take the risk of being seen and of being destroyed. But how did
one go about finding out how to do this in real life? And where
did the courage come from? I knew, but shook my head.

I noticed, now, that the darkness and shadows of my earlier
window paintings were not present. Rather there was a lightness
and fresh "outsideness." A true freedom had begun to creep into
my work from somewhere else deep inside my mind and heart.

It was a strange experience to watch these things flow out of my
hidden self onto the canvas and to realize that they might be only
the front edge of a wave of life which could carry me up the shore
to some unknown place where I might be at home. Everywhere
in my work now was primal nature—the waves crashing together
in a violent painting of the sea, a lone person standing on a cliff
offering a prayer.

At times in my excitement, I was working on as many as five
paintings at once. Several times I would wake up in the middle of
the night, particularly as I was doing the painting of the sea,
to go and add color to the waters that crashed together. And as
the waves burst, I knew that the source of energy at the core
of me that had begun uncoiling when I became a Christian was
about to break loose. I had the incredible expectation that something new was coming into my life, though I still didn't know what
it was—something I had feared yet longed for, but never understood.

One painting called "The Way" was of two Indians traveling
with everything they owned on their backs. I too was on that
journey. I had left the past, and everything I valued was with me.
The future was ahead of me as I traveled with those Indians.

Then there was the painting of a tired old man working with
clay. One sensed that he had the wisdom of the earth about him.
He had been to hell and back and now was simply working with
his hands. He reminded me of some of the older men at the carnival. But in my heart I knew that I was that old man. The wisdom
that I hadn't been able to get at with my mind was in his blood-

stream. I felt it in the basement of my own soul, pressing to get out and lead me to life. I too was saying with my hands what I could not yet grasp with my head.

And finally, I painted a stone wall, grey and weathered. Everything beside it was growing in one direction, except one small daisy. The painting was called "Turning Loose," and I was that daisy. Although I had no idea where God would take me, I knew that in some absolutely critical sense I was in the process of breaking out of the prison I'd stayed in all my life.

As I drove back to Chicago, I began to prepare mentally for the new show. I was going to call it "From the Door Within." Whereas my last show, with wine and cheese, had been an emerging *from* a pious cocoon, this show represented a glorious announcement of a new future that God was nudging me *toward*. I didn't understand what was going to happen, I only knew that something was already beginning to bubble up in me. And it seemed very good and authentic. But instead of a hope for growth and change, the expectancy was one of a whole new chapter that was about to begin in my life. It was as if my "person" were about to be born. I was almost afraid, yet excited to be where I was. And I felt that I could almost watch and feel a stirring of the Holy Spirit, a preparing within me.

It still seemed like a paradox that just when I had cut through the trappings of religion, rebelled terribly from the unreality of institutional programs and decided to be honest at all costs—just then I saw *my own* tendency to hide my true feelings and play God by trying to be everywhere at once and have all the answers. And I hated myself for having adopted a stance of "victorious perfection" which separated me from people and God. I began to see that the church's problem is people like me who will not risk being real.

Now, because of my month at the beach, I could see how I had misunderstood what living the Christian life meant. I had put the "dressed up" image and the victorious witness in the place of the blood and guts of the struggles of living which I was now convinced would always be a part of life.

I still didn't know what to do about my discovery. And I didn't know who I might be able to discuss it with. But I knew God was forcing me to be ready to risk everything for Him and to find His will for my life. The people at the church were sincere. But somehow, what *I* had become in the fellowship smacked of death. And I knew that where God is present, real and full *life* is taking place, with all of its creative and earthy implications.

At the beach I had tasted a new kind of reality. I knew it was from God, and it sounded and felt like Jesus, but it didn't have a religious label. I had been in touch with a loving, healing Spirit of Creativity, which I knew must have been the Spirit of the living Christ. The experience was so real and so close and total that I had no words to express it. But I felt that there was more to come. First, however, I was going to have to bury the past and make an honest beginning.

In the headiness of my decision to be honest, my first reaction was to break my old dishonest religious mold, to say to the world in clear terms, "I am trusting God and the process of living toward freedom in Christ." So for this art show, I had a costume made that would be unbelievable to my Christian friends. It was an Indian costume in a way, with beads and feathers hanging down from a little leather band in front, over a bluejean half bib. With this went bluejeans. Hedy Robinson, artist.

This girl with her hair down and her eyes shining was living in the "now" between the past and the future. Since life was free and uncontrollable, like the sea and like the Holy Spirit, I was being free and uncontrollable in the way I dressed. I realize now I might have chosen a more mature way to make my announcement. But I wanted to let this be a beginning for living. I didn't want to be immoral or evil, I just wanted to be free from stuffiness and enjoy the life God had given back to me. And in my proper "victorious" stance I had never let myself be free enough to do this. I continued to get my pictures framed and ready for the show—not thinking that God might be preparing to call my bluff about my commitment to pay any price to find honesty—and intimacy.

41. Out of the Mouths of Children

During these days and weeks, my children became very worried. They didn't know what the change in my feelings about life and Christianity meant. Being committed to God and regular members of North Shore, they felt I should do whatever God wanted me to do. But Susan couldn't see how God would think painting was more important than public witnessing. Since both of them believed totally in my faith, they just loved me and prayed for me, but they were confused.

I'd never been able to tell them when I had any problems, since I'd felt I had to be strong and "handle" everything. I'd been afraid I might lose their confidence and respect if they knew I was often weak and anxious. But something had happened to me at the beach which unexpectedly spilled over into our life together.

About a week before the art show, I went into their bedroom one evening. Though I was afraid to tell them about my dishonesty and fear of showing any weakness, I couldn't hide myself from them any longer.

After a few minutes I said, "Girls, I've been having some problems I don't know what to do about. I know God's going to help me. But I'd like for you to pray for me, that I'll be strong enough and smart enough to find His will and do it."

293

Then quietly I told them how I'd been afraid to let anyone down or let them know I got tired and discouraged. I told them I thought what I'd done in faking it was sinful and proud, that I was sorry, and that I needed their help and their prayers.

Deep down inside I expected them to be disappointed in me. But instead they just looked at me a few seconds to make sure they had heard correctly. Then they both hugged me and said, "Oh, Mom, we love you so much!" And I saw that there were tears— of happiness—in their eyes. My gosh, they had been waiting for me to tell them! Of course, they had known all along I'd been troubled and not honest. But when I finally had the courage to confess my weakness to them, then they relaxed and could love me! And we began the most intimate discussion we'd ever had, as I told them something of my struggles. They responded by telling me something of theirs. It was warm and loving and strangely secure as we sat close to each other propped up in bed.

The fact that the men in my life were still pressing me and demanding total attention had disturbed Susan and Janie. They hadn't understood the pressure I'd been under. They had wondered why I'd been so frantic, and couldn't see that all I was trying to do was to find the space to be Hedy, the artist, the person God had made. All they'd seen was that somehow people weren't giving their mother any peace. And I hadn't known how to handle the relationships and end them in healthy definite ways when it was necessary. So I'd tried to ignore the sticky situations and escape rather than hurt or disappoint people.

Finally, Susan said to me, "All I hear when they're here with you, is what *they* want, particuarly the men. But Mom, what is it that *you* want out of life? It seems like people are taking things from you, all your time and energy for them, and you're letting them." She stopped and was thoughtful before going on. "But, Mom, is that the same thing as *giving* things to people the way Jesus did?"

Her words brought me up short. That's what Pepper had told me, wasn't it? My best friend and now my child! But it was true. Where Jesus had said, "They do not take my life, but I give it,"

I was letting people *take* my life, a piece at a time, out of guilt and fear of disappointing them. How could this be really Christian when it wasn't following Christ's example? How many Christians, how many ministers, thinking they were doing God's will, had let people pull them apart for their own use and own selfish interests—and then had no energy left to offer their life to Christ to be used in *His* strategy? I realized I'd have to be honest and admit I wasn't God with boundless energy. Directly and honestly I'd have to cut off some of the counseling I'd been doing and some of the speaking—with no excuses, no games.

My life was spread out in a hundred directions. Out of pride and ignorance I'd let people take it away from God, from me and from my children. Susan was right. It was almost as though I'd been sitting in front of a very powerful fan that had been blowing me almost to pieces. And I hadn't had the courage to be honest and turn off the switch. There was only an emotional skeleton left when I had started being reborn.

That night the girls and I talked about how we could change things. Who could help us? God? His angels?

"Could we pray, Mom?" Susan asked. I nodded and she began: "Dear God, Mom is hurt and confused. Please send her an angel to tell her how you want her to live so she won't be so lonely inside and so miserable." Then Janie prayed for me. I felt so close to them and could tell they sensed the closeness too. Why had I waited so long to be human with my children? Because I was afraid they would reject me, of course. But I saw now that this kind of honesty was the basis for intimacy in families—even though it was very threatening.

I saw, too, that I needed to discover what it means to be God's kind of honest person, in fact what it means to be a person at all. I had "performed" all my life, first for the world and then for God. My performing had been with conscious integrity mostly, but *performing* was very different from *living*. And now I wanted to learn how to *live* for God.

My children's insight amazed me. The problem of pride in not letting anybody know that I had any needs had kept me from asking for help until it was almost too late. But Susan and Janie had known all along.

That first hesitant confession, which seemed frightening and risky to me, since I'd always been the strength of my family, opened many doorways I'd never even suspected were there into my children's hearts.

During the next few days we began to have very personal talks about hopes, dreams and fears that each of us had, but had never been able to share. It seemed so strange that confession to another human being of one's real self with the unresolved problems and weaknesses—the *last* thing I'd been willing to believe would lead me to intimacy—should have done just that with my children.

The following week on Thursday I was coming in from my studio, tired but happy, when Janie called from her bedroom, "Hi Mom, Lucy called!"

Lucy. What in the world did she want? She had almost never called me. And my father never had. I dialed and then heard Lucy's voice.

"Hedy, Paul wants you to come out here in the morning at nine."

I couldn't imagine what he wanted, and immediately thought about what I might have done wrong.

"Lucy, do you know what he wants?"

"No, he just said to tell you to come out here at nine."

"Well, O.K., tell him I'll be there."

I didn't eat much dinner that night and was so preoccupied I had trouble listening to the children's chattering at the table.

That night I lay awake a long time propped up in my bed. The only light was the glow from my cigarette as I thought about my daddy and the fact that he still didn't know how much I loved him. What in the world did he want?

The next morning I was up early and, after getting the kids off to school, was on my way to Libertyville by 8:15 to make sure I got there on time.

Daddy opened the door himself.

"Hello, Paul. Lucy said you wanted to see me." My stomach was fluttering just as it had when I was little and was afraid I'd done something wrong. I knew it was dumb, and I hoped I looked calm and relaxed.

"Sit down, Hedy." He was dressed in a new suit which looked very good on him. I mentioned it. He glanced down at the suit.

"Oh yea, Lucy's been after me to wear it, but I never have." He looked at me obviously ready to get on to the business at hand.

"Hedy, you shouldn't be smoking. It's stupid with your throat. I want you to meet a man who can help you quit. He's one of my customers." He looked at his watch and then started to get up.

"You mean right now?"

"Of course right now. That's why I asked you to come. We've got an appointment at ten."

I couldn't believe it! What was going on? How did he know what the doctor had said? Findley, of course. I followed him out the back door and got in his car with him feeling just like a little girl again. Neither of us said anything during the thirty-five minute drive toward the city.

Finally we pulled into the parking lot of an office building in Evanston.

"This is his office." Paul said.

When we got to the office door it read "United Smoking Center." It was one of the most expensive and successful centers for helping people who wanted to quit smoking. Daddy's friend was the director. When he came in, Paul shook his hand.

"Hello, Ben, this is my daughter, Hedy. She needs to quit smoking. I don't know what you can do with her. She's as stubborn as a mule and doesn't have a lick of sense. But her doctor says she really needs to stop."

I felt my face turn red. He was treating me like a rebellious ten-year-old.

The director was very gracious and seemed interested in helping me. He explained a little about the program.

After asking him some questions, I said, "How much will this cost?"

"Three hundred and seventy-five dollars."

"Can I pay it out over a period of time?"

Daddy interrupted, pulling his checkbook out of his pocket.

"Here, Hedy, I'm making this check payable to you, because I think the program will mean more if you give him the money."

"Paul, when do I have to get this paid back to you?" I asked.

He said, "Well, it damn sure is a *loan*." Then he pursed his lips and went on, "But if you aren't smoking at the end of two years you don't have to pay me back."

After making an appointment for my first session, we left. When we got back to Libertyville, I stood by the car and felt tears welling up inside. "Thank you, Paul."

He said gruffly, "Would you like to see my garden?"

"I'd love to."

He showed me his beautiful vegetable garden. Then we came back to the car. I turned to go. But after a few steps I turned and ran back to him and threw my arms around him, burying my face in his chest.

"Oh thank you, Daddy!"

He stood stiff as a rod with his hands at his sides and didn't say anything.

As I drove home, I cried. Maybe I was worth something to him. I doubted if he'd ever call me again—or rather have Lucy call me. But God had really been neat to let me know that somehow my daddy did care. As I thought about his crusty frown when he signed the check, I felt the tears coming again.

But I didn't have any more time to think about it right then. Because all this was happening as I was very busy getting ready for the show "From the Door Within" and making out the invitation list.

As I was going through some boxes, I found the name and address of "Dr. Arthur Parker." *Art!* On the card with his name and address in Omaha, Art had scribbled, "Let me know when you have your next art show, Hedy. I'd be very interested." I smiled.

What a statement of faith. I'd hardly been able to move when he'd written that.

As I looked at this man's name, I realized that he just might have gone through the same thing I was going through in attempting to be honest. I remembered again how he'd talked about having pressures in the church and feeling "too busy doing church work to be a Christian." Out of all the people I knew, Art just might understand what was happening to me. He certainly wouldn't be intimidated by my Christian experience or treat me like a saint. As I sat there looking at the card, I knew somehow that he *was* going through the same thing—or had already. I wondered what he had discovered to help him get through the frustrating and lonely experience I was having.

It was totally safe to write him a note, since he was happily married and had a full life of his own. So, I did. I simply told him that this had been the roughest year of my life, and I wrote it on an invitation to the art show, not dreaming he would come.

42. The Tint of Sunrise

THE SHOW OPENED on June 15 at a fashionable gallery near Jacques Restaurant. I not only served champagne at the opening, but I drank it, just like the guests. I welcomed the people to show them what God had brought out through the crack in the doorway to my soul. I was really enjoying my own party and wasn't the least bit worried about selling the paintings. This was a whole new experience for me, since I'd always been very careful to keep a cautious reserve so that I was in control. And although I wasn't out of control, I was certainly free. It was a great party and I felt young and happy.

Some of my friends had laughingly started calling me "Mrs. Billy Sunday" during the height of my witnessing. But today, in my self-designed Indian outfit, I was anything but Mrs. Billy Sunday. And a strange thing happened.

Several members of a Christian women's study group were at the opening. As I handed each of them a glass of champagne, I looked them squarely in the eye and said, "How have you been?"

Most of them replied with the usual polite, "Oh, just fine, how have you been, Hedy?"

I smiled. "This has been a hell of a year!" I told them. "The worst year of my life in many ways."

Each one looked at me a moment, sort of shocked. Then a smile spread across their faces. And without exception, they nodded their heads and said that this had been an awful year for them too, and they wished they'd had the courage to admit it. And these were all women who claimed to have "the victory"!

As we talked, they confided that trying to hide their problems and project the victorious life had exhausted them. It seemed unreal, and separated them from God and from the people in their families. One said, "I'd like to get out of all the organizations I'm running myself ragged with and begin to walk with the Lord again." I felt a greater kinship with these women in having admitted the hell we'd been through than I'd ever felt when we shared "the victory." As I moved on, I silently said, "Thank you God." This was another confirmation that what I'd been looking for in terms of intimacy of relationship with people might begin with confession, rather than ability, beauty, or even witnessing about the triumphs of God.

My "unnatural" behavior drew a strange reaction from the people who were closest to me. My mother kept wanting me to tie my dress up tighter so that I would be more of a lady. Harry, who was still my most frequent date, kept being suspicious when I'd talk very long to any other man, even if it was about a painting. He kept urging me to go and stand by the door.

Those in the inner circle of my life, who should have loved me and been rejoicing with me, could not tolerate my being myself. I realized that my behavior was certainly different from the conservative Christian stereotype, and maybe a little bizarre and immature. But I also realized that those closest to me wanted me to continue being the superpious but unreal Christian I'd tried to be—though ironically *they* were not that way themselves. As a guilt-ridden and proper, rigid Christian, I had been predictable, and thus controllable. And now my freedom seemed to be a threat to everyone.

As I went through that day, I wondered: "Who besides my children would love me if I were really truthful about my pain, loneliness and fears? Would anybody who really knew me love me?" It was an old question with new meaning that haunted me at a semiconscious level through those days following the opening.

What kind of a world had I gotten myself into? My own dishonesty had evidently led me into relationships which demanded that I be St. Hedy, that I be things I wasn't and in fact had never been—though I couldn't think of a time since I'd been a Christian that I hadn't been sincere about my faith in God. But who was *I*, really? And who could I now relate to honestly so I could find out? I was just beginning to know myself. Although I had talked to a lot of Christians about their lives, I didn't know any adult I thought could understand what I was going through now. It was very sad. But I still felt the underlying hope that God was taking me somewhere I was almost destined to go.

The show was very successful. Opening day, Sunday, I sold three-fourths of the paintings. On Monday and Tuesday, I came back, arriving at ten o'clock in the morning and staying till eight or nine at night. Wednesday morning, as I arrived at the gallery, I was tired but grateful. There were only three paintings left to be sold and I'd made up my mind to work long hours that day and the next and close the show by Friday. It was scheduled to run for two weeks, but I was too tired and couldn't make it.

When I reached the top of the stairs that led to the gallery, I stopped. Down the long hall in the shadows a tall man was sitting in a chair by the wall. I barely recognized the profile against the window at the end. But though I hadn't seen him in four years, I knew in a split second that it was Art, the doctor I'd written the note to on the invitation. And I also knew that it was he God had sent to me. Even then I couldn't have guessed what a revolution this meeting might begin in my life.

I started walking down the hall. When I'd gone about two-thirds of the way, Art turned and saw me. He stood up and started walking toward me. He looked much older than he had four years before. Then he smiled. I tossed my purse on the couch by the wall and spontaneously put my hands up on his shoulders, and he hugged me.

I can't remember what I said, but I'll never forget his words,

"Why you're *beautiful*, Hedy." The last time he had seen me was in my cast in the hospital.

I took him by the hand and led him straight back to the room full of my paintings. Mother had arrived earlier to lay out extra brochures. After introducing Art to her, I showed him my paintings. I knew he understood as he looked at each one carefully and nodded his head. Then I asked mother if she could stay for a while as he'd asked me to lunch. Mother said she would. As Art and I stepped outside, the sunshine was warm and the air clear.

Suddenly, I was feeling happy and excited. I took his hand once again and led him out to my car. This was unusual behavior for me, but I knew there was something very important about our meeting. Somehow I knew we wouldn't be back within the hour. And deep down inside I didn't care if we ever came back. Something told me this was a special time, that the plot of my life was unfolding, and I just might find out who I was.

I'm not sure what happened during those next few hours. We went to a patio restaurant and sat at an outside table under the trees. Having always been very careful about revealing my true feelings, I was amazed at what started happening.

"Hedy," Art told me, "I was really surprised to get your note, especially since you said this had been the worst year of your life. Because it's been the worst year of mine too, even though my vocational dreams are coming true." And he started talking very openly about the personal agony and discouragement he'd been through in his practice and especially in his personal life.

As Art talked, I could feel a vibrant quality about him. His whole body was in everything he said, but I especially noticed his hands. He was very tanned and his hands looked strong, yet flexible and gentle. He spoke of his discouragement with the church and the anger and frustration he had felt about the dishonesty in institutions. Then he described the disillusioning realization of his own dishonesty, his own phoniness and vanity in the midst of all his witnessing for Christ. He'd seen that he manipulated people as a doctor, as a lay witness in the church and as a person in his own home.

"Talk about the heart being deceitful and wicked, I wouldn't have believed it, Hedy," he said. "I actually believed I had almost total integrity until I began to succeed. But then everybody seemed to expect me to be more than I was. And I was crushed when I heard myself lying, even to people I loved, in my desperation, rather than face hidden conflicts which might let them see my fears and inadequacies." He said he'd found that he couldn't hide the unreality in his life from himself any longer. As he talked, I felt like I was hearing an almost perfect echo of my own life during the past two years.

He smiled, and I suddenly realized he had an attractive smile. And his eyes were unbelievably expressive. As he confessed his true feelings and failures to me, the atmosphere changed in a way I can't describe. I felt the thing happening between us which I'd sensed in the fire at the beach and then with the children, and the Christian women's group ladies, as I'd told them last week how I really was.

And yet I felt safe with this man who, like me, wanted to love God and wanted to find life and reality in relationships. He too found himself being phony and afraid to risk being hurt at close range. After an hour I had relaxed and was neither uncomfortable nor guarded as I had always been with men, for fear they would try to take something of my life from me without my permission. My protective shell almost disappeared during the next two hours. Because I felt secure, I wanted to comfort him in his misery. And because he had confessed to me and become vulnerable, he'd made it safe for me to think about giving him my secrets.

My first thought was my lifelong response, "No, don't tell him anything about your fears or weaknesses. He won't like you." But I could almost hear God saying, "This is not a love affair, Hedy. This is the chance to be yourself you've prayed for." Very tentatively I began to tell for the first time about the hiding I had done in my life—particularly from men—for fear I wouldn't be acceptable.

And as I began to talk to him, I felt the warmth of a relationship I'd dreamed of when I looked into the fire those nights at the beach at Sister Bay. Only now that we were each vulnerable, this flame began to include us both. It was what I'd wanted with my father and with Buzzy, Danny and Findley, and with Pepper. I could see it in his eyes and feel it in my own. It was a unique experience. It was not like being in love, it was like being close. Love was involved, but I realized that this could happen between two women or two men.

But as we continued talking, I realized suddenly that I was starting my old pattern of getting emotionally involved with a man all at once when I saw safety and gentleness in his eyes. I had done that with Buzzy, with Danny and even with Findley—blocking out anything negative and exaggerating the aspects of the man which promised to fulfill my dreams, my needs.

But just as I was slipping into feelings of loving Art and wanting to own him as mine, a warning light went on inside somewhere, and I could almost hear God's voice saying, "Hedy, I've been trying to tell you that My kind of intimacy doesn't come in *owning* someone but through being *open* with them!"

Yes, I was still thinking that intimacy always included the total physical and emotional joining of two people, even though my closeness with Pepper had showed me that wasn't true. I didn't know what was happening, but I knew I was in uncharted waters for me. It was scary as well as exciting.

We were just two persons sharing simply and directly at a deep level—gradually taking off the religious, the formal, the armor of stereotyped language, and of background differences. And yet he was a man—and I'd always been terrified of being vulnerable to any man. We were like two trusting children, sharing together what life was for us during that hour. We expected nothing from each other in return. And neither of us was demanding or offering anything for the future.

It was a paradox. I was looking into his laughing eyes one minute. And the next we were both on the verge of tears. Though our conversation was deadly serious and we were reliving the hell we had been through during the past year, a great sense of happiness had settled over me. I laughed more than I had in several years, as we identified with each other and the stupid mistakes we'd made because of our awful pride, by trying to protect ourselves from God and people. And suddenly the grayness I had experienced about God was gone. He seemed real and present again with us both.

Oh, the relief of really being myself! I couldn't believe I was telling a man my hurts, and confessing my fears of life, my thoughts of suicide. As I looked at him, I wondered if I could tell him about being raped. But I didn't.

I laughed out loud when I realized that I wasn't having to be "Mrs. Billy Sunday" with this man. I also didn't have to prove I wasn't, although he was very committed to God himself. He'd taken off the jacket to his light summer suit and seemed very relaxed. Although he too was always surrounded by people, he evidently didn't feel that he needed to be anything for me other than a person struggling with the problems of his life—each of which seemed familiar enough to be a piece of furniture from my own soul.

"Maybe," I thought, "it's at this level of personal difficulties, hopes and dreams that we're all brothers and sisters—instead of at the level of our intellectual assent to certain theological propositions." In any case, for a woman who'd been trying all her life to win her father's (and the world's) love by perfect performance, these three hours of being able to sit and relax and feel accepted with even a few problems and failures in full view—this was like a miracle.

Finally, Art looked at his watch and said he had to start for the airport to catch a plane to Omaha. "I'll drive you out," I said. As he was paying the check, I wondered how many hundreds of thousands of Christians had been through the process of making a commitment to God, working hard in the church for years, and suddenly finding themselves in the midst of a discouraging grayness. How many were still smiling till their faces ached, but were discouraged and lonely in the midst of a congregation?

The two of us had only touched the surface of true intimacy, but the grayness was gone. Yet we both knew that we had begun to experience something which was deeper than we could verbalize.

As we pulled up to the airport, Art asked me, "Do you suppose two people like us could be *totally* honest with each other and with God? What would happen? Would we find a new beginning? A new way to live openly as free people under God? Could we find a way to share with God, so that *He* could teach us about His kind of freedom?"

I didn't know, but I was quiet now. Talking to this man alone for three hours and experiencing something of the miracle of intimacy was one of the most remarkable things that had ever happened to me. When the conversation started, it had seemed safe to be together because he was a happily married man. But I was no longer safe. One of the agonizing things which had happened to him the past few months was that he and his wife had been divorced. He was just beginning to come back to life after working through his grief. I'd known nothing of this when I'd written the note.

But when he had told me about the death of his marriage, I was gripped with my old fear and uncertainty. Suddenly I was not safe at all. He was an attractive man with whom I was sharing at a deep level, approaching a depth of intimacy in which I was very vulnerable and frightened. Revealing myself to a well-known layman who was a professionally trained doctor interested in the psychological aspect of medicine would have been one thing. But what if I revealed myself with my secrets and my insecurities and were rejected by a man who was really available to accept or reject me *as a woman?* I withdrew into the protection of my own silence.

And now, as he was sitting with the car door open at the airport, we were discussing the possibility of continuing this conversation, betting our lives that God would lead us to the truth about ourselves and the consequences of being truly open with another person.

Suddenly the secret search of my whole life for intimacy was on the line. Could I really risk being open with a man as we searched for the truth. What if he saw my unconscious games and called me a phony? And what if he were right!

I knew again how much I'd always been afraid that way down at the center of me underneath all my performance and appearance, there might be nothing at all—like the "center" of an onion if one peeled back all the layers. I felt a light perspiration on my temples. My mind left the conversation for a moment. "God, what are you doing to me?" I thought, "What on earth are you doing to me?" I didn't know. Suddenly I was on very uncertain ground. And yet I knew this was what God had been driving me quietly but relentlessly toward.

Almost all my life since Buzzy I had been in control of situations where there were men. They might reject me in ways no one knew about, but *I* did the leaving. And as I looked at the man beside me, I realized that he also had always been in control in situations involving women. But what if he found out that I wasn't the self-contained woman, artist and semisaint? Would I be shattered when he saw that I'm only a weak and vacillating person—a frightened little girl who wants to love and be loved?

I looked at Art. I knew that I wanted to talk to him again more than he could possibly know. But I was afraid.

He seemed to be as desperate as I was to find out if life were real. And he was honest about his own anxious feelings. But he had already made the decision that whatever the cost, he was not going to settle for a life that was phony, a life that was safe, a life that was covered with the trappings of reality without the guts of reality. But he was also on uncertain ground, and he didn't know anyone he could find out about himself with. I could tell from his eyes that he had the same fear I did about being known—and that he saw me as an attractive woman.

He glanced at his watch. Then, after looking steadily into my eyes for a moment, he reached over and gave me a very gentle kiss. Then he was gone, running toward the terminal door, shouting over his shoulder, "I'll call you, Hedy!"

Driving home I was in a daze. After living all my life in a carefully protected shell, I had in three hours simply laid it aside and come out in the warm sunshine of personal intimacy—and with a man. This whole experience was so different from any of my past relationships with men that I felt dazzled by the personal thing that had taken place between us. It was not a game.

But I knew that, in reality, we had just begun to reveal our true selves. There might be all kinds of pain and confrontation if we were really honest. And I knew Art would confront me about any dishonesty he found. I was afraid of criticism and sensed that he was too. Yet I knew he was kind and that he cared.

"But what if I fall in love with him?" I cried out to God. "Why am I so terrified of the intimacy I crave?" I remembered one of the first times I'd heard an inner voice that I thought was God saying to me: "If you try to do My will, Hedy, I'll love you and I'll take care of you whatever happens." But I was afraid to trust God with this part of my life.

With that awareness came the shocking realization that intimacy was more important to me than God! My mind fought against accepting that, but it was evidently true. Maybe that's what God was trying to tell me: that I had to quit insisting on my way and trust Him with the outcome of my closest relationships. If I tried to find His will, then true intimacy might reveal that Art and I were very different and *didn't* belong together. But I saw that I could only find out by wanting God's will more than my own preconceived schemes.

I remembered Art's serious, thoughtful face as he'd said, "Hedy, there must be thousands, maybe millions of people like us for whom life has turned gray. And all the prayer, all the religious good works, the witnessing or ecstatic gifts in the world, as valuable as they are, won't replace the intimacy we've begun to experience here in a couple of hours by beginning to be who we really are."

He had stopped and looked at me very thoughtfully, his eyes narrowed and his head slightly cocked. "Hedy, are you up for trying to be totally honest with me in these conversations?" He waited.

I simply couldn't answer him.

Finally he said, "Well, think it over, and I will too. Two weeks from next Saturday, I'm coming back to Chicago for the rest of the summer to do some research. I'll call you at six o'clock. If you want to be a part of this crazy experiment with me, you can let me know and we'll start meeting and getting to know each other."

It sounded so matter of fact, but for me it felt like an invitation to turn loose and jump off a forty-story building.

43. Please Love Me

I HAD AGREED TO DO a show for the Canadian government in the fall and was planning to be in town all summer painting, so I had no excuse for not seeing Art. On the other hand, it was probably going to be one of the busiest and most productive times of my life. I told myself I simply didn't have time to spend hours and hours talking to a man I'd barely begun to know. But I knew that I was already deeply involved with Art. That's what terrified me about being in a continuing relationship with him. Would we just talk? Would I tell him of my hidden shame? I never had told *anyone* my whole story, even Danny. All week my lifelong fear of being known battled my desire for it.

I began to pray and confess specific fears to God. I asked the children to pray for me about what to do during the summer. As I got more specific with God, because of my having been specific with Art, the grayness between God and me began to dissolve.

On the Friday before Art was due back, I woke up realizing that I had been crying out to the world all my life to "Please Love Me!" But I couldn't believe the love when it came because I knew that I'd always hidden my true self. And my only hope to receive love and believe it would be to let my real self be known! If someone loved me then, I might be able to accept it. I knew God wanted me to be myself, but my fears of rejection were blind and total. How could anything so painful be God's will? I cried out to Him for a sign.

I wanted with all my heart to be God's person and to do His will again. But He would not, it seemed, give me an answer about Art. I'd have to make my own decision. All I seemed to hear echoing down the halls of my soul was God's voice saying, "Hedy, will you trust Me to make you whole and happy? Will you trust Me? Trust Me? Trust Me?"

By Saturday evening, the seventeenth, I was a wreck. I had watched myself use all my old tricks of finding fault with Art so I could push him away. After all he was too intense, too probing. That would drive me crazy. Also, women were attracted to him. Could I trust him?

But then it was as if God said to me: "You're not agreeing to *marry* him, Hedy, just to find out with him about My kind of love and intimacy." But I felt a sick feeling in my stomach, the terror of being known just as I was and being rejected if I were really vulnerable, or of having to change in a way I couldn't. And in that moment I knew that *that* terror was the reason the church was so often impersonal, the reason so many marriages were phony. And that was why I was phony. What if I showed Art my secret real self and he didn't love me? Could I possibly risk it—even if it were God's will? No, I just didn't think I could do it, even though I knew now that He would be there to pick me up.

The telephone startled me. I looked at my watch. Six o'clock on the dot. I stood with my hand on the receiver as it rang, one, two, three, four, five times. Finally, I picked it up and heard myself saying in my hoarse whisper "Hello . . . yes, Art, I'd . . . I'd love to go with you."

And then silently, but with my heart in my throat, "All right, God, I'm coming with you whatever happens. But if I tell my whole story and there's nothing there that's lovable, please, Lord, please love me!"

EPILOGUE

THE WAY IT IS
by Keith Miller

The Way It Is

As HEDY ROBINSON finished telling me this story, I was almost awed by her honesty. Suddenly I realized why my life might have turned gray, why I had wanted to withdraw from teaching and speaking as a Christian. I had been resisting facing my own unconscious manipulative psychological games. I was afraid to trust God with the very personal areas of my own life, and consequently I'd become afraid of honest relationships.

As I saw Hedy wrestling with these same problems, I heard God pointing me to a new willingness to face myself in relation to those close to me so that I wouldn't hurt and stifle them. I saw the need for the church as a fellowship of risking, open people who want to quit playing games and to make a place for all the lost and searching Hedys—male and female—all over the world, who are crying out, "Please love me!" in the midst of the loneliness and fear of being known.

As a matter of fact, I realized that the church may be the only institution in which this openness can happen. We can admit we've failed because we have forgiveness and new chances built into our life together.

Hedy discovered that God's gift is not success but rather the amazing hope which comes through trusting Him with the outcome of our relationships and our lives—the knowledge that He will be with us all the way, teaching and healing us whatever happens—as we search for intimacy with Him and each other.

Hedy says that in many ways she's happier than she's ever been. She's back in the church now with a new enthusiasm. And she's with her children, painting and loving God very much, as she tries to be real with herself and those around her.

As I thought about her story, I realized that God is calling me at this time in my life to tell the other people in the world with a new conviction about Jesus Christ in and through His church. And that's where I am in my own journey—back home with His people in the church.

And I want to take the risk of betting my whole life that God can give us all the love of a Father and the courage to find His kind of openness and intimacy. But it's very threatening to open oneself to other people. And the search for honesty, it seems, has got to be tempered by the awareness that every person also has a very important need for privacy.

In fact, the thing which probably impressed me most about the miracle of what God has done in Hedy's life is that in spite of a lifetime of extreme privacy and feeling rejected and being hurt by people who even came close to knowing her, Hedy actually found the courage through Christ to risk telling Art the story you have just read. As I said in the beginning, all the names and some of the events and vocational identities were changed. But I know that she told it all to him, and that it changed his life . . . because . . . I am Art.